MEDIA POWER IN CENTRAL AMERICA

THE HISTORY OF COMMUNICATION

Robert W. McChesney and John C. Nerone, editors

A list of books in the series appears at the end of this book.

RICK ROCKWELL

AND NOREENE JANUS

Media Power in

Central America

UNIVERSITY OF ILLINOIS PRESS

URBANA AND CHICAGO

Library of Congress Cataloging-in-Publication Data
Rockwell, Rick J., 1958–
Media power in Central America / Rick J. Rockwell
and Noreene Janus.
    p.   cm. — (History of communication)
Includes bibliographical references and index.
ISBN 0-252-02802-3 (cloth : alk. paper)
1. Mass media—Political aspects—Central America.
2. Mass media—Economic aspects—Central America.
3. Democracy—Central America.
4. United States—Foreign relations—Central America.
5. Central America—Foreign relations—United States.
6. Central America—Politics and government—1979–
I. Janus, Noreene. II. Title. III. Series.
P95.82.C35R63   2003
302.23'09728—dc21   2002010964

To John and Isabelle

—N.J.

To the memory of Greg Weisz,

for putting me on the path

—R.R.

We journalists believe in the rather Jeffersonian ideal that if we unearth the facts, and give people in a free society the information they need, democracy will flourish.

—Philip J. Trounstine, *San Jose Mercury News*

Contents

Acknowledgments

We wish to acknowledge the role Sanford Ungar played in shaping this book project. While he was the dean of the School of Communication at American University, Ungar secured a project to review aspects of Central American media. This project brought us together as researchers for the first time and laid the groundwork for this book. Ungar was also instrumental in helping us find a publisher interested in our work. Thanks, Sandy.

We also want to thank our editor, Dick Martin, at the University of Illinois Press, for his patience and encouragement.

In addition, we thank Albasari Caro, who exactingly translated many of our interview tapes and gave us helpful advice as we wrote the book, as well as providing research assistance. We want to acknowledge the research work of Dylana Segura, at *La Nación* (San José), who helped us shape the sections of the book dealing with Costa Rica by sharing her interview tapes. We want to thank Kristin Neubauer for her help in Nicaragua. We also wish to thank André Verlöy, Juan Cristobal Villalobos, and Gloriana Guillen for their research assistance.

This book was produced after eight trips to Central America from 1998 through 2001. During those trips we conducted more than 250 interviews. We wish to thank all those interviewed for giving their time and their thoughts. For his advice on interview subjects, Bill Douglas, of World Learning, deserves special recognition. We thank Bill for his interest, participation, and logistical support.

Noreene wishes to thank Harold Moore, who gave us the keys to the Nicaraguan media world in the form of Roger Solarzano Gaitan. Noreene wishes to acknowledge the memories of Herb Schiller and Jorge Schnitman, who were there at the beginning and who would have loved this book; they were always deeply interested in the people, issues, and struggles it covers. Noreene also wishes to thank John Clark for his love, enthusiasm, and encouragement.

In addition, Rick wishes to thank Wendy Swallow and Wendell Cochran, of American University, who were extremely understanding about balancing research needs against the needs of the institution; Rodger Streitmatter for his sage advice; and Patricia Aufderheide for her counsel. Rick also wishes to credit Declan MacManus for the inspiration and Amy Luther for her eternal patience and love.

Abbreviations

AOL	America On-Line
APES	Salvadoran Press Association
APG	Association of Guatemalan Journalists
ARENA	National Republican Alliance (El Salvador)
Banaico	Panamanian Agro-Industrial and Commercial Bank
CANATEL	Costa Rican National Chamber of Television
CBS	Columbia Broadcasting System (U.S.)
CNN	Cable News Network (U.S.)
CONATEL	Honduran Communications Commission
COSUFFAA	Honduran Supreme Council of the Armed Forces
CPJ	The Committee to Protect Journalists
CVP	Cellular Vision de Panama
ESPN	Entertainment and Sports Programming Network (U.S.)
FCC	Federal Communications Commission (U.S.)
FIU	Florida International University
FMLN	Farabundo Martí Front for National Liberation (El Salvador)
FRG	Guatemalan Republican Front
FSLN	Sandinista National Liberation Front (Nicaragua)
HBO	Home Box Office (U.S.)
IAPA	Inter-American Press Association
IMF	International Monetary Fund
IPI	International Press Institute
MCRL	Free Costa Rica Movement
NGO	Nongovernmental Organization

NPR	National Public Radio (U.S.)
OAS	Organization of American States
PAN	National Advancement Party (Guatemala)
PDC	Christian Democratic Party (El Salvador and Panama)
PLN	National Liberation Party (Costa Rica)
PRD	Democratic Revolutionary Party (Panama)
PRI	Institutional Revolutionary Party (Mexico)
PUSC	Social Christian Unity Party (Costa Rica)
PVP	Popular Vanguard Party (Costa Rica)
SIN	Peruvian National Intelligence Services
TCS	Telecorporacion Salvadoreño
TVN	Televisora Nacional (Panama)
UCN	National Union Center Party (Guatemala)
UHF	Ultrahigh Frequency
VHF	Very High Frequency

MEDIA POWER IN CENTRAL AMERICA

Introduction

The cycle of history is at low tide in Central America: the small nations of the land bridge between North and South America were the strategic focus of cold war policy makers in the 1980s, but today they have seemingly dropped from the radar screen of our conscience. Notably, however, the region's civil and guerrilla wars have left an uncertain future as their legacy. With all these countries at peace, and with dictators removed from the scene, the United States has moved its attention elsewhere, to Kosovo, to Colombia, and to China.

But U.S. policy in the region has itself sown the seeds of future problems. Rather than view all U.S. meddling in Central America as inappropriate, this book will argue that once it became intricately involved in the workings of these nations, the United States had a responsibility to help with a transition toward peace. Instead of shouldering this responsibility, the United States continues to do what it has too often done before in Central America: tinkering until business interests and capitalism are served without addressing the fundamental reasons that guerrilla wars erupted in the first place. Once trade and profits are ensured in the region, the United States moves its attention elsewhere, only to return to tamp down the fires that inevitably spring up again and again.

The cycle of U.S. involvement during the past two centuries certainly constitutes one of the region's unique characteristics, an element of media and governmental development that distinguish the area from all others. The United States' attempts to protect its market interests in Central America through military intervention under the guise of constructing democracy are too numerous to document here. But these interventions continue to affect the perceptions of current U.S. programs to promote democracy and civil society.

This time, in the region's important postwar era, before relegating Central America to its usual place on a dusty back shelf, the United States blithely ignored fundamental concerns for free expression in the Information Age as it rushed to shore up incipient democracies throughout the region. Although democratizing the world has been a cornerstone of U.S. policy in the 1990s, in the Information Age Washington has seemed uninformed or inept in the way it approaches policies to encourage free expression and the flow of information as it tries to support so-called emerging democracies or emerging nations. With the United States' role as global supercop expanding rather than shrinking, and the trend toward U.S. sponsorship of democracy movements, the Central American experience in the 1990s can perhaps teach us a lesson.

We have focused on communications systems in Central America because they present a unique model as nation building and democratization become more important in U.S. and European foreign policy. The intriguing part of this model is that each country acts as a separate building block in creating an image of the entire region. Within each country one can detect different stages of development. Each media system differs from the others. Each of these six countries has a unique history and personality. Each occupies a different location on the spectrum of economic and political development: from the sophistication and longtime democracy of Costa Rica to the corruption and fear in Honduras, a nation still trying to rid itself of a political system dominated by the military. One of the interesting aspects of examining the media in these countries is discovering the ways in which state and corporate interests have developed sophisticated means to manipulate media content now that the days of heavy-handed military censors are over. In addition, we have focused on the media of these nations because their roles in the region's politics have been universally ignored.

It is important to note that the United States is just one factor in the way these countries have developed, but it has often been the most important hegemonic factor governing how these nations formed their political systems after independence from Spain. Nonetheless, the United States has not always sought to promote the same freedoms guaranteed by its constitutional system. Likewise, local elites have often used U.S. intrusions in Central America for their own ends.

For too long those who sought to bring real democracy to the region have neglected to build the systems of communication and free expression that would allow democracy to flourish. In 1858 the philosopher

J. S. Mill wrote, "The time, it is hoped, is gone by when any defense would be necessary of the 'liberty of the press' as one of the securities against corrupt or tyrannical government."[1] The example of Central America shows that Mill's optimistic view has not yet been universally realized.

Authoritarianism may have been removed from the power equation for now, but tacitly republican forms of government in the region are still using tactics honed by authoritarian regimes of the past to maintain their control. In this way a type of semiauthoritarianism has settled over many parts of Central America. Its media systems have been warped by their authoritarian and violent pasts, often becoming corrupt centers of political polarization bent on the personal agendas of elite owners or colluding with government in an attempt to cloud public perception. Those who resist this prescribed pattern of behavior still encounter the strong-arm tactics of military and paramilitary forces. As the Latin American scholar Silvio Waisbord notes, "Recent episodes of violence against journalists show that ideological persecution and the ambivalent stands of government officials on the defense of freedom of expression still persist."[2]

One might argue that the flaws in the communication systems of Central America merely show how capitalism is a higher priority there than true democracy. Although a few genuine programs to bolster democracy in Central America became a strong part of the foreign policy of the Clinton administration, advancement of business interests in the region remained central among Washington's goals. Further, many Central American leaders were happy to comply with these policies as long as their own economic needs were met.

Some may see this as a universal rather than a regional problem. As Upton Sinclair wrote: "Journalism is one of the devices whereby industrial autocracy keeps its control over political democracy; it is the day-by-day, between-elections propaganda, whereby minds of the people are kept in a state of acquiescence, so that when the crisis of an election comes, they go to the polls and cast their ballots for either of the two candidates of their exploiters."[3]

Sinclair was writing about the United States, a maturing democratic system with a cultural and political history different from Central America's. Journalism developed in Latin America altogether differently than it did in the United States. As Waisbord writes: "Simply, none of the crucial developments that permitted the rise of a market-oriented press and the ideal of objectivity in the United States existed in the region."[4] Thus the imposition of a system with capital as its primary priority rather than the development of democracy will surely affect not just a nation's political system but also the way that the political and economic system employs communication to do its bidding. If he were alive today, Upton Sinclair would surely note the capitalist imperative in U.S. journalism has only worsened its quality and that the nation's plutocracy continues to employ the communication system as a measure of control, albeit of a system that has a democratic foundation.

Those who see capitalism and democracy as happily existing coequals in national development should perhaps consider that capitalism and authoritarianism have coexisted in the Latin American model for most of the twentieth century. In her work on Latin American communication systems, Elizabeth Fox notes that "free markets do not guarantee democracy or the open marketplace of ideas when faced with domestic authoritarianism."[5] Chile under General Augusto Pinochet is just one example. For another example, consider how Panama spent a generation under dictators but became one of Latin America's largest banking centers. In our view the true competitive marketplace of ideas is an essential factor for constructing a media system that supports pluralism and perhaps eventually democracy. This has been absent from much of Central America, and as our profiles of each country demonstrate, to some extent the region still suffers from this affliction.

In the latter sections of this book we will analyze these trends and their meaning for the further development of these countries. We will examine both the theories of Thomas Carothers and others who analyze these nascent democracies as they sometimes slip into semiauthoritarianism and the implications of such developments for key media outlets. Strong central governments often maintain rigid control by colluding with powerful elites who control important sectors of the nations' media operations.[6]

Building on what Fox, Waisbord, and others have written about the interplay among politics, media systems, and attempts to foster democracy in Latin America, this book will focus on the nations of Central America to construct a model for analyzing the development of media systems in emerging nations generally. One of our central tenets will be that in the Central American context, lacking strong historical roots in democracy, media systems tend to support and reflect a country's oligarchic tendencies. Furthermore, the owners of media systems tend to protect their market interests in a nation, which usually means providing support for an institutionalized hierarchy or oligarchy rather than opening the market to nation building, democratic forces, or the true marketplace of ideas. What initially appears to be competition may reflect only inter-elite battles within an oligarchic system undergoing change. The dream of the media as a democratizing force thus crashes against a larger system.

We believe these ideas can also be used to gauge the progress of Eastern European, Russian, and other systems making the transition away from authoritarianism; to do so, media analysts need to uncover the connections among the media, government, and large business concerns in each national system and thus to analyze the ruling hierarchies. For instance, even Central European nations with robust economies, such as the Czech Republic or Poland, must deal with media-related problems inherited from the communist era, while media systems in the Balkans are dealing with fissures in civil society based on racial and ethnic tensions predating communism.[7]

Central America, too, is receding from its role as one of the main stages where the cold war played out its last act. Although Nicaragua never developed a fully centralized, state-run economy, the transition of its media system may prove a useful example to compare to those of Eastern Europe or Central Asia.

In this analysis we will profile each individual country and then compare them to gauge their progress in this post–cold war era. Although we believe this style of analysis has universal applications, we must also acknowledge the forces of globalization and media convergence, trends that began before the twenty-first century but that will surely shape media systems in Central America for the foreseeable future. Both globalization and convergence will certainly affect our model for reviewing these emerging nations. Globalization, one might contend, can greatly affect a small, compact media system undergoing major redevelopment and change in a shifting political atmosphere such as that of Central America.

Nonetheless, we take a different view. Compare such systems to large markets such as those in the United States or Western Europe, where politics and media systems are relatively stable yet globalization has made major inroads. From the viewpoint of media entrepreneurs, available capital and market resources clearly constitute the main accelerators behind globalization and convergence. Market size and political instability are less important. Our analysis will show that media owners in Central America tend to exaggerate the factors of small market size and instability for their own ends. In fact, Central America's shortage of capital and historical lack of resources may actually slow globalization in the region.

A casual observer who can sample the satellite services and cable television readily available only to the elite of these countries may perceive the globalization tsunami that appears already to be crashing ashore in Central America, with all the fears of cultural imperialism that the phenomenon may bring. As Waisbord has noted, however, intrahemispheric cultural crosscurrents in television programming and other interchanges had an impact on television network content and other media long before the term *globalization* became fashionable.[8]

Like Waisbord, we will argue that Central America's shared tongue and political history created buffers to slow the process of globalization and retain some of the region's various national characters. Many Central Americans remain relatively isolated and poor, so that the giant cable and satellite communications revolution that has swept most of the developed world has had little impact beyond the elite of these nations. For now, these outside influences have merely helped elites to communicate better within their class. In the poor countries of the region, such as Guatemala, where fewer than 15 percent of the populace own a telephone, let alone a cell phone, cable television seems an almost unachievable luxury. So far the satellite and telecommunications revolution has done little for the region except to provoke owners to further consolidate media properties in anticipation of the seemingly inevitable invasion from beyond. The few who do not fear the future have nevertheless laid out a similar course toward diminishing domestic competition, laying the groundwork to strengthen their market positions. We will examine the specifics of these reactions in the chapters that focus on individual countries, because the reaction has been different in each country. We will also underscore the influence not only of U.S. firms but also of other broadcasting concerns based elsewhere in Latin America, such as Mexico.

After the initial wave of influence from the United States, Mexico has become one of the primary exporters of programming to the region. This is a natural development considering Mexico's position as an exporter of television product on a worldwide scale.[9] We will document the spread of Mexican ownership in the region. Further, we will show the reactions that Mexican purchases of Central American stations have caused in the region.

We believe globalization and the international trend toward media concentration and consolidation only reinforce the media owners' backlash tendency to erect walls for protecting their interests in these small markets. This is in keeping with the work of Joseph Straubhaar (regarding Brazilian television) and others who have noted local and national responses to the spread of global media.[10] When selling unprofitable or marginal media concerns to investors from outside the region, Central American media owners have often sparked controversy or even action to close down international investment in their nations' media systems. Globalization and its implications for ownership of media outlets by foreign nationals or international conglomerates also further undercut attempts to build democracy by forcing oligarchic small market systems to create barriers to new owners, thus reducing the possibility of adding external competition for the entrenched media owners inside these nations.

This tendency suggests one of this book's basic tenets. In Central America, historical political developments matter more than current global forces or external pressures for democratization in shaping a country's media system. That is not to say that global forces, external pressures, U.S. foreign policy, international economic shifts, and other factors do not affect the development of these nations and their media systems. We view these systems as multidimensional, however, developing with strong foundations set first by domestic concerns, culture, and politics. Fox certainly makes a similar argument while rejecting various one-dimensional approaches toward theorizing how Latin American broadcasting systems evolved.[11]

Fox rejects Marxist, liberal, and realist theories for defining the shape of some Latin American media systems. We agree: a more holistic approach, one that looks at the media system historically and then through contemporary political and economic prisms, is essential for analyzing these nations' media. Economic aspects of these capitalist systems are an extremely important section of this model because of their impact on the end product, as has been noted by Sinclair earlier and more directly by Waisbord in his analysis of journalistic trends throughout the hemisphere. As Waisbord notes, journalistic autonomy from the political and economic sectors is "inconceivable when newsrooms have a limited degree of independence vis-à-vis owners' economic and political interests. The latter regularly and unmistakably impregnate daily reporting and, consequently, trump allegiance to the rules of objectivity."[12] Economic pressures, too, restrain or propel journalists within these systems and act as an invisible editor. When the political and economic pressures coincide or, in some cases, originate in the same external source, journalists are often forced into a system of self-censorship, a closed loop that chokes off free expression before it can begin.

This is perhaps the chief difference between the media oligarchies of Central America and the media oligarchy of the United States, which has evolved during the past forty years. In the United States this concentration of the media and the suppression of alternative voices is certainly a concern for democracy.[13] The media concentration in the United States, however, much like the capitalist system of journalism criticized by Sinclair, grows like a mold on a maturing democratic system with strong roots. Central American democracy is a transplant that may fail to take root in the region's rocky soil.

Central American media oligarchies exist in a system where the state, in the form of a strong central government, is more comfortable with media it can control either through direct censorship or through strong economic limitations on press freedom. This is one of the primary reasons the states in most of the region have not curtailed their advertising or media budgets. These budgets help to prop up much of the media system, which the state sees mainly as serving its interests in disseminating information from the ruling oligarchies downward to the masses. We will demonstrate how most Central American countries subsidize the media in a variety of ways and use those subsidies as a mechanism of control. The tens of millions of dollars spent on what amount to sophisticated government propaganda campaigns could be used for more pressing and obvious needs, such as eradicating poverty, starting job programs, or providing basic universal literacy education.

Because the evolution of Latin American media has often been tied to state support of the media, political and economic concerns are often more intricately intertwined there than in other regions of the world, such as the United States. This book thus revolves around issues of political and economic censorship. Because strong central governments often employ tactics that threaten the safety or livelihoods of journalists, we also explore the important issue of self-censorship in Central America.

In addition, we analyze the dominance of the state-controlled advertising systems that prop up much of the media in Central America, as seen in Guatemala in the late 1990s when the state intervened to shuffle media ownership. Guatemala exemplified a fundamental rule of media control: when faced with the power of state-dominated ad systems, the media either accept the conditions laid down by the state or close.[14] In very few instances do the media have a third option: take the large monetary losses and seek other ways to survive. We argue that only when a media outlet's profitability is uncoupled from state sponsorship and subsidies, when the outlet exists as an independent force in the marketplace, with the citizenry supporting it through subscriptions, sales, or other means— *only then* will it have the ability to change the overall media climate. Media systems where most individual media outlets require state financing to be profitable tend to support authoritarian or oligarchic regimes.

This shifting of sensibilities toward less state support and control can even be seen in the writing from the region, such as this snippet of an editorial from El Salvador's newly modernized newspaper *El Diario de Hoy:* "Up until now our media have been aligned with official power, with political cronies, with economic interests, and with ideologies, in an almost feudal style of journalism. But it is time to get rid of our fear of offending the almighty advertiser. The advertiser should see that his interests are best served in the medium that sells the most copies, not the one with the most biased news. That is the law of the market."[15]

Another law of the market is that success breeds imitation. Certainly some of the vertical integration in the Central American marketplace has been copied from successful models in the United States and elsewhere in Latin America. Many of the changes in the region's media have swept in on the heels of U.S. foreign policy: much of the improved quality of television broadcasting in El Salvador and Panama is directly linked to the intervention of the United States in those nations during the Reagan and Bush administrations, which focused U.S. and worldwide media attention on those nations. The subsequent concentration there of international media, which did not have to deal with government attempts at direct censorship (as did reporters covering the Contra War in Nicaragua), affected the level of reporting and inevitably the overall quality of presentations by national broadcasters. In El Salvador the protracted nature of the civil war may have expanded those changes beyond broadcasting and into a variety of media outlets.[16] Certainly El Salvador's newspapers have recently undergone face-lifts that have not only made them at least comparable to any newspaper in the hemisphere but also placed them, along with newspapers from Costa Rica and Panama, in the vanguard of the Central American press.

Nonetheless, the press in El Salvador remains overwhelmingly conservative and generally supports the right-wing governments that have dominated the nation in the postwar years. Similar trends show up throughout the isthmus, with the media supporting established, well-entrenched conservative oligarchies in their grip on state power. Such a system will be difficult to change, despite attempts at democratic reform. We devote considerable effort in the coming pages to analyzing these difficulties.

We believe that the forces threatening the primacy of existing state relations with media owners will invoke a backlash in the system that may result in violence or in the state's use of mechanisms to control media output, especially during transition periods. The history of censorship and violence against the media in Central America points to these findings, and our detailed analysis and profile of each country will bolster this important point. Lacking democratic traditions, few in these nations may notice the subtle strangulation of opposition voices that has continued through a variety of different methods in the postwar period, but the choice to ignore these developments could contribute to a wide-ranging political disaster in an area struggling after decades of armed conflict. As one UN review noted: "In no other part of the world has the career of journalism become so dangerous or so psychologically debilitating as in Latin America."[17]

In the coming pages we use anecdotal examples, historical data, and key interviews with media leaders to profile the media in each of these nations and then create a comparative analysis of the situation across the region. We define the major players who make up the various portions of each country's print and broadcast media. In so doing, we illuminate the various niches of these media markets. This entire picture and the interrelationships and competition among the various media outlets, along with the relationships among the media and the forces of the government, business elites, and the military, constitute what we call the country's media system.

Beyond focusing attention on an important and often neglected region, this examination of media power has more universal applications. As we have stated, using Central America as a laboratory to examine unique media systems will let us draw conclusions about similar systems and the transition toward democracy in other parts of the globe. As politics evolve in the Balkans, in Southeast Asia, in the islands of Indonesia, and in other nations moving away from authoritarianism, especially where media systems have depended directly on state support, such a model can become a useful tool for defining the shape and progress of nations beyond Central America. We believe that the character of Central American media allows us to sketch with great detail the media evolution of the past decade in the crucial post–cold war period.

In the end, our model for examining these media systems shows that the true nature of the media's interplay with democratization can be found only through examining the political and economic structures that surround the media in these individual nations. More important, in nations where the disparity between rich and poor citizens is growing and media owners constitute a small, closed circle, media ownership will only enhance further vertical integration of the economic power already concentrated in the hands of a few. The media reflect the rulers or the media oligarchy speaking to the ruled (the classes below the top echelons of political and economic elites) rather than the free exchange of ideas between disparate classes and forces necessary in a democracy. Media monopolies have tended to impede the freedoms necessary for long-term sustainable democracies. We thus examine how the oligarchies in many of these nations have used monopolistic media systems to maintain their power and dominance in the region. Furthermore, Central American media monopolies have constructed a subterfuge, selling the idea that by increasing their power through concentration and vertical integration in these markets, they are in fact serving the growth of democracy.

Instead, the record shows that despite some journalists' efforts to open the media to a broader range of opinions, a select few retain control. The record also shows that for every trend toward increased media freedom touted by observers inside and outside the region, there are powerful contrary forces that have continued to limit the alternative media and the distribution of alternative messages to a populace quite accustomed to receiving the short end of the stick in this sort of power equation. All too often, under the cover of peace accords or masked by the hype that comes with more commercial systems, the media in Central America have only superficially appeared to be changing in ways that would bolster democracy. All is not bleak, however, because progress has been made. Nevertheless, as these nations struggle to find new approaches to having the media and government support pluralism, elites often cannot resist the temptation to use repressive methods that recall the authoritarian past. In the spirit of Mill, who hoped for an end to authoritarianism in a struggle for liberty, this book takes on the responsibility of watching the watchers: casting light on media practices that have colluded with state and economic powers to undercut the very ideas at the core of free expression.

1 Honduras and the Media Oligarchy

In Honduras Rafael Nodarse is known impolitely as "the pirate." This is just one of the nicknames that the Honduran establishment hung on this media owner, but it is telling, because it reveals what many think about the methods Nodarse used to obtain his media properties and to keep them afloat. The nickname is revealing also because it casts Nodarse as someone operating beyond the accepted rules of commerce in Honduras.

Nodarse owns broadcast and cable television operations based in San Pedro Sula, a commercial center and the nation's second-largest city. Nodarse's Canales 6 and 69 (operating on VHF and UHF, respectively) and his cable company began operations with the help of the Honduran military, until recently an unchecked force in the country's political, commercial, and even social development. One of the ways Nodarse earned his nickname was by using his political connections with the military to obtain the operating permits for his television properties, much to the disapproval of his competition. In Honduras, a country regarded as the prototypical banana republic, the shady backroom political dealings of an earlier era often continue to shape the landscape.

Mountainous and rugged, Honduras is a developing nation about the size of Louisiana. The country is struggling to overcome major setbacks during the 1990s. In 1998 Hurricane Mitch rampaged across Central America, and Honduras bore the brunt of its destruction: many experts said roads, bridges, and other important infrastructure in the country would not be replaced for a generation.[1] Entire villages and towns were wiped out. Even before the hurricane, the country was struggling with an economic depression that had hit in 1994. The country's boom-and-bust economy is often tied to its chief exports, bananas and coffee. With those exports drawing lower prices on the world market in the late 1990s, the nation struggled just to replace what it had lost in the devastating storm.

As is common across Central America, a small group of families and a few giant companies have historically dominated the economic landscape of Honduras. During the twentieth century the United Fruit Company controlled more than vast plantations of bananas, the country's largest crop. United Fruit had built the nation's railroads and retained control of that transportation system, along with a string of diversified businesses. In the 1950s United Fruit and the Standard Fruit Company accounted for more than 90 percent of the government's tax revenues, showing their central importance to the nation.

United Fruit had backed the electoral success of the National Party and Tiburcio Carías Andino in 1933. A typical Latin American *caudillo*, Carías managed to rewrite the constitution to allow his reelection, guaranteeing sixteen years of continuous rule.[2] United Fruit was happy to see its hand-picked candidate evolve into a dictator. Before his rise to the presidency, Carías had gained notoriety as a general who used ruthless means to quell dissent. In 1923 he became one of the first military leaders ever to order the aerial bombing of civilian areas to snuff out support for rebels allied with the Liberal Party.[3]

For most of the twentieth century, the country was ruled by military dictators, military juntas, or generals who wielded power from behind the facade of presidents and popularly elected representatives. In 1957, after the National Party had used congressional maneuvers and questionable constitutional rules to keep itself in power despite losing the popular vote in the 1954 elections, the military took control of election oversight. By 1963 the military was ruling the country directly.[4] Many Hondurans mark the true beginnings of their democracy from the 1986 elections, when the military oversaw the peaceful transfer of presidential power from the National Party to the Liberal Party, the first such peaceful transition of civilian rule in thirty years. In reality, however, the Honduran military was still running the country.

During the 1980s the military controlled the national police and large portions of the country's economic infrastructure. In the United States, under the Reagan administration, U.S. policy called for supporting Honduras's military as a way to help the Nicaraguan Contras, who were active in the southern border regions, and as a way to provide a backstop for U.S. military advisers operating in El Salvador during that country's long civil war. At the midpoint of the Reagan administration, American military aid to Honduras hit $77.5 million.[5]

The 1980s may have marked the height of military power, with Honduras playing the important role of bulwark for U.S. Central American policy. The 1990s, however, saw evolution toward civilian control of the central government. With the demise of the Sandinista regime in neighboring Nicaragua and the end to the Salvadoran civil war, U.S. policy sought nonmilitary means to support democratic development in the region. By the end of Honduran president Carlos Reina's administration, U.S. military aid had shrunk to $400,000.[6] Reina terminated military control of the Honduran telecommunications system, the immigration department, the national police force's investigatory arm, and the merchant marine. The military still controls a bank, insurance companies, and one of the country's two large cement companies.

With civilian control of telecommunications came a new interest in the operations of Rafael Nodarse, in part because one of his stations caused broadcast interference for two television channels based in Tegucigalpa, the capital. These stations, Canales 5 and 7, are owned by José Rafael Ferrari, a member of the country's powerful media establishment.

The new Honduran Communications Commission (known as CONATEL) began a review of Nodarse's broadcast license once the primacy of the civilian government was established in the late 1990s, but no one in the central government was daring enough to criticize the way Nodarse used military influence to cut through government red tape and avoid oversight mechanisms. Asked about the matter, Norman Roy Hernandez, CONATEL's chairman, responded with the following oblique comment: "Frankly that came at a time when communication oversight was not taken seriously and when there may have been other priorities."[7]

CONATEL and Nodarse had been at odds almost since civilian control of the broadcast airwaves began. Thumbing his nose at any controls, Nodarse opened television operations in Tegucigalpa and the southern city of Comayagua in 1997 without approval from the government. These so-called pirate television stations not only reinforced Nodarse's image as an owner beyond the control of the law but also spread the use of his nickname in the media. CONATEL asked a judge to have Nodarse arrested and sought to fine him $250,000.[8] Nodarse successfully blocked the government's move to regulate him in the nation's Supreme Court for many months, but ultimately he was fined and forced to shut down his nonlicensed operations.[9]

The civilian authorities in Honduras were not the only ones concerned with Nodarse's television operations. The U.S. government pressured Honduras to rein in the rogue television owner. It was concerned that Nodarse was using copyrighted material from the United States without paying the proper royalties. The State Department wanted Nodarse to stop using illegal means to obtain programming. It was concerned that he was stripping satellite signals to provide his stations with Hollywood movies and even English-language news. News programs from Denver's KUSA-TV were often shown on Nodarse's stations.

During a trip to Honduras in 1998, Assistant Secretary of State Jeffrey Davidow pressed the Honduran government on the issue. Such bilateral issues as immigration, the drug trade, and the United States' military presence in Honduras captured the headlines during Davidow's visit. The popular anchorman and commentator Rodrigo Wong Arévalo, however, who is known in Honduras for his stands against U.S. interference in regional affairs, openly discussed the pressure Davidow and the United States were placing on the Honduran government to curtail Nodarse's practices. Importantly, Wong Arévalo made his comments on his news program, "Abriendo Brecha," which is broadcast by Nodarse's main competitor, Centroamericana de Television, owned by José Rafael Ferrari. Such uncommon support of Nodarse resulted mainly from Wong Arévalo's long-held beliefs that the United States exerts too much influence inside the Honduran political system and that Hondurans should work out their problems free from such outside influences.

Wong Arévalo's comments also opened up discussion about Nodarse's background and the way he had obtained his broadcast licenses. Nodarse fled Cuba in 1962 in the wake of Fidel Castro's revolution. He obtained U.S. citizenship and moved to Honduras in the late 1960s.[10] This is why he is often called "the Cuban" as well as "the pirate." Honduran commentators such as Wong Arévalo have often mentioned Nodarse's anti-Castro sentiments and his strong ties with the Honduran military as a way to link him to the U.S. security apparatus. Nodarse's ability to run roughshod over the weak Honduran regulatory environment for broadcasting and the long delays in getting him to comply with the edicts of CONATEL also fueled speculation about the Cuban broadcaster's special connections.

Whatever Nodarse's connections to the United States had been, the State Department decided it would no longer ignore the blatant disregard for copyright law and moved to stop the Cuban American media owner. A month after Davidow's visit, the United States suspended $5 million in Honduran tariff benefits and threatened to impose further economic sanctions unless Nodarse was stopped or began paying for retransmission rights for U.S. programs.[11] Quickly responding to the economic pressure, CONATEL fined Nodarse $37,000 for his practices and ordered his broadcast operations closed for a week.[12]

As a subtext for CONATEL's intervention, one of his competitors had to file a complaint against the controversial station owner. Samir Kawas, the owner of Canal 21 in San Pedro Sula, officially sought the legal action against Nodarse, alleging that his use of unlicensed films and other programming gave him an illegal competitive edge. CONATEL ruled that Nodarse should pay his fine directly to Kawas.[13]

On its face this action appears to be strictly a matter of Honduras's justice and regulatory bodies acting against a media owner who has defied legal mechanisms established to oversee commerce. In addition, because the United States has a long history of intervening in Honduras and other parts of the region to protect its commercial interests, the request for action and subsequent economic pressure seem to be in character. Beyond the historical context, however, it can be argued that the request was justified: Honduras's legal and regulatory systems ruled that Nodarse's stations were in fact pilfering satellite signals and rebroadcasting programming in clear violation of international copyright law. Nevertheless, the system had done little to rein in the Cuban media owner before outside pressure was applied.

Nodarse's clever response to this pressure was to use his broadcast properties to rally support for his cause and brand the government as a puppet of the United States. Although many in intellectual and media circles realized that Nodarse was ignoring his own image as someone who had benefited from the past interventionist policies of the United States, this tactic allowed him to generate some populist support for his cause. Relying on the fact that few people would know how he had used his own influence and connections to obtain broadcast licenses, Nodarse portrayed the government as a giant force aligned with the country's business elites to crush his independent voice.

Before the government could fine him and close his stations, Nodarse organized protests against its actions. In March 1998 Nodarse staged a rally in San Pedro Sula's main square, where protesters chanted slogans against the United States and the Honduran government. Speakers at the rally said the Honduran government responded to Washington as if it were connected by remote control. President Carlos Flores Facussé and Rafael Ferrari, who had lodged the interference complaints against Nodarse, were portrayed as willing stooges of the United States. Speakers also portrayed the United States as using imperialist policies to muzzle Nodarse and his station, the sort of theme that often excites crowds in Latin America.

Nodarse's national outlets broadcast live coverage of the rally and subsequent march for several hours, repeating the coverage in its entirety during the next few days. The rally was also expertly photographed, so that three hundred people who blocked one street and filled up one corner of the city's central square appeared to fill the entire square. With a flourish, the event was capped with a march to the statue of Francisco Morazán, Honduras's national hero.

Although Nodarse's stations used propaganda techniques in an attempt to amplify their owner's complaints, the message resonated with some in the audience. Nodarse's advocates portrayed him as a rebel standing up for free speech against controlling elements in the Honduran government. Typical Hondurans saw the government and Nodarse's competitors as trying to strip them of the ability to see popular movies and other programs supplied by Nodarse's stations. Often Nodarse's advocates portrayed President Flores and the media mogul Ferrari as representing a media monopoly.

In this way Nodarse's fight, which centered on his need for economic survival and thus his illegal practices, struck a chord with some Hondurans. Although Nodarse and his advocates warped the fight for free expression to fit their propaganda protests and oversimplified the full situation in their portrayals, they were not far from a reality that most Hondurans understand: a handful of powerful people control the media system in this small country, and those who do not conform to the limits and messages cleared by this small group either have no way to communicate or are relegated to the fringes. Nodarse, with his colorful nicknames, is branded as an outsider in the Honduran system: not only a media owner who clearly sided with the military authorities for decades but also someone from another part of Latin America who is not accepted by the dominant culture of media owners in Honduras.

Five families control most of the media outlets in Honduras. These powerful media moguls—the Canahuatis, Sikaffys, Rosenthals, Ferrari, and President Flores's family, the Facussés—have managed to combine control of communications media with political and economic might. Most, if not all, of these families have large stakes in other Honduran industries.

For instance, the Canahuati family owns the newspaper with the largest circulation, *La Prensa* (this is a popular name for newspapers in Latin America and should not be confused with the Panamanian or Nicaraguan papers of the same name), based in San Pedro Sula. They also own *El Heraldo*, in Tegucigalpa. (Again, this is a popular name for newspapers in the region. This publication should not be confused with *El Heraldo* of San José, Costa Rica.) The family owns businesses outside of the media as well, including a home furnishings company. Because lumber and wood products are among the country's leading exports, the newsprint and furniture that the Canahuatis use and sell show that they have carved out an important niche in the Honduran economy. The Canahuati family also owns companies that sell insurance, bottled water, and soft drinks.[14]

These families with major media holdings seem to have intertwining interests. For instance, in 1998 Jorge Canahuati III, who had been in charge of his family's home furnishings business, was being trained in the intricacies of media operations at VICA Television, the property of another prominent family with media holdings, the Sikaffys.[15] The Canahuatis and Sikaffys do not compete directly in the Honduran system because the Canahuatis do not own electronic media properties and the Sikaffys do not own newspapers. In the 1970s the Sikaffy family had diversified beyond its mercantile holdings, investing in a cement factory and construction firms.[16] The Sikaffy family also controls Tegucigalpa's Canal 9 and an AM-FM radio combo in San Pedro Sula called La Voz de Centroamérica.

The chummy climate among most of the media owners in Honduras, exemplified by the Sikaffy-Canahuati alliance, may result from their generally shared political beliefs and cultural backgrounds. Many of the media owners belong to successful Arab Honduran families called *turcos* in the local slang. Many of these families immigrated from Lebanon and Syria to Honduras at the beginning of the twentieth century. These immigrant families intermarried, helped one another prosper in their new homeland, and became proponents of the country's Liberal Party.

Unlike El Salvador, Nicaragua, and Guatemala, where elite families rose to prominence on the strength of agro-exports, mainly coffee, Honduras followed a different path of development. In the 1890s banana farms were held mainly by small middle-class ranchers, and bananas constituted only 11 percent of the nation's exports. By 1930 that had changed. In the intervening years United Fruit and Standard Fruit had bought banana plantations, and millions of other acres were transferred to banana production. By 1930 bananas constituted 84 percent of Honduras's exports, and the country produced one-third of the world's banana supply. More than 75 percent of the nation's banana-producing land, however, was owned by three companies from the United States.[17] The benefits of the banana boom did not create a banana oligarchy but instead reinforced U.S. firms' abilities to dabble in Honduran politics. For decades Honduras had a one-crop economy. Coffee was introduced as an export crop in the mid-twentieth century, but this happened much later than it did in the rest of Central America and was not accompanied by the rise of a coffee elite.

The lack of an agricultural elite left the way clear for the *turco* immigrants to vault to prominence based on the success of their investments. By the 1960s the Adonie, Kafie, and Facussé families provided the leaders of Honduras's mercantile class, skilled entrepreneurs who began investing in the nation's incipient manufacturing projects.[18] When these prominent immigrant families prospered, they invested heavily in the country's media as a way to promote their products, businesses, and ideas.

So it was not unusual for these families to close ranks to oppose someone seen as an interloper, such as Nodarse. When CONATEL needed someone to file a complaint against Nodarse, Samir Kawas, a *turco* competitor, led the charge. (It may come as no surprise to learn that Kawas is part of the Sikaffy television clan; his full name is Samir Kawas Sikaffy.) Rafael Ferrari, another powerful *turco* media owner, had opposed Nodarse for years, not only because the Cuban's stations caused broadcast interference for Ferrari's television holdings, but also because Ferrari was generally opposed to opening the television spectrum to new competition, and Nodarse had pulled influential strings to get his broadcast license.

Ferrari controls a four-station TV group in Tegucigalpa and Canal 7 in San Pedro Sula. He also owns one of the nation's largest media production centers and headquarters for various radio networks, a media complex known as Emisoras Unidas in Tegucigalpa. Emisoras Unidas is home to Honduras's most popular radio news programs on its flagship radio station, HRN, as well as several radio programs in popular music formats. Ferrari founded HRN in the mid-1950s and is considered the country's leading radio pioneer.[19] Ferrari also owns one of the nation's more popular soccer teams.[20]

In addition, Ferrari is a powerful politician who maneuvered unsuccessfully for a presidential nomination from the Liberal Party in 1997 (he may well try again in the future). Ferrari eventually supported President Flores, the winning Liberal candidate, a move that may have come at a price. Ferrari was vilified at the pro-Nodarse rally in San Pedro Sula not simply because he was a powerful competitor but because many felt that Ferrari made a bargain with the president to close Nodarse's television operations or at least pressure the Cuban media owner. Some Hondurans saw the pressure from CONATEL and the United States as a convenient cover for a backroom political deal meant to boost the profits and power of these successful *turco* media owners.

President Flores is also a media owner. His family, the Facussés, owns the newspaper *La Tribuna*, which is based in Tegucigalpa. (Like *La Prensa* and *El Heraldo*, this is a popular name for newspapers in Central America. This paper should not be confused with *La Tribuna* in Managua, Nicaragua.) Flores's success inside the Liberal Party stemmed in part from the support of this newspaper and of other *turco* media owners.

By the time of Flores's presidential victory, the Facussé family was one of the most powerful *turco* clans. After *turco* families turned from mercantile businesses to manufacturing and industry, the Facussé family became known for its holdings in chemical firms. By the 1970s the Facussés were investing heavily in agribusiness concerns. In a way they had reversed the usual Central American success formula, turning to agricultural businesses as a means of diversification instead of fundamental investment.

Flores got his start in politics thanks to the intercessions of his uncle Miguel Facussé. Miguel Facussé served as the chief economic adviser to President Roberto Suazo Córdova in the mid-1980s. Eventually Facussé helped Flores gain a position as one of President Suazo's political advisers.[21]

This is the most obvious example of media oligarchy on display in Central America. In other nations media barons have used their broadcast and newspaper holdings to promote their other businesses, their political causes, and their own social agendas. In Honduras, however, a small group of families used their control of information flow and their muscle inside one of the nation's leading political parties to ratchet up media power and ultimately take control of their country's presidency.

Important members of the Flores administration also trace their roots to *La Tribuna*. For instance, Edgardo Dumas Rodriguez, who was the first Honduran ambassador to the United States in the Flores administration, is a minority investor in the newspaper.

Rodolfo Dumas Castillo, the ambassador's son, who is a prominent lawyer and served as an aide to President Flores's election campaign in 1997, noted that without *La Tribuna* and the support of other media, Flores would probably have lost the election.[22] Dumas Castillo noted that the reach of the media in Honduras, starting with newspapers, is important and has changed markedly in the past generation. With prominent newspapers controlling the message, a political candidate can set a political agenda or at least insert ideas into political debate. Because many Honduran radio and television news broadcasts merely repeat items from the nation's newspapers, controlling the editorial content of newspapers, the source of much of the elite debate in Honduras, became a key to Flores's victory. Moreover, Dumas Castillo indicated, this subtle control of the campaign coverage and message allowed Flores more flexibility in his campaign: unlike the other candidates, he was not forced to stump around

the country to get out his message. Although Flores employed traditional campaign tools, he was able to reduce his personal exposure because
he was guaranteed daily coverage through the media and his Liberal Party contacts to key media owners, such as Ferrari. Not only did Flores's
opponents have to struggle for positive media coverage; in addition, they
were unable to run their campaigns in the same way. These candidates
had to make the traditional campaign stops around the country while
Flores was able to run a more centralized operation. Of course politicians
everywhere have learned how to use the media in a campaign, but being
a politician, a media owner, and part of a powerful clique with similar
economic interests takes the ease of using the media to a new level.

The success of the *turco* media owners and that of the Liberal Party
are so interconnected in Honduras that mostly media owners were considered the strongest contenders to succeed Flores as president. For instance, Jaime Rosenthal Oliva, another leading media owner, was Flores's
chief competitor within the Liberal Party for its presidential nomination.
Rosenthal has plenty of political experience. He served as vice-president
in the administration of President José Simeón Azcona Hoyo in the late
1980s, and he was Azcona's chief economic adviser.[23] Rosenthal challenged Ferrari for the Liberal Party leadership in 2001, but neither won
the nomination. Ricardo Maduro of the National Party won the recent
election.

A successful banker, Rosenthal heads a family that owns one of the
nation's most respected newspapers, *El Tiempo,* based in San Pedro Sula.
Although Rosenthal is often lumped in with the *turco* Liberal media
owners, his family has different origins. Rosenthal was born in Honduras, but his mother is from El Salvador, and his father immigrated from
Romania.[24]

At times Rosenthal has competed hotly with the *turcos* in the separate fields of politics and the media. Against Ferrari's protests, in 1993
Rosenthal obtained the broadcast license for a new Channel 11 in Honduras. Rosenthal has yet to invest in the infrastructure to operate the
channel. He has been approached by the Sikaffy family and the prominent Mexican broadcasting company TV Azteca to sell his license rights.
As the 1990s came to a close, however, Rosenthal still retained the rights
to the channel.[25]

Politicians outside the *turco* media circles have certainly noticed the
immigrant media owners' successful political tactics. Bracing himself for
a run at the top of the Liberal Party ticket and preparing to run a campaign in the style of President Flores, one of Honduras's top congressional
leaders, Calvin Weddle Calderón, formed a syndicate of investors to buy

control of one of the nation's newspapers, *El Periodico*.[26] (Again, this is a popular name for newspapers in Latin America. *El Periodico* of Tegucigalpa should not be confused with a publication with a similar name based in Guatemala.) Ironically this newspaper had been founded by a group of investors from the National Party, the chief conservative opposition to Weddle's Liberal Party. Former Honduran president Rafael Callejas had headed the original investment group that started the newspaper, and he used it as a launching pad for his presidency. Weedle was not so lucky in 2001.

Turco media owners who have not gravitated toward the Liberal Party have nevertheless parlayed their media and business success into political muscle in other parties. For instance, Miguel Andonie Fernandez, a prosperous real estate investor who also owns medical production companies and a chain of pharmacies, owns one of the country's most popular chains of radio stations, Radio America. Andonie Fernandez is also a leader in a minor Honduran political party, the Unity Party.

Another member of the Andonie clan is a media owner of note. Abraham Andonie, who owns significant holdings in a chain of drug stores and a medical supply export company, heads a group of investors who own the newspaper *El Nuevo Día*, based in San Pedro Sula.[27]

With *turcos* owning most of the nation's newspapers, along with the most popular radio and television operations, it is easy to see how a maverick Cuban broadcaster such as Nodarse could feel isolated and beset not just by the political system but also by his brethren in the media. This does not excuse Nodarse for using his stations to broadcast propaganda in defense of his commercial and political interests, nor does it justify his abuse of copyright laws. Nonetheless, his case highlights an important phenomenon, for the media and political systems closed ranks to pressure Nodarse when his tactics could no longer be excused or covered up by his patrons in the military. It nicely illustrates how the Honduran communications and political systems react to outsiders who do not accept the social, political, and legal norms and cover their reactions under the guise of attempting to regulate competition.

For example, when Nodarse staged his protests in San Pedro Sula, much of the country's media ignored the gathering and subsequent march. This ran opposite to the tactic used by Nodarse: pouring hype on a march that he had staged and pumping it up into a satirical antigovernment circus. By ignoring the protest, much of Honduras's media establishment was refusing to acknowledge this debate over control of the nation's airwaves and its political implications. Thus not only were they fighting his attempts to use the media to foment a populist response against tighter civilian control of the nation's broadcast system, but they also were exhibiting a type of control over content much more common in capitalist systems. No formal censorship system is necessary in these systems; rather, the common cultural and commercial concerns of the media system dictate which stories will be covered and which will be ignored.[28]

Edgardo Benitez, the editor of *El Nuevo Día*, said he felt covering Nodarse was a waste of time, and he refused to give the story any space. He viewed the protest and Nodarse's tactics as mere showmanship and not worthy of coverage.[29]

Although this sentiment prevailed among Honduras's media gatekeepers, the country's conservative newspaper of record, *La Prensa*, a Canahuati publication, decided to give Nodarse's protests some coverage: five paragraphs. Coverage of phony passport rings, drug dealers, union activists, and debates over road construction consumed much of *La Prensa* on the day after the protest; meanwhile, the discussion about federal control of the media and its consequent political fallout was confined to one small corner of an inside page.[30]

The story of Nodarse's fight against the Honduran media establishment exemplifies some of the central tenets of the ideas we are advancing for the analysis of media systems in this region. As we have stated, the owners of media systems tend to protect their market interests. This means they will usually support an institutionalized hierarchy or oligarchy rather than open the media system to nation building, democratic forces, or the true marketplace of ideas. Media owners from outside these nations or closed systems must appear nonthreatening to the oligarchic forces before they will be allowed to make major inroads in the changing national character of the nation's media system. Without his patrons in the Honduran military, Nodarse would likely not have a broadcast license in Honduras's media system, which has evolved to exclude almost any major player who is not linked in some major way to the tight circle of *turco* media owners. The fight against Nodarse, thinly veiled behind CONATEL, the stalking horse for the Liberal Party forces of the president and Ferrari, surely reveals a system working to purge an outside force that has refused to conform to the norms set by the *turco* media oligarchy.

In a unique fashion, the Honduran media owners have not only evolved as part of the nation's business elites; they have also crossed over to become political leaders. Instead of a three-tiered system—where media owners are linked on the one hand to business elites, who provide their advertising livelihood, and on the other to political elites, whose activities they both mirror and affect—the Honduran system has fused all these structures onto the economic base created by the oligarchy of *turco* families.

The political ascendancy of President Flores also shows how systems without strong historical roots in democracy tend to have media that support and reflect a country's oligarchic tendencies. This is relatively easy to see here because the media *are* the oligarchy in Honduras. Although Flores was not the first Honduran politician to use a newspaper as a platform for a successful candidacy for president, he was the first member of the elite *turco* media class to use this method, and his successful campaign showed that most of the other media owners would fall into rank behind him, supporting his political cause.

Those who have not supported Flores in the media have faced various repressive responses from the media hierarchy. Individual cases that highlight these problems are discussed in detail in chapter 7. In general, however, the Committee to Protect Journalists (CPJ), an international organization that reports on the climate of media freedom worldwide, has criticized Flores. The CPJ cites various critics of the president who say he has personally phoned other media owners to have reporters dismissed or demoted or to have their stories spiked.[31] The CPJ also notes that Flores has rewarded his supporters in the media with political perks. For instance, acting much as he did with Edgardo Dumas Rodriguez of *La Tribuna*, the former Honduran ambassador to the United States, Flores named at least twenty other journalists to diplomatic posts. This carrot-and-stick approach has created a system in which journalists censor themselves as a means of survival, measuring their stories to make sure they have not strayed into a dangerous zone that may upset Flores or other members of his administration.

Some members of the media dismiss this view. Raul Valladares, the news director at HRN, the Ferrari flagship radio station, noted that sources often pressure journalists to put a certain spin on stories. He said that members of the military who wanted to comment on stories called him even while he was vacationing in Miami. He felt that calls and comments that may disagree with a journalist's view are not undue pressure but just part of the job; indeed, they largely go unprinted and unbroadcast, even if they come from high government offices.[32]

Juan Ramon Martinez, a prominent columnist at *La Tribuna*, the president's newspaper, takes a moderate view of the situation. He acknowledges that having a president with significant influence in the media sphere creates a chilling effect among many Honduran journalists, especially when it comes to criticism of the president. Martinez did not discount or discredit the stories that Flores would phone other papers and ask for retribution against his critics. Nevertheless, he said that Flores had left journalists at his own newspaper to their own devices. According to Martinez, since Flores wanted to avoid the conflict of interest charges that might ensue were he to appear to run his opinions in the newspaper, journalists at *La Tribuna* were actually some of the most unhindered in the nation.[33] Regardless of Martinez's opinion, the CPJ characterized the coverage in *La Tribuna* as "uniformly favorable" to the president.[34]

Because of his connections inside *turco* media and political circles, President Flores enjoyed an unusual ability to shape the boundaries of political discourse inside Honduras. The one media owner whom the president seemingly could not corral, however, was the renegade Nodarse. Other media outlets met Nodarse's criticism of the president, his protests, and his flouting of the law in the face of CONATEL with stony silence or heated criticism. On the surface Nodarse's battles with the *turco* media establishment and the president appear to have grown out of the commercial competition in Honduras.

A closer examination of the situation, however, suggests that what appears to be a struggle among competitive elements in a media system may actually reflect inter-elite battles inside an oligarchic system undergoing change. Nodarse's clash with the media establishment reflected a deeper tectonic shift in Honduran politics, because Nodarse's patrons were members of the country's powerful military.

The battle for civilian control of broadcasting in Honduras was being fought just as Flores was struggling to become the first president in recent history to control the military directly. The local media missed much of that power struggle, however, because journalists had surrendered their watchdog role, not wanting to fall victim to the president's systematic way of weeding critical voices from the nation's media outlets.

Although the Honduran system masquerades as a constitutional democracy, for much of the twentieth century the country has been ruled by military dictators, military juntas, or generals who wielded power from behind the facade of presidents and popularly elected representatives. Flores's predecessor, President Reina, also of the Liberal Party, had declined to exercise his constitutional power to appoint a commander of the armed forces and thus exert control over the country's military. Under Reina the Supreme Council of the Armed Forces (Spanish acronym, COSUFFAA) was the real power in the country, and that body had appointed General Mario Raúl Hung Pacheco to head the military until his retirement in 1999. President Reina's balancing act with the military did include several acts of independence, though, including disregarding COSUFFAA's recommendations for defense minister.[35] During the early days of the Flores administration, the new president boxed with COSUFFAA and Hung Pacheco over a variety of issues, including promotions, military pay, amnesty for human rights violations, and even the times when COSUFFAA would meet with the president.

A few months after Hurricane Mitch devastated the country, Hung Pacheco retired and Flores created the Civil Defense Ministry, through which he assumed total control of the military, power no Honduran president has held since 1956. Flores moved Edgardo Dumas, his partner from *La Tribuna* and his representative in Washington, into the difficult job as civil defense minister. In the summer of 1999, less than a year after assuming control of the military, Flores fired four top commanders, including the vice-minister of civil defense and the head of COSUFFAA. At the time Flores had to deny reports that the military commanders were plotting a coup.[36]

Honduran journalists who attempted to dig into the political intrigue behind the president's problems with the military were met with intimidation. For instance, television reporter Renato Alvarez escaped from an attempted kidnapping. The incident occurred after Alvarez had explored and reported the possibility of a coup.[37]

In this atmosphere the government was also moving aggressively to rein in Nodarse. The renegade broadcaster lost his appeal to Honduras's Supreme Court and was forced to pay a fine of $250,000 to CONATEL for extending his stations' signals through illegal transmitters in Tegucigalpa and Comayagua.[38] Nodarse's ability to ignore dictates from the civilian government was slipping away just as civilian authority was displacing control of the military. Again, what appears to be merely competition between the *turco* media forces and Nodarse, the outsider, actually reflects the deeper political struggle for civilian control of Honduras after decades of military dominance.

The nascent civil society in Honduras and the entrepreneurial class were pushing military leaders aside because of their feeling that the country's economy would respond better to a more pluralistic system, even if that system retained the dominance of a certain oligarchic class. As John Shattuck and J. Brian Atwood write: "Political pluralism, including a free press and a political opposition, generates more and better information for use in economic decision-making."[39] Although Honduras was far from approximating this ideal, the same forces were at work. Nodarse's problems with the Flores administration simply showed which way the current was flowing.

During the decades of military dominance, the country's communication infrastructure had improved. By 1997, the beginning of the Flores era, 185 radio stations were operating in Honduras, a 23 percent increase since 1980.[40] The country's mountainous geography and low literacy rates make radio the most important medium there. Surveys of the population showed that only 8 percent read a newspaper on a regular basis, and about 32 percent are illiterate.[41] "Even people who do not have a proper bed own a radio," Rodolfo Dumas Castillo noted proudly.[42]

Although radio stations and radio programming multiplied in response to the country's growing information needs, many of the additional stations were merely repeaters for stations in the capital or San Pedro Sula. For instance, Radio America, generally regarded as the second-most popular network in the country, is broadcast nationwide on a series of seven different repeater stations.[43]

As the country's political history shows, no matter who is in power—the military or civilian politicians—messages flow from the centralized locations of Tegucigalpa or San Pedro Sula, the bases of politics and commerce in the country. Both electronic and print media based in these cities reflect the centralized and oligarchic nature of the Honduran media scene. Although the Honduran education system has significantly cut illiteracy rates in the past generation, some of the lack of newspaper readership can be traced to tumult in the marketplace.[44] For instance, the two leading newspapers of the 1970s, *El Día* and *El Cronista*, do not exist today.

Honduras is undergoing a transition away from a system controlled by the military—a rather closed autocratic oligarchy—to a system controlled by media elites. The military-run system did not allow much space for criticism by the media. In some ways the decades of military dominance affected—and impeded—the development of the media. For example, the prominent media outlets in 1950s Honduras reflected the split between the nation's main political parties, the National and Liberal parties. Each party had a prominent newspaper that served as its voice: the Liberal Party owned *El Pueblo*, and *El Nacional* was the National Party's outlet. The military pressured the parties to close those newspapers in the 1970s. Now, with the passing of another generation and the receding power of the military, another group of newspapers has replaced the favored newspapers of the 1970s.

Although media elites, such as Flores, are now taking control of Honduras, they too have exhibited little patience with those who criticize the system of power or try to reveal too much about its inner workings. Flores faced some criticism in the Honduran media system, but the pressure he applied against his critics, through his connections inside the country's media circles, curbed the usual watchdog role the media need to play in a democracy.

Eventually such a closed system of media control only stifles debate and confines the political spectrum. Honduran politicians say they are working toward democracy in the transfer of power away from the military, but are they really replacing the old system with a new twenty-first-century media junta? In the end, this media system does not bolster democracy but merely supports the transfer of power from military elites to civilian elites in a country that has rarely opened power to truly democratic forces or given voice to the dispossessed, the underemployed, or the uneducated.

Who speaks for the 3 million Hondurans—roughly half the population of the country—who are officially recognized as living in poverty? When the information system converts into a cartel of families with similar interests—groups that are all too willing to censor information for the sake of business interests or personal political goals—those who are not part of that group become dispossessed of their rights in an information society. When Elizabeth Fox wrote about the development of Latin American broadcasting and media systems, she noted: "In those cases where an authoritarian state reached an accommodation with a domestic industry, a strong, monopolistic and increasingly politically autonomous broadcasting industry emerged."[45] In a way Honduras is an aberrant version of that development theory, as families with similar cultural, economic, and historical backgrounds took control of the nation's media system and made some accommodation with the ruling military forces. What they have developed is not democracy, however, but rather a new form of Central American oligarchy.

2 El Salvador's Newly Respun Corporatism

In 1999 El Salvador elected a young new president, and many wondered whether a new generation of leadership would help the country forget its bitter civil war. When he was inaugurated, thirty-nine-year-old Francisco Flores Perez of the ARENA party (the Spanish abbreviation for the National Republican Alliance) pledged a new economic future for the impoverished country.

On the night of his election victory, however, he also wanted the country to remember the past. On that night he invoked the name of his party's founder, the controversial Roberto d'Aubuisson. D'Aubuisson was an ally of the Salvadoran oligarchy who had organized death squads during the civil war and planned the slaying of Archbishop Oscar Romero in 1980.

"Is this a transformation or is he a professional at the service of millionaires?" asked the Reverend Jose Maria Tojeira of President Flores in the *New York Times*. Tojeira is the rector of the Central American University (known as UCA in Spanish) in San Salvador, the country's capital. "ARENA is more moderate than in d'Aubuisson's days. But it's in the hands of rich people who don't favor social change."[1] The same questions might be asked of the new generation of Salvadoran media leaders, and the same doubts would probably be voiced.

When more than thirteen years of war came to an end in the early 1990s, the country moved to remake itself. The media were no exception. The most obvious example of a media organization remaking itself in the postwar era came at the daily newspaper *El Diario de Hoy*. This conservative publication, with a daily circulation of 100,000, embarked on a modernization program in the mid-1990s. Under its executive director, Fabricio Altamirano, the third generation of Altamiranos to lead the publication, *El Diario de Hoy* has become one of the most lively publications in Central America. The newspaper's remake included adding new sections—"Economy and Business," "City News," and "Life," a section for soft news and features—creating a new layout design, and reworking the newspaper's content so that it was less obviously slanted in favor of ARENA.

In 1998 Fabricio Altamirano was the driving force behind the launch of *Mas,* an Altamirano family publication emphasizing sports and entertainment news and aimed at a younger reader. Altamirano's goal was to appeal to young readers who would not read the family's flagship publication. With the country's population getting younger and with young readers spurning newspapers, this was a bold initiative by the U.S.-educated businessman. And the move paid off. Within a year *Mas* became the third-largest newspaper in the country, circulating about 30,000 copies daily.[2]

Just underneath the surface at *El Diario de Hoy,* however, lies the publication's past, represented by Enrique Altamirano, Fabricio's father (the paper was founded in 1936 by Enrique's mother, the matriarch of a prominent family that owned cotton and coffee plantations). The elder Altamirano was a vocal supporter of d'Aubuisson. He often used the paper's editorial space to condemn ARENA presidents for being too moderate. During the worst period of repression in the civil war, several prominent members of opposition groups were killed after being denounced in the columns of *El Diario de Hoy.* Meanwhile, Enrique Altamirano spent much of the war running the paper and filing editorials from the safety of Madrid.

Enrique Altamirano has approved the changes in *El Diario de Hoy* and the launching of *Mas,* but he wants limits to the modernization trend. In his view the publications will continue to support the family's conservative agenda. He compares the publications to a McDonald's franchise: just as the people who buy hamburgers from the fast-food chain cannot impose changes in the company's business practices, the newspaper reader cannot impose changes on his publications' editorial practices.[3]

Altamirano made his comments in direct reference to a proposed law giving people covered in the newspaper the "right of reply," as it is referred to in Central America. Many of the nations on the isthmus have such laws, which allow public figures or others mentioned in news stories some leverage to get their point of view into the newspaper. Most newspaper journalists see such laws as intrusive. Conservative newspaper owners such as Altamirano opposed the law because they thought it would let the country's left wing publicize its views more widely. For years Altamirano opposed any coverage of the nation's left or former guerrillas except in the most negative light.

Such rigid conservatism is common in the political and economic atmosphere of El Salvador, a country ruled by an oligarchy that became notorious during the nation's civil war. El Salvador's elite class, which built its fortunes on the profits of coffee plantations, was known as the Fourteen Families.[4] The name is derived from the fourteen families who were the major landholders at the time of the country's independence from Spain in 1821. Today the Fourteen Families have expanded to include at least 250 distinct groups as part of the oligarchy. When the civil war began, these families, representing about 2 percent of the country's population, controlled more than 66 percent of its land. Many believe the country exploded into civil war because those families refused to reform the oligarchic system and share land and power with the rest of the nation.

Some histories of El Salvador trace the country's land problems back more than a century, to the 1880s. As occurred in Honduras, the economy was shifting in this period to become dependent on one agricultural crop. The Salvadoran economy, however, came to depend on coffee. By 1901 coffee constituted 76 percent of the country's exports. That total continued to grow until 1931, when coffee peaked as the primary crop, accounting for more than 95 percent of El Salvador's exports.[5]

For centuries the oligarchic property owners had moved to repress the nation's indigenous groups and take their land. This process accelerated at the end of the nineteenth century as coffee plantation owners usurped political and judicial power from the colonial village hierarchy imposed by Spanish rule. To back up their seizure of land and power, the coffee oligarchy established a mounted police force in 1889. This was followed in 1912 by the establishment of the National Guard.[6] These police and military organizations eventually evolved from the oligarchy's hired goons into a separate force, although one aligned with the powerful landowners. When a military junta seized control in 1931, the coup marked the transition from the oligarchy's direct control of the presidency to a system of military dictators ruling with the assent of the large landowners.

Members of the oligarchy did not endorse freedom of the press. For instance, in 1960 Ricardo Quiñonez wrote the *New York Times* to complain about that newspaper's characterization of the Salvadoran agricultural elite. In his letter Quiñonez railed against the "unrestricted liberty" of the press.[7] The Meléndez Quiñonez family had ruled El Salvador from 1913 through 1927, more or less as an economic dictatorship cloaked in the powers of a democratically elected presidency. The family had maintained its rule through electoral fraud, economic coercion, and the support of other powerful agricultural families.[8] Eventually the Meléndez Quiñonez family's hand-picked presidential successor tried to stage a fair election. He failed, and the transition to military rule quickly followed.

During the years of military dictatorship, some families of the agricultural oligarchy, such as the Altamiranos, began supporting the military power structure through newspapers. The Altamiranos also linked with successful immigrant families such as the d'Aubuissons and Sols to form political alliances on the far right of the political spectrum. The d'Aubuissons and Sols were part of a wave of wealthy immigrants from France, Germany, and other parts of Europe who settled in El Salvador before the coffee boom of the nineteenth century. These immigrant families invested wisely, prospered, and were accepted as part of the Salvadoran oligarchy.[9]

In the early 1980s, as El Salvador eventually turned to more moderate leaders, some members of the oligarchy moved to form the conservative party ARENA. CIA and National Security Agency reports from the 1980s reveal that rich expatriate Salvadorans in the United States and Guatemala helped finance ARENA, as did ultraconservative elements of Guatemala's agricultural elite.[10]

The class divisions and polarized nature of Salvadoran society were reflected in the media, especially the country's newspapers. During the war years and until its modernization efforts, *El Diario de Hoy* was known as a corrupt, poorly designed propaganda sheet for ARENA's far-right elements. Of El Salvador's top two newspapers, both of which supported ARENA, it was regarded as the ugly sister. Journalists who worked for the paper were often subject to censorship, either from editors who were looking out for the economic and political interests of the oligarchy or directly from government elites. Before its reformation, the pages of *El Diario de Hoy* were like a direct link to the opinion of the Salvadoran army, the conservative legislature, or the d'Aubuisson tendency of ARENA.

Recognizing that Salvadoran readers wanted something different in the postwar era, and reacting to changes at competing newspapers, Fabricio Altamirano brought in a professional from outside the country to give *El Diario de Hoy* a face-lift. Lafitte Fernandez, a Costa Rican, was given the editor's chair and sweeping powers to make changes. As Fernandez said, the younger Altamirano may not have understood journalism—that would be Fernandez's department—but he did understand good business. And his business sense dictated that it was time for generational change.[11]

Instead of simply redesigning the paper, Fernandez first changed the staff. This let him use ideas from the new staff instead of merely imposing his will and thus build team spirit. He began by methodically clearing the newsroom of most of the midcareer journalists, sacking many of them for ethics violations. Most of the replacements were fresh from the university or journalism training programs and in their twenties. The so-called *empiricos* they replaced had little formal training; the *empiricos* had learned the ropes of Central American journalism on the job, and they had been corrupted by the casual bribery rampant in the system years earlier. Fernandez likewise gave pink slips to most of the paper's editing staff, retaining only one of the older editors. Again, he replaced the editors with young, twenty-something upstarts. Some of these new editors and reporters came from outside the country, untainted by the polarized politics of the civil-war era. News staffers began to refer affectionately to the remade organization as "the kindergarten," emphasizing its youthful and fresh approach.

The Altamiranos and their young staff set themselves a goal. Instead of shilling for the oligarchy, the paper would strive to be one of the best in Central America, with a new move toward objectivity. Not only did the Altamiranos buy technology to improve the newspaper's graphics and allow full-color printing; more important, the publication's columns were opened to a wider view of ideas. Stories became more balanced. Themes and personalities that had been banned in the past now appeared on a regular basis.

Like much of the apparent generational shift toward more pluralism and openness in El Salvador, however, the actual aperture for change was smaller than it appeared. When examining the current state of El Salvador's changing media climate, it is important to remember our method, which calls for an examination of the historical context. This history will prove to be the most important factor shaping the country's media system, more important than external pressures. Of course, in the Salvadoran context it may be impossible to untangle domestic forces for change from external forces, usually tied to policy interests of the United States.

During the Reagan administration El Salvador was a focal point of U.S. policy, as Washington overlooked the human rights abuses of right-wing death squads and massacres at the hands of the Salvadoran military to ensure that a leftist insurgency was snuffed out. During the civil war 75,000 people were killed in a small country—about the size of Belgium—with a population of 6 million.[12] The United Nations brokered a peace agreement in 1992. The leftist guerrillas, the Farabundo Martí Front for National Liberation (Spanish acronym, FMLN), became the main opposition group to the conservative ARENA.

When the civil war began, El Salvador's president was General Carlos Humberto Romero. At that time the country had only two television news programs, both of which were tightly controlled and repeated only what General Romero and his associates deemed to be appropriate. For the most part, the definition of news in El Salvador, even in the country's newspapers, was limited to social and commercial news: weddings, birthdays, or store openings. This type of news carried little to no information about the conflict that was engulfing the nation.

There was a twofold reason for this weak news culture. First, the nation's three largest newspapers in the late 1970s (the same top newspapers as today) were owned by families who supported the military government. Also, the news media were accustomed to state censorship. In 1955 the regime of Colonel José Lemus had instituted a program for military censors to review material for use in the newspapers or broadcast media.[13]

That changed in 1984, during the presidency of José Napoleon Duarte, a Christian Democrat (Spanish acronym, PDC) whom Washington backed strongly as a moderating force. During the Duarte era the media began carrying more detailed reports on local and national politics. This reflected the Duarte government's new strategy to control public opinion by offering structured news rather than openly censoring information. This freedom remained limited, however. The government dictated just how far reporters could go and how far publications could push the ideological boundaries.

Journalists nevertheless welcomed even this limited freedom as an improvement over a period when government or military censors actively screened news stories and let only the most innocuous items pass. During the Duarte era the leading newspapers, which were aligned with ARENA, took advantage of the reduced censorship. These papers attacked the Duarte administration for its ineptitude and strongly criticized the way the war was waged. Public support for Duarte, whom many viewed as the Reagan administration's errand boy, began to slip away. Veteran journalists from the civil-war era vividly recall this open period because it was followed by the presidency of Alfredo Cristiani of ARENA, who promptly revived censorship for much of the media.

Some veteran journalists thus fear another retrenchment, despite the current era of openness and change. Some see the current era as a fragile period that will crumble again with the political tides of the country. To these veteran journalists, the changes at *El Diario de Hoy* are merely cosmetic shifts; they do not reflect competition or an opening for freedom of expression but rather stem from political divisions inside ARENA. The changes at *El Diario de Hoy* that allowed for more open discussion of politics in the nation may merely be fallout from these intraparty squabbles. This view seems to support our theoretical approach: what appears to be competition may actually reflect interelite battles inside a changing oligarchic system.

Recent events and reaction to the editorial changes appear to substantiate this view. When the Altamiranos first launched their editorial makeover, other powerful elements in ARENA reacted negatively. Former president Armando Calderón Sol phoned the Altamiranos and accused them of having hired communists as they restaffed the newspaper. The former president and others in ARENA pressured them to remove Fernandez as chief editor and send him back to Costa Rica, but the Altamiranos held firm.

This pressure on *El Diario de Hoy* may have led Enrique Altamirano to have his publication back the Christian Democrats in the presidential elections of 1999. This move belied the popular conception, widespread in the media, that the Altamiranos would always support ARENA and the most conservative candidates. Even though the paper's new leadership sought to create a more objective media outlet, the elections showed retrenchment on that front. Most of the newspaper's positive election coverage still landed in ARENA's column and supported the man who would be president, Francisco Flores, but more than 26 percent of the favorable articles run by the paper seemed to support the Christian Democrats, a ratio far out of proportion to the minor party's showing in the elections.[14] In direct contradiction to the positive coverage given ARENA, and perhaps as a reflection of the divisions inside the party, most of the negative coverage from *El Diario de Hoy* was also aimed at Flores.

The presidential election made it apparent that, despite the modernizing changes of the 1990s, the elder Altamirano would still step into the editorial content of his paper and adjust its spin when he felt like it, just as he had in the past. His fingerprints might be harder to find in the redesigned product that his son's team had created, but they were there.

One of the top editors at *El Diario de Hoy*, Juan Bosco, said that he had to interview Flores secretly during the campaign, because Enrique Altamirano would have been infuriated to discover his journalists reaching out to the ARENA candidate. Bosco divulged that he had to go to the candidate's house late in the evening to ensure that no one learned he was gathering background information on the campaign directly from the ARENA candidate.[15] He also recounted how the elder Altamirano actively worked in the newsroom, reducing the coverage of ARENA and the FMLN.

One reason for the elder Altamirano's decision to intensify the coverage of the Christian Democrats and lend them his support was his own personal animosity toward Flores. On the night of Flores's election victory, the elder Altamirano came to an editorial meeting in an attempt to block a picture of the new president from the front page of *El Diario de Hoy*. Enrique Altamirano argued instead for a front-page picture depicting ARENA supporters celebrating. After much heated discussion, the paper's owner backed down and let his editors run a picture of the new president.

The fight for objectivity had not been easy and was not over. Editors such as Bosco were chastened but still respected the owner, despite his attitudes toward inserting his political views into the newspaper's coverage. "Enrique Altamirano is a person who goes with his principles even if they are not popular," Bosco said, "which is good." But the incident also showed that the days of owners who use their media properties to amplify their personal views were far from over.

During the campaign Flores, a former philosophy professor who had served in the Calderón Sol administration, found himself without many friends in the media. *El Diario de Hoy*'s main Salvadoran competitor, *La Prensa Grafica*, another generally dependable voice for ARENA, became a harsh critic of the candidate.

In 1998 Cecilia Gallardo de Cano, the former ARENA minister of education, was installed as the chief editor of *La Prensa Grafica*. Although she was a highly regarded government minister, she had no background in journalism. Her appointment to the post signaled that she would infuse her positive views on ARENA into the daily coverage. She was also angling for her own presidential bid. When the party denied her the candidacy in 1999, however, she turned on Flores. As with *El Diario de Hoy*, an analysis of the political coverage in *La Prensa Grafica* showed a decidedly split personality. Although the paper gave ARENA more than twice the amount of favorable coverage it gave the FMLN, most of its negative coverage was aimed at ARENA as well.[16]

This was a significant break with the past. Like its main competition, *La Prensa Grafica* had been a reliable supporter of ARENA, a paper where the party's presidential candidates could expect to see only positive coverage. Although the coverage was still mostly positive, the paper's criticisms came as a surprise. Unlike its major competition, however, *La Prensa Grafica* did open its columns to paid editorials placed by ARENA. These so-called *campos pagados* allowed the party to get its unfiltered views into a publication that had once been virtually an intraparty newsletter.

For the better part of a century, *La Prensa Grafica* had been the oligarchy's unfailing mouthpiece. Founded in 1915, the paper had been a

bastion of conservative thought steered by the country's successful Dutriz family. In 1979 the family's holdings, including the newspaper, comprised eleven different companies collectively valued at $1.7 million, and
the Dutriz family was listed among the country's longtime elite.[17]

The family decided to scale down the paper's ideological tone immediately following the civil war. Since 1992 it has undergone its own reform campaign to include more objective reporting, a modern design, and
color printing. The paper owns the largest printing press in the region.
These business changes arguably spurred a reaction from the Altamiranos. Until *El Diario de Hoy* launched its own modernization campaign,
La Prensa Grafica had been considered the country's leading newspaper.

In 1996 the Dutriz family sold its control of the publication, with its
circulation of 100,000, to a group of conservative investors, although the
family retained a minority stake. The Dutriz family still exerts considerable influence in the paper's editorial direction. In 1997 the paper endured a strike by journalists who sought more independence from the
ARENA party line.

Again, the changes at and competition between *La Prensa Grafica*
and *El Diario de Hoy* appear to be the results of political battles inside
the dominant party, ARENA. This supports our belief that competition
may simply reflect a changing oligarchic system and the inter-elite battles within that system. This is not to judge the competition as positive
or negative for El Salvador's media system. (We view competition as a
generally positive factor for the media, except in situations such as the
overcrowded radio spectrum in Central America.) Instead, we hope to
analyze the economic competition for what lies underneath it: the battle for political power inside a nation's oligarchic system. The battle for
change at El Salvador's largest newspapers, for example, reflected internal weaknesses inside the country's dominant political party.

Without a solid wall of support from the nation's two leading newspapers, ARENA lost ground in the legislative elections of 2000. The
FMLN took a slight majority in the country's unicameral legislature.
Consequently, the beginning of the feared retrenchment phase may now
begin as the Altamiranos and Cano both consider how their publications
can best serve the political causes that seem to provide these papers their
raison d'être.

Indeed, some early signs are not positive. In 2001, after a series of
earthquakes rocked the country, *El Diario de Hoy* fell back into an older
pattern of behavior, attacking FMLN politicians and media outlets that
were not solid supporters of ARENA (see chapter 7). Uncharacteristical-
ly, Enrique Altamirano set aside his personal animosity toward President

Flores and became one of the president's strongest backers for his handling of the earthquake crisis. As they had in the war period, *El Diario de Hoy*'s editorial columns became required reading because of Enrique's barbed attacks on the opposition.[18]

Despite that turn toward partisan behavior, political polling in El Salvador since the civil war has consistently revealed the media to be the only institution in the country that has retained some degree of credibility with the populace. Also, despite undercurrents of polarization left over from the civil war, the media are seen as a mechanism for communicating the needs of the wider populace to the oligarchy and the country's political leadership.[19]

Perhaps this trust stems from the complexity of the media scene in El Salvador, which has advanced beyond the level of some of its neighbors. The rich and diverse media landscape allows the populace to sample opinions from more than just the two dominant newspapers.

For instance, the afternoon daily *El Mundo* was founded in 1966 by the Borja family, which has large agricultural holdings and is known for coffee production. In 1971 the family's land holdings comprised 14,591 acres. In 1979 the Borja family, including its branch with the surname Nathan, owned thirty-three Salvadoran companies. The total worth of the Borja/Nathan corporate holdings was listed at $13.3 million.[20]

With a circulation of only 28,000, the Borjas' newspaper took a more centrist, moderate tack to distinguish itself from the larger morning publications, *La Prensa Grafica* and *El Diario de Hoy*. Trade unions, which the morning papers considered to be part of the country's opposition forces during the war, found that *El Mundo* was a receptive site for their advertising and *campos pagados*. As the Dutriz and Altamirano publications became more open to a wider array of opinions, however, *El Mundo* became increasingly conservative. For instance, in the 1999 presidential elections, *El Mundo* surpassed both morning papers for being outwardly pro-ARENA, and it ran twice as many negative pieces about the FMLN as its morning competition did.[21] The paper now tends to reflect the Borja family's political ideals more than when it was founded more than thirty years ago.

The other afternoon paper, *Co-Latino*, is El Salvador's oldest daily, founded in 1890. This publication breaks with the Salvadoran tradition of aligning with the conservative oligarchy and consistently represents left-wing ideology. In 1989, facing mounting debts (which were partially accumulated backing the unsuccessful presidential candidate Julio Adolfo Reyes Prendes), the newspaper's staff formed a cooperative to keep the paper afloat and bought the controlling interest. Since that time European foundations and the FMLN have all contributed to keep *Co-Latino* publishing. The publication has a poor distribution network, however, and may circulate only several thousand copies each day (no reliable figures are available).

The reduction of the left's ability to publish freely in El Salvador was an obvious legacy of the civil war. During the war's early years, the government and military targeted media outlets labeled as helping the opposition. Journalists were hunted by death squads, and the military regarded some publications as enemy installations. Although the Salvadoran civil war boasts a rich history of underground radio stations and publications, the central government first moved to shut down newspapers that merely failed to give their total backing (like the ARENA-inspired morning papers) to the government's antiguerrilla efforts. In 1980 government security forces murdered the editors and staff of *La Crónica de Pueblo* and mutilated their bodies. In 1981 the Salvadoran army destroyed the publishing plant of *El Independiente* and arrested many members of its staff as guerrilla collaborators. After the assassination of Archbishop Romero, the army used dynamite to destroy Radio Católica YSAX.[22]

Co-Latino continued publishing throughout the war and survived as the lone government critic. Nonetheless, the paper's headquarters still show damage from a 1991 firebomb attack at the end of the war.

The reduced influence of leftist and moderate views in the Salvadoran press underscores what we have outlined in our theoretical approach to the media landscape of the region: political developments are the primary factor determining how democratization will shape a country's media system. How can the FMLN hold a slight majority in the nation's legislature yet be vastly underrepresented in the columns of Salvadoran newspapers? Were it not for the systematic destruction of outlets for left-wing and moderate voices during the war, perhaps there would be more equilibrium in the nation's press.

La Prensa Grafica and *El Diario de Hoy* certainly changed their unwavering support of ARENA in the postwar years, but overall they still tended to support the conservative lead of the nation's oligarchy and their conservative owners, despite attempts at modernization. The Dutriz and Altamirano families, although competitors, seemed to buy into the philosophy of Shattuck and Atwood as stated in the previous chapter, namely, that political pluralism, a free press, and space for opposition comments generate a better economic atmosphere and thus a better atmosphere for decision making by entrepreneurs.[23] They were willing to ignore that philosophy when it suited them, however, especially in times of electoral change.

Because only 7 percent of the Salvadoran population get information from the newspapers on a daily basis, these publications reflect the concerns of the nation's elite. As Edward S. Herman and Noam Chomsky note: "The media will depart from elite consensus only rarely and in limited ways."[24] Although there have been changes and controversies within the Salvadoran media, these changes seem to conform to this view, for they have occurred within limited and prescribed contexts. The system of power and dominance is evolving in El Salvador, as it is elsewhere in the region, but the evolution is still guided by factions that held power at the end of the war. In such dynamic systems the media are far from a group of static organisms. The media outlets change, reform, and evolve again because of a multitude of economic, political, and even security factors. Many of these same factors, however, are transforming civil society and the political sphere as well.

Overall this examination of the Salvadoran media tends to substantiate one cornerstone of our model: media systems tend to support and reflect a country's oligarchic tendencies, especially when the nation lacks strong democratic roots. The Flores administration may represent a new generation trying to separate itself from the bloody policies of the conservative oligarchy during the civil war, but it is in fact the third ARENA administration since 1989. Although some factions of ARENA, represented by the major morning papers, were unhappy with Flores, in the end he triumphed. In the overall analysis, most of the nation's newspapers still supported his candidacy, even if they did so grudgingly. ARENA, the party of the conservative oligarchy, still dominated the electoral and media processes, despite the criticisms of a few powerful media owners and managers. This support shows that media owners and leaders are part of the elite group that has pledged itself to support the country's economic oligarchy.

But what of the country's electronic media? A legendary group of underground radio stations operated in El Salvador during the war years: Radio Venceremos, Radio Doble Efe, and Radio Farabundo Martí, among others.

Radio Doble Efe converted into a cooperative run by its workers and various nongovernmental organizations after peace accords were signed in 1992, while the other stations became more traditional commercial concerns.[25] Sinking into the morass of stations—168 stations share the AM and FM radio frequencies in El Salvador—the former supporters of the FMLN soon began to lose their underground and alternative sound, which once catered strictly to the left-wing views that mainstream stations suppressed during the war. To be economically viable in such a competitive atmosphere, the former rebel stations were soon accepting paid announce-

ments from the government and all political parties. Formats were changing too: protest music gave way to mainstream commercial rock.

Radio Sonora, now one of the top three radio networks in the country, was an alternative station during the war. Although not an underground or illegal network, Radio Sonora gave voice to university students,
independent journalists, labor activists, and others who could not find
space in the mainstream media outlets sanctioned by the nation's establishment. Founded in 1961 by Roberto Castañeda Alas, the radio chain
has often opened the airwaves to the full spectrum of political viewpoints
in the country. For disseminating these controversial viewpoints, however, Castañeda was forced to live in exile during the worst part of the
war, although his stations were allowed to continue broadcasting.

Nevertheless, like many opposition elements in El Salvador, after the
war Radio Sonora found capitulating to the powerful to be more profitable
than retaining its earlier philosophy. The corporate approach of ARENA,
which often called for buying out opposition voices in the postwar era,
came knocking on Castañeda's door, especially during the 1999 presidential election. Although Castañeda claimed to program one of the more
independent radio outlets in the country, in the end, he said, he had to
face economic realities.[26]

Flores ran a closed camp during the 1999 elections, avoiding direct
interviews and media coverage at every turn, partially as a reaction to the
critical coverage he received from the country's top daily newspapers. As
a counterweight, ARENA bought coverage on radio stations.

Radio is one of the most cost-effective mechanisms in El Salvador
because 70 percent of Salvadorans get some news, information, or entertainment from the radio on a daily basis. Rates are also relatively cheap,
ranging from two to twenty dollars per minute. Taking those statistics
into full measure, the Flores campaign bought *campos pagados* on the
most popular radio networks but asked the station owners to shield the
fact that the time had been purchased by the party or the campaign. Listeners thus had difficulty distinguishing real news from paid advertisement masquerading as news.[27]

Because ARENA and the Flores campaign purchased large blocks of
time on Radio Sonora, public perception of the station shifted. The station was viewed as pro-ARENA, and indeed, it ran twice as many information programs supporting Flores and ARENA as it did for the FMLN.[28]

In addition, economic concerns beyond the sale of airtime caused
some of the top radio stations to tilt ideologically. Even for popular networks such as Radio Sonora, profit margins are tight. Only 8 percent of
the nation's advertising goes to radio, and it must be shared in an over-

saturated and underregulated environment of 168 different stations. According to Castañeda, media owners predicted that an FMLN victory in the presidential elections would prompt pro-FMLN pirate radio stations, still operating in the countryside after the war, to come down from the mountains.[29] Those stations would inevitably seek legal status and frequencies in the capital, further overcrowding the nation's airwaves.

Some of these fears resemble those expressed by conservatives after the FMLN's first postwar electoral successes in 1997, when the left won control of the mayor's office of San Salvador and first began to loosen ARENA's grip on the legislature. After those wins at the ballot box, various Salvadoran media sources reported some members of the conservative oligarchy had approached military officers about staging a coup, but the generals who had been approached refused to budge.[30]

Media owners had other concerns about the FMLN's electoral advances. Owners are not taxed on profits from their media enterprises in El Salvador, but Castañeda said that many feared an FMLN presidential victory would lead to a series of taxes and other regulatory restrictions of the media. Corporate concerns thus became paramount in the way the electronic media portrayed the election battle.

On popular network Radio YSKL those concerns combined with the *campos pagados* to skew coverage of the election: ARENA and Flores received more than seven times the coverage of the nearest competitor, the FMLN. Some critics in the print media complained that YSKL had sold out its ideals. It was certainly the most egregious example, but no worse than other stations that were similarly willing to take ARENA's money and hide the fact from the public. YSKL news director Nery Mabel Reyes said that at least 80 percent of all her station's coverage of ARENA was due to contractual arrangements with the party.[31] In her opinion it seemed logical that the party willing to pay for coverage would be the party that received special concessions from Radio YSKL, regardless of ideology.

Reyes also said ARENA had a party functionary who worked part-time in the network's news department. Although Reyes said that she recognized the conflict of interest compromising her department, the network's owners had encouraged close cooperation with the party because of its large advertising outlay. The network's owner asked her to overlook the problem. Owner Guillermo Flores, who built the network on sports coverage, is known as a supporter of conservative causes, but in the past he had opened YSKL to a variety of viewpoints.[32]

At RCS Radio one might expect coverage of ARENA to dominate, because members of the Dutriz family, the driving force behind *La Pren-*

sa Grafica, were the principal owners, along with key partner Abelardo Torres. When it was founded in 1996, however, RCS received quite a bit of notice because it combined viewpoints from a wide political spectrum: former guerrillas shared airtime with former army commanders, and editorial views ran the gamut in between. During the 1999 election, however, ARENA received 50 percent more coverage than any of the other parties. Ignacio "Nacho" Castillo, the Chilean-born news director at RCS Radio, argued that the ideological views and business fears expressed by others were not at work at his radio network. Rather, he said, ARENA ran an extremely organized campaign and notified news departments of events, speeches, and rallies days in advance, while the FMLN and the minor parties sometimes gave stations only a few hours' notice.[33] Other news directors gave the same reasoning for some of the imbalance in radio coverage. Whether the reason was organization, economic fears, or monetary enticements, it is hard to ignore how the major radio networks became the voice of the oligarchy during the 1999 campaign. When confronted with this reality, many news leaders in El Salvador merely shrug and say it has been this way for decades.

In a country where only 8 percent had a phone in 1997, and the waiting list for installation bore 300,000 names, radio and television constitute extremely important voice communication media.[34] In El Salvador television has the same penetration as radio, connecting daily with 70 percent of the population. Conservative forces were able to secure the support of the most popular radio stations through a variety of means during the 1999 presidential elections, but they had no such concerns when it came to television, for the dominant broadcaster in El Salvador is Boris Esersky, a longtime supporter of the nation's anticommunist and conservative causes. Esersky opened the first television outlets in 1950, only eight years after Radio YSKL went on the air. He now owns Telecorporacion Salvadoreño (TCS), which includes a three-station group of the country's most-watched television channels.

Esersky and his stations are dominant forces in the media scene in El Salvador. Together his three VHF stations control 90 percent of the nation's viewing audience, leaving his competitors to pick over what little is left. The other two VHF channels in the country, independent Canal 12 and government-owned Canal 10, must cope with single-digit ratings.[35] El Salvador also has six UHF stations, which compete for less than 5 percent of the viewing audience and can be seen only in San Salvador and the city's suburbs.

Media observers in San Salvador compare Esersky to old-school Latin American media titans such as the late Emilio ("El Tigre") Azcarraga

Milmo, who built the Televisa empire in Mexico. As did El Tigre, Esersky pledged himself and his stations to helping his nation's oligarchy preserve its grip on power. Esersky is known for giving large amounts of free television time to his friends in ARENA. He has also ordered his news departments to be responsive to the calls of government officials, who have a virtual veto over the stories to run on Esersky's stations.

Boris Esersky's conservative roots in El Salvador run deep. The Araujo Esersky family has been part of the country's elite for more than a century. (This also connects Esersky to one of ARENA's new generation leaders, Walter Araujo, the majority leader in the country's legislature.) Boris Esersky began as one of the country's radio pioneers. His station, YSEB, was one of the most popular in El Salvador in the 1950s.[36] In 1979 the Araujo Esersky family was listed as owning fourteen Salvadoran companies, with a combined capital worth of $5.3 million.[37] Since that time Boris Esersky has continued to expand the family's media empire.

Esersky's power in the media system is amplified by his ownership of most of El Salvador's leading advertising agencies, public relations firms, and cable television franchises. Esersky also publishes the Salvadoran version of *TV Guide*, along with other specialty magazines. Chemical laboratories (for photo processing) and radio stations round out Esersky's Salvadoran media empire.

Although cable penetration was estimated at only 3 percent in 1997,[38] Esersky removed competitors from the nation's cable systems at his discretion. Esersky's main VHF competitor, Canal 12, does not get access to Salvadoran cable, and neither did Canal 33, El Salvador's all-news channel. Problems with cable access contributed to Canal 33's eventual failure. Through his control of the nation's main advertising agencies, Esersky was also able to ration and squeeze his competitors' access to advertising revenue.

In later chapters we detail how Esersky has used the Salvadoran broadcast system to manipulate the nation's economic and political system. A few remarks are in order here, however, because it is important to understand how Esersky operates to fully understand the Salvadoran media scene. Esersky is one of the major television owners in the region, and his actions have been key elements informing our approach to analyzing the media systems of Central America. Like other media owners, Esersky has tried to protect his media properties against the effects of globalization and international media concentration. By doing so, he has concentrated power in his own nation and tried to create barriers to new owners. His efforts have curbed competition and also undercut democratic forces in El Salvador.

For example, Esersky has tried to stop Mexican investors from expanding their media enterprises into El Salvador. So far his efforts have produced mixed results.

In the latter part of the Calderón Sol administration, when Mexican broadcasters made a bid to buy control of an unused state television frequency, Esersky exerted his political influence, and his political associates blocked the sale.[39] Although El Salvador's former president Armando Calderón Sol promised to bring the station on-line as a state educational channel after the controversy over the blocked sale, nothing happened during his administration.

Nevertheless, Esersky was unable to block the sale of Canal 12 to a consortium headed by Mexico's TV Azteca. Ricardo Salinas Pliego, who owns TV Azteca, has worked to expand his broadcasting empire beyond his home country almost since he entered the Mexican media scene in the early 1990s. Salinas not only succeeded in sparking competition with media giant Televisa in his home country, but he also invested elsewhere in Central America. He became a minority investor in one television channel in Guatemala, and he brought the Mexican media baron Angel González, who controls a monopoly of commercial television stations in Guatemala City (see chapter 5), into his original investment consortium to run Canal 12. Canal 12's founder, Jorge Zedan, and the Salvadoran entrepreneur Armando Bukele became minority shareholders of the station when the sale was structured.[40] González sold his initial stake in the station, but the Mexican television network had firmly won a foothold in what had been exclusively a Salvadoran enclave.[41]

Once the Mexican ownership group was in place, speculation immediately turned to what would happen to Mauricio Funes. Funes is like the Ted Koppel of El Salvador, an analytical journalist with a gift for interviewing who runs the nation's premier morning news interview program. Some in El Salvador call Funes "the national conscience," and with good reason. Funes pioneered the early morning news interview format on Salvadoran television when Canal 12 was founded in 1984. His program featured high-ranking local and national officials along with the nation's leading doctors, teachers, and other professionals. Funes's hard-hitting and lively programs often brought together political enemies in a type of televised debate. The most famous of these programs pitted ARENA's d'Aubuisson against other national political leaders. TCS eventually copied the successful format, and now such programs are a fundamental part of the television scene in El Salvador.

Some of Funes's fans have worried that the tone of his program, which in the past was often critical of the government, softened after the Mexican investors bought Canal 12. Funes, however, has said that criticism is baseless: "There was fear that we would not be as aggressive in our coverage and that we wouldn't criticize certain sectors. But fortunately that didn't happen." He added: "After we signed the strategic alliance with TV Azteca, there has been no instance in which they tried to limit our coverage. We have had complete freedom."[42]

These claims seem to be borne out in the coverage Funes and his program provided during the 1999 presidential election. During the pre-election period, Funes's program gave twice as much positive coverage to the FMLN as it did to Flores, ARENA's victorious candidate.[43] Nevertheless, some media observers in San Salvador believe that Funes has softened his critiques, despite statistical evidence showing that he remains a critic of conservative causes.

These observers see TV Azteca as being more interested in profits than in controversy. They claim that Canal 12's founder, Zedan, turned Funes loose during the civil war years primarily to provide a source for criticism of the government. Zedan's instincts that such a different viewpoint would attract viewers were correct, because despite the dominance of the TCS empire, Funes tends to win his time slot in the ratings. (Zedan, Funes, and TV Azteca further exhibited signs of their motivations in an incident we outline in chapter 7.)

Perhaps the critics are reacting to the other programming moves the Mexican investors made at Canal 12. Controversial programs that once surrounded Funes's interviews have been dropped in favor of Mexican soap operas (*telenovelas*) and other mass entertainment from Mexico City. These programming moves need not indicate sinister designs, because Esersky's TCS has always imported Mexican entertainment programming (which many consider to be richer and more sophisticated than that produced in El Salvador or the rest of Central America), something that Canal 12 could not afford in the past. Some of the criticism aimed at the new Mexican investors may also have resulted from the fact that they were making programming changes for business reasons in a culture that often assumed such changes to have political motives. It soon became apparent, however, that different motivations drove the programming decisions of Canal 12's new owners, who were somewhat oblivious to the political context.

What is also apparent is that the Mexican investment in the Salvadoran system has failed to change the basic equilibrium between stations and their ratings. The most popular stations still reflect the conservative philosophy of Esersky. Programs critical of ARENA and the conservative government are confined to Canal 12, which gets low ratings. Although

Funes's programs gain attention and higher marks, they are still only a minor piece of the broadcast landscape when compared to the hours of conservative thought programmed at TCS. If anything, the Mexican investors have reduced the number of news and information programs on Canal 12, which may have contributed to the perception that the channel has become less controversial since its sale to investors from outside the country.

All of this supports the method we have sketched for analyzing these media systems. As we have noted, owners of media systems will tend to protect their market interests in a nation. This usually means supporting an institutionalized hierarchy or oligarchy rather than opening the media system to nation building, democratic forces, or the true marketplace of ideas. Esersky certainly exhibits these tendencies, both in his support of the conservative oligarchy and ARENA and in his use of those political allies to block competition from outside the nation. This competition posed an outside threat to his comfortable position as the primary broadcaster and, given the penetration of television and his stations' ratings, possibly the most powerful media owner in the Salvadoran system.

We have also noted that transnational media owners must appear nonthreatening to authoritarian or oligarchic forces before they can make major inroads in the national character or ownership structure of a particular nation's media system. The Mexican investors who acquired Canal 12 certainly fit that description. González, who owns considerable media enterprises in Guatemala, has a reputation for befriending powerful conservative oligarchic forces as a way to maintain control of his broadcast properties. (We deal with the details of González's media empire in later chapters.) Likewise, Salinas, the owner of TV Azteca, strongly supports Mexico's Institutional Revolutionary Party (Spanish acronym, PRI), which represented Mexico's oligarchy and ruled that nation for more than seventy years, being toppled only recently. In Mexico Salinas has followed in the wake of Televisa, steering his channel to support the PRI as well. As he sees it, television has no place criticizing the central government. "Television is mainly for entertainment and for women, who belong at home," Salinas said when he acquired TV Azteca in 1993.[44]

In its programming moves TV Azteca has not upset the equilibrium established by Esersky's dominance of the Salvadoran market. It has not muzzled Funes's critical voice, but it has reduced the number of information programs that might have supported similar viewpoints. In the end, TV Azteca's presence has not been a catalyst for change in the system. Until it threatens the primacy of Esersky or his political patrons, it will likely continue to have a presence, albeit minor, in the Salvadoran system.

Esersky's TCS retains its dominance not only because it carries the best Spanish-language syndicated fare, such as the *telenovelas* and dramas from Mexico's Televisa, but also because the three-station group coordinates its program schedule: Canal 2 specializes in *telenovelas*, Canal 4 relies primarily on sports, and Canal 6 airs movies and music events. Each channel has its own unique news programming, but the TCS network news is simulcast on all three channels. TCS can thus bombard Salvadoran viewers with a heavy dose of news skewed toward ARENA, supportive of the government and the status quo. During the recent elections, especially the presidential election of 1999, TCS clearly used these methods in its continued support of the conservative cause.

The media portrayed the 1999 elections as ushering in a new generation of leadership for a country still bearing the scars of a brutal civil war. Although change was the dominant theme in the passing of the baton to young President Flores, his victory actually reaffirmed the oligarchic system that has ruled the country for more than a century.

The Salvadoran media system and its interactions with the nation's political elite suggest new, divergent trends and a move toward diversity in some quarters. Questions remain, however. Will the politicians who claim to support democracy be honest brokers of change, as was the former Mexican president Ernesto Zedillo, or ruthless powerbrokers, as was the former Peruvian president Alberto Fujimori? How will the media owners who support the oligarchy react to a president with sincere intentions to eventually share power with the country's left?

The dynamic fluctuations in the media system result from both internal and external factors. There are generational shifts in leadership both in political entities and at longtime publications such as *El Diario de Hoy*. There are struggles between journalists who want more voice and owners who want those voices to conform to a particular message. There are also generational struggles between the younger journalists who follow the new objective journalism of Lafitte Fernandez and the *empiricos* who remain in the system and who are happy to slant their views. There are competitive struggles between native media and Mexican investors. There is the struggle to realize at least part of the promised democracy, which in turn confronts conflicting market forces. Finally, there is the push and pull between the nation's right and left, the very forces that sparked a civil war. All this is in motion in El Salvador; nothing is static. Yet which of these changes matter? Which new trends will bring an open democracy to this land of uneasy peace?

In the end the violent forces unleashed in the civil war have been penned. The country has donned a business suit and gone off to raise capital. This new corporatism of the government and the conservative right has purchased the souls of some former leftists. Rebel radio is now playing corporate rock, and the populace doesn't seem to mind. The dominance of conservative media means those who refuse to buy into the new corporatist mode are relegated to the fringes of the country's media system.

A full 70 percent of the Salvadoran population are either unemployed or underemployed, however, and the government admits that at least 30 percent of the country live in extreme poverty, without electricity or running water. How long will it be before the old problems explode again, ruining the party for those dressed up in their new corporate suits? Its high murder rate keeps El Salvador among the most dangerous countries in the hemisphere. Such are the signs of the slowly dissipating frustration left over from the last war.

The faux democracy of ARENA and the oligarchy masquerades as pluralism to tamp down dissent, just as the *campos pagados* in Salvadoran election coverage pass as real journalism, real news. This is what Michael Shifter criticizes when he speaks of the anemic qualities of protodemocracies that have sprung up in Latin America. Elections may be held regularly, but when it comes to practicing the rule of law, opening the system to free expression, and facing the critics of government with accountability while inviting the participation of the masses, the new democracies of the region, including El Salvador, come up wanting.[45] With regard to the media, the Salvadoran system must find a way to allow alternative voices a bigger role instead of stifling them in the haze of commercial media owned by large corporate forces; only then will the media become the chorus of divergent opinions that makes up a true democracy.

3 Panama's Media Civil War

The mean season was in full roar in Panama during August 1998. In some parts of the tropics, the mean season is what locals call the rainy season, a time of daily thunderstorms. Each day a drenching storm pummels the region. After the clouds clear away, the country steams under intense sunlight.

During this uncomfortably sticky season, the Panamanian government was exhorting voters to change the country's constitution. Raul Perez Balladares, then the president, was hoping to run for a second term of office, although the constitution prevented it. Pushing through the constitutional change, political operatives reasoned, would give him momentum in the 1999 presidential race.

Evoking the mean weather of the campaign season, Panama's politics are thick with secret agendas, overheated rhetoric, and vicious vendettas. Barely more than a week before the referendum, the mean season came calling for Juan Luis Correa Esquivel, the general manager of Panama's most profitable paper, *La Prensa*. Federal police raided Correa's home and searched his business car. They confiscated an Uzi submachine gun and other weapons during the search. The authorities said the search had been sparked by a formal complaint from Correa's wife, who accused her husband of domestic abuse. All this was splashed across the front page of Correa's main competitor, *La Estrella de Panama*, just a week before the election.[1]

A casual observer might have seen a sensational story and nothing more. Critics of the Perez Balladares administration, however, noted the way *La Estrella,* Panama's one progovernment newspaper, handled the piece: it took up most of the front page, was accompanied by two images (one a manufactured photo collage that layered a picture of *La Prensa's* offices, a profile of Correa, and a modeled photo of a handgun), and included a front-page editorial condemning Correa. The entire affair could have been coincidental, but many Panamanians recognized the story and the search as a political cheap shot. They knew that Perez Balladares's Democratic Revolutionary Party (Spanish acronym, PRD) was once run by the dictator General Manuel Noriega. They also remembered that Noriega's party has a reputation for playing dirty. Correa's reputation thus became a casualty in the rough and tumble of the campaign.

The sensational story and federal raid were suspect because of their timing as well. Two weeks before the plebiscite, polls showed the proposed constitutional change losing popularity with voters. With Perez Balladares's shot at a second term looking dimmer, the president decided to lash out at his media critics. *La Prensa* was at the top of his list. Perez Balladares had accused *La Prensa* of manipulating the news to campaign against the referendum. These charges came just a few days before the raid on Correa.

This was not the first salvo the Panamanian president had fired at the media during the campaign. He was not above using his allies at *La Estrella* to organize his own media campaigns to sway the nation's opinion.

The nasty rivalry between *La Estrella* and *La Prensa* is an intense feud that reflects both the deeper, polarized nature of Panamanian politics and the way the media were treated during the years of dictatorship and earlier. As we have noted before, a nation's political history is the primary force shaping its current media climate and level of democracy. In the case of Panama, the Noriega dictatorship and subsequent U.S. invasion, dubbed Operation Just Cause, still loom large in the nation's politics and media.

Nevertheless, the polarization in Panamanian politics, society, and media stretch further back in the nation's history, at least to the 1960s and one crucial event. In 1968, just eleven days after he was elected president, Dr. Arnulfo Arias Madrid was overthrown by General Omar Torrijos and the Panamanian National Guard. Although this was the third time Arias had been deposed by military forces, it would not be his last attempt at a political comeback. Torrijos's successful coup, however, and the intervening decades of military power resonated through Panama's political structures and media, as the military built a political party to support its cause and aligned itself with conservative members of the nation's oligarchy, who in turn controlled key media outlets.

The Torrijos coup was a major milestone in Panama's history, a record littered with military takeovers, political assassinations, riots, and instability before the decades of dictatorship. The Torrijos regime attempted to enforce stability on this roiling political scene and end the political career of Dr. Arnulfo Arias. Arias was a populist politician who dominated the Panamanian political scene for a generation. He was a major candidate in five presidential elections, losing two of those contests in a clouded atmosphere of fraud.

The Arias family was regarded as a cornerstone of Panamanian society. The family played a key role not only in the revolt that broke Panama from Colombia in 1903 (and let it become a pawn in the United States' plans for a transoceanic canal), but also in the country's oligarchy.[2]

Like the *turcos* of Honduras and the so-called Fourteen Families of El Salvador, the Panamanian oligarchy had a popular moniker: the Twenty Families. Although the number of families sometimes came into dispute, the list always included the Arias clan, with its holdings in cattle and coffee. The Arias family produced leaders in society, business, and politics, and it eventually branched into media holdings, setting the tone for the future in that field, too.

Besides practicing law, Dr. Harmodio Arias Madrid invested in a Spanish-language newspaper, *El Panamá América*, in 1928. The paper was partially a translation of a now-defunct English-language newspaper, *The Panama American*, which began publishing in 1925. As a prominent lawyer and publisher, Harmodio Arias launched a successful bid for the country's presidency. During his presidency Harmodio Arias renegotiated Panama's status so that the country at least temporarily avoided the status of U.S. protectorate. At the end of his presidency, in 1936, Harmodio Arias officially retired from politics, and turned his energies to his newspaper. By 1938 the Arias clan had bought out Nelson Rounsevell, the English-language paper's founder, to begin expanding the family's media holdings.

Harmodio Arias used both newspapers to support his brother, Arnulfo Arias, in his 1940 bid for the presidency. In his short time in office, Arnulfo Arias tried to remake the Panamanian government. He pushed through constitutional reforms, created a social security system, strengthened labor laws, and gave women the right to vote.[3] Arnulfo Arias also championed new laws with racist intent, however, and worked to block expansion of U.S. military bases beyond the Canal Zone in the tense period before the United States entered World War II. Some members of the Panamanian elite, upset with the reforms, felt Arnulfo Arias had fascist leanings, although the president had pledged to reform and reduce the influence of the nation's military.[4] As was inevitable, the military, some factions in the Panamanian elite, and Arias's political enemies conspired to overthrow him, nine months after he took office, with the blessing of the U.S. State Department.[5]

In an election marred by fraud and violence, Arnulfo Arias again won the presidency in 1948. Rioters, spurred on by thugs paid by his political opponents, then protested the victory by attacking the offices of *El Panamá América*, his brother's newspaper. The Arias family's opponents and the military conspired to keep the family out of the presidential palace and anointed Domingo Diaz Arosemena, Arias's opponent and the preferred choice of the United States, as the victor. When Diaz Arosemena died, his coalition collapsed amid violence and political infighting, and Arnulfo Arias returned from exile in Costa Rica to regain the presidency in 1949.[6] In 1951, however, another military coup again unseated Arias.

Colonel Jose Antonio Remón, who pushed Arias aside, went on to win the nation's 1952 elections but was later assassinated at a Panamanian dog track. One of Remón's vice-presidents, Jose Ramón Guizado, was implicated in the shooting, but the Panamanian Supreme Court set aside his conviction. In the tumult Ricardo Arias Espinosa (who was not directly related to the Arias Madrid branch of the family) assumed the presidency.[7] As president Ricardo Arias loudly protested U.S. moves to block Panama from international conferences, especially those relating to political issues involving the Panama Canal.[8] President Arias had little international influence, however, and the original 1903 canal treaty gave the United States sovereignty over the waterway.

During the 1950s the Arias Madrid branch of the family was expanding its media enterprises. Dr. Gilberto Arias, Harmodio's son, started Panama's most popular newspaper, the tabloid *Crítica*. Rosario Arias de Galindo became the clan's media leader in 1962 when her father, Harmodio, died and she acquired control of his shares in the publishing company.[9]

In 1968 Arnulfo Arias again decided to run for the presidency. General Bolivar Vallarino, the commander of the National Guard and a leading member of one of the Twenty Families, organized a campaign to harass Arias's supporters and substitute fraudulent ballots at the polls.[10] Arias nevertheless won by a landslide, despite General Vallarino's plans. Only eleven days after taking office, Arias was again deposed, this time in a coup organized by Omar Torrijos.

With the coup by Torrijos and the National Guard came wrenching change. Members of the Arias clan were forced into exile, and the government seized control of the family's newspapers. Military dictatorships held the family's property for the next two decades. The military also closed two radio stations with close business ties to Arnulfo Arias.[11]

The Torrijos regime extended its control of the media throughout the country. After the coup Torrijos issued an emergency decree establishing media censors and ordered the closure of two non-Arias newspapers. The government also reserved the power to select editors for privately held media companies.[12] In 1975, when commentators at Radio Impacto tried to test the limits of free speech, the Torrijos regime shut down the radio station as well.[13]

In the late 1970s, however, as his regime renegotiated the Panama Canal Treaty with the United States, General Torrijos created openings for the country's political opposition. In part a public relations gesture to give the dictator leverage in his negotiations with the United States, the move nevertheless created a real political opening. Opposition parties were allowed to form, their rallies were tolerated, and the media were freed to voice more criticism. The country saw an influx of returning exiles, including Roberto Eisenmann Jr., the principal founder of *La Prensa*. Eisenmann formed an investment group comprising representatives of various opposition political factions, including Ricardo Arias Calderón, a leader of the country's Christian Democrats (PDC), and Ricardo Alberto Arias.[14]

Torrijos did not move to block the new paper because he felt it would fold after its first year. He needed to let Eisenmann and his investors work at founding the paper to give the illusion that a free press could exist in Panama. Torrijos intended to play a hidden ace, however: the government, the nation's largest advertiser, would refuse to do business with the fledgling paper. Panama's *Editora Revolucionaria*, the official government newspaper, was losing about $1.2 million annually at the time. Torrijos's math told him that without key advertising support, Eisenmann's investment group could not bear such financial losses for long. The *La Prensa* group had managed to raise more than $1 million to start the paper, however, and they had set aside $250,000 as an emergency fund to deal with losses.[15] This was enough to keep the paper afloat until its second year of operation, when it began to make a profit.

In 1980 the paper emerged as the key voice of opposition to the Torrijos regime, and for the next eight years the battle was joined. Not surprisingly, the pattern set by the Arias family's *El Panamá América* was repeated in the clash between reformist ideas, represented this time by *La Prensa* and its political backers, and the conservative elites maintained by the military. Politically motivated mobs (known as *turbas* in Central America) organized by the PRD attacked the newspaper's offices and employees on a variety of occasions. The newspaper was also harassed by paramilitary groups aligned with the National Guard. The National

Guard occupied the newspaper on numerous occasions, installed military censors to screen its stories, and shut down its operations for extended periods. Finally, in a crackdown by the Noriega regime in 1988, the paper was closed altogether, and by that point many of its owners, editors, and writers had been forced back into exile. (Even from exile in Miami, however, Eisenmann put together a network of people willing to receive and copy a special version of *La Prensa*. He distributed this clandestine newsletter via computer modem and fax machine.)

During the same period the military was cracking down on radio operations as well. The Torrijos and Noriega regimes closed various stations for criticizing the government. During the Noriega era Radio KW Continente, the main opposition voice on the radio waves, was bombed by the military and subsequently closed.

After the United States invaded Panama in 1989 and arrested Noriega, the media climate was again transformed. It is no wonder that Panamanians tend to mark most events as happening either before or after the invasion, because it was the catalyst for major political and social shifts. The Arias family regained control of its newspapers; *La Prensa* was allowed to print again; and the Correa family, one of the nation's broadcasting pioneers, rebuilt their bombed-out studios, restarted their transmitter, and again took to the airwaves on Radio KW Continente.

Key media outlets had openly sided with the military regimes during their two decades in power, however. The Duque family's *La Estrella* had become the primary voice supporting the Torrijos regime in the 1960s. In addition, the families controlling the nation's main television outlets, Canales 2 and 4, had supported the military governments. These media outlets continued to support the PRD and became staunch competitors against the rejuvenated voices of the previously suppressed media outlets.

These political divisions among the media have continued through the present, even though more than a decade has elapsed since the U.S. invasion and both sides—the promilitary PRD and the various opposition parties—have shared electoral power. The media were not the only sector that had been shaped by the divisive preinvasion climate. Despite the invasion, Panama's politics continue to resonate with the polarization of the past. Sometimes it is difficult to separate the media from the politics. For instance, Juan Luis Correa Esquivel, the general manager of *La Prensa,* was a former leader in the underground opposition to General Noriega.[16] For years after the invasion, Correa said, he received threatening phone calls from backers of the military regime who did not like his paper's editorial policies. This might explain why he possessed various firearms and became the target of the previously mentioned federal police search during the 1998 referendum campaign.

To show their continued resentment of *La Estrella* for its support of the military regimes, for years the staff at *La Prensa* has refused to interact with journalists from the pro-PRD publication. For example, in Panama's informal baseball league for journalists, *La Prensa*'s team refuses to take the field against players from *La Estrella*. Editors at *La Prensa* have openly cheered *La Estrella*'s circulation problems since the invasion and publicly voiced hopes that the paper would disappear. Those same editors have accused *La Estrella* of giving voice to promilitary or fascist elements in Panamanian society even today.

But it seems that as long as the Duque family, which owns *La Estrella*, continues to reap political benefits from the publication, it will continue to publish the paper. The oldest paper in the country, *La Estrella* is generally regarded as a publication meant to support the political views of its owner, Tomas G. Altamirano Duque, who served as a vice-president in the Perez Balladares administration.

La Estrella, founded in 1853, was part of a corporation that also published the now-defunct English-language *Panama Star and Herald*. Jose Gabriel Duque became the paper's publisher and principal owner in 1894. The newspaper has been in the Duque family ever since and was once Panama's premier publication. Since the invasion, however, *La Estrella*'s circulation has shrunk to less than a third of what it was during the Noriega era, printing only 6,000 copies daily.

Although the paper's popularity problems have been tied directly to the sinking electoral fortunes of the PRD, the party it unflaggingly supports, *La Estrella*'s editor, James Aparicio, blamed his paper's problems on what he called anticompetitive business measures instituted by his competition.[17] Aparicio claimed that his competitors get advertisers to sign exclusive contracts that block the firms from advertising with *La Estrella*. Aparicio further believes that some advertisers have signed partially restrictive contracts allowing them to place ads in a variety of media outlets but not *La Estrella*, thus steering advertising revenue away from his paper "like a boycott." This advertising war is just another example of the rancor left over from the politics of the preinvasion era.

The ultracompetitive advertising climate does not fully explain *La Estrella*'s circulation nosedive, however. Many news distributors in Panama refuse to handle the paper because it was seen as the voice of the unpopular Perez Balladares administration and the military regimes. The paper's managers admit that not all their problems are tied to advertising practices and realize that they must fix their distribution and circulation problems if the newspaper is to be anything more than a media front for the political ambitions of Altamirano Duque.

The newspaper nevertheless retains a core audience because a sizable portion of the population has traditionally supported the PRD and dictatorships. PRD supporters view the various opposition parties as a rabble of confusion and disarray with no coherent central voice, said Aparicio: "If you listen to the opposition, you can go mad with all their different directions and theories." PRD supporters complain about the slow speed at which democracy works, and they long for a strong central figure to take decisive measures. This is why Perez Balladares consistently maintained the image of a strong, uncompromising leader. No wonder his nickname was "El Toro," the bull.

Some of *La Estrella*'s advertising and circulation problems have resulted from increased competition in both the Panamanian market and the PRD. A moderate faction of the Duque family (led by Juan Carlos Duque, Carlos Duque Zerr, Tomas Gerardo Duque Zerr, and others) decided to start its own publication, *El Universal de Panamá*, in 1995. (Although some in this faction are now regarded as moderates, they were considered close associates of General Noriega during the dictatorship.) With the growing popularity of *El Universal*, the fortunes of *La Estrella* began to wane.

Instead of taking a partisan line, the Duques who started *El Universal* wanted a paper known for its objectivity. Slowly, once the journalistic community realized that the paper would not be simply another party mouthpiece, they began to attract some of the country's top journalists to their new publication. In a move unusual for a Central American publication, the Duques also brought an ombudsman aboard the newspaper.

As in many Central American countries, however, newspaper readership here is low—only about 10 percent of the population read a paper on a daily basis—making it hard for *El Universal* to make inroads in the market. With their paper's circulation ranging between 7,000 and 10,000 copies daily, the Duques sold the controlling interest to entrepreneur Martin Rodin. The family kept a minority stake in the publication, however, and many family members retained management positions.

The Duque family's principal rivals in the newspaper business are the same rivals they have faced for the better part of a century within the country's oligarchy: the Arias family. In the postinvasion years the Arias family's two papers, *El Panamá América* and *Crítica*, regained their strong circulations, and *Crítica* (briefly renamed *Crítica Libre* after the postdictatorship government restored the publication to the family) became the country's highest-circulation newspaper, serving 40,000 readers daily. *Crítica* is one of Panama's low-brow tabloids, but the Arias family uses profits from it to keep the flagship paper, *El Panamá América,* afloat. *El Panamá América,* with a daily circulation of about 19,000, is a venerable newspaper of record and tends to steer politically into the progressive reformist politics the family has promoted for decades. Rosario Arias de Galindo, the publisher responsible for both publications, feels her newspapers are popular because the population trusts them as a source of information.[18]

When it comes to circulation, the Arias family faces stiff competition from the tabloid *El Siglo,* which depends heavily on sensational fare along with occasional investigative reports. This newspaper, started by the Padilla family in 1985, was also shut down during the Noriega era. The Padilla family claims that their publication circulates at least as many copies as *Crítica,* if not more, but most observers believe *El Siglo*'s circulation figures are inflated to attract more advertising. (This is a common practice in Central America. The Panamanian market has no single independent arbiter of circulation figures.) Most observers peg *El Siglo*'s daily circulation at 25,000 copies.[19]

The leading newspaper for investigative reporting is certainly *La Prensa,* which was often named one of the best newspapers in Latin America in the 1990s. The paper was the first Panamanian daily printed in color and the second daily in Central America with an internet site. During the past decade *La Prensa* has won numerous Central American journalism awards for the work of its investigative team. This team has generally focused on detailing human rights abuses during the Noriega regime. *La Prensa*'s management credits the newspaper's current popularity with its criticism of the dictatorship during the Noriega era (just as the Arias family publications and other media outlets enjoy popularity because of their strong stand against the dictatorship). The paper circulates to 35,000 readers daily and sells more advertising space than any other periodical in the country. "Some days the paper looks like the yellow pages, it is so fat with ads," noted Jaime Padilla Beliz, the publisher of *El Siglo.*[20] Envious journalists and media observers have compared *La Prensa*'s success to the popularity of Coke in Panama; like the soft drink, the newspaper can apparently do no wrong.

La Prensa is fairly unusual in Panama and in Central America because it lists more than 1,300 shareholders as its owners. Shareholders are prevented from owning more than 1 percent of the paper. This unique structure has freed the paper from many of the economic conflicts that plague other papers. Without a strong owner tied to other enterprises, as are the media owners of Honduras, the journalists at *La Prensa* theoretically have more liberty to write about and investigate the nation's businesses and entrepreneurs. The company proudly boasts of its profit-sharing and stock-ownership plan for its regular employees, who make the highest salaries in the market. Indeed, salaries are high enough to attract employees from radio and television. The paper also provides insurance and other benefits, which is uncommon for dailies in the region. Finally, the paper's management and board of directors have tried to practice a form of civic journalism in Panama. In the charged Panamanian media climate, however, this style of activist journalism—controversial in the United States—has often been viewed as activism for the sake of the powerful on the newspaper's board of directors.

La Prensa's management has often portrayed the paper's content as some of the most objective journalism available in Central America. Because the paper does not have a single owner, the management frequently characterizes it as being beyond reproach and above the political fray, but some in the government and at *La Prensa*'s competitors see it differently. Aparicio, the editor of *La Estrella*, still one of *La Prensa*'s intellectual adversaries, accused his competitor of warping news or ignoring items that reflected badly on the nation's opposition parties during the Perez Balladares administration.[21] Nevertheless, Indalecio Rodriguez, the ombudsman at *El Universal*, defended *La Prensa*. "I think they would oppose whoever is the president, whoever is in power, no matter what the party," he said. "Isn't that the role for a leading newspaper in a democracy?"[22]

In fact, it is not always easy to analyze *La Prensa*'s role in Panama's media system from its content and its management's statements of editorial philosophy. Former reporters for the newspaper have criticized the publication's powerful board of directors for sometimes steering coverage to support their political and economic concerns, despite representations to the contrary. Many of the paper's founders and board members have played key political roles in Panama. For instance, Ricardo Arias Calderón, a PDC member who served as a vice-president in the administration of President Guillermo Endara immediately after the invasion, was a founding member of *La Prensa*'s board, although he resigned that position before taking office (the paper was closed at the time because the Panamanian National Guard had damaged its printing plant). In 1994 *La Prensa* strongly backed the unsuccessful presidential bid of one of its board members, Rubén Darío Carles.[23]

While in exile during the Noriega era, one of the paper's founders, Roberto Eisenmann, certainly went beyond the typical role of a journalist by lobbying members of the Reagan administration to intervene militarily in Panama.[24] As a journalist in exile, Eisenmann had every right to lobby for a return to freedom of expression and other civil liberties in his homeland, but members of the U.S. government saw him as a political activist and businessman first and only secondarily as the leader of an anti-Noriega newspaper.

Although Eisenmann has severed his official ties with the newspaper he started, he remains influential there and respected by the paper's management. Eisenmann went on to serve as a key adviser to President Mireya Moscoso, an ardent opponent of the PRD.[25]

The newspaper sector of Panama's media landscape clearly reflects a divided oligarchy. Part of the oligarchy pressed for various reforms, including more democratic forms of government, and stood against the country's militarization and tyrannical dictatorships. Today's popular publications in Panama likewise express those views. Powerful elements in the nation's oligarchy nevertheless continue to support political elements that backed the dictators and militarism. Some of the nation's newspapers continue to express those views. The account thus far shows that the oligarchy has included—and continues to include—leaders of the nation's media, not unlike the *turcos* of Honduras. The Panamanian system seems more advanced, however, and less closed to entrepreneurs and business leaders from outside the ultraelite. Thus the Padilla family and businesspeople such as Eisenmann have left deep marks on the system. Again as in Honduras, a faction of the Panamanian media leadership aligned itself politically with elements prone to supporting the nation's military; as were their counterparts in Honduras, these elements were treated with disdain and contempt from other sectors of society. The staff of *La Estrella* thus became media pariahs because of the Duque family's support for the dictators and the PRD.

The Panamanian context differs, however, in the way both the civilian government and the United States reacted to this polarization. Since the invasion Panama has disbanded its military. Some would say this was Arnulfo Arias's dream realized almost sixty years later. No such move is underway in Honduras. Similarly, the United States, although drastically reducing its support for the armed forces in Honduras, has not moved to crush the military as it did in Panama.

Some might see the United States' direct intervention in Panama as disproving the principle we have advanced, namely, that political developments matter more than external pressures in shaping a country's media system. As stated by the administration of President George H. W. Bush, the goal of Operation Just Cause was to restore democracy in Panama and bring General Noriega to justice for his role in the international drug trade. Certainly the invasion has done more to resurrect an atmosphere of freedom among the media in Panama than has any other single event, allowing a critical opposition press again to function in Panama.

If anything, Panama helps us further define our meaning in regard to these external pressures. One might reasonably argue that U.S. foreign policy has been the most important factor in the region's history, especially since this policy was often backed by the unparalleled might of the U.S. armed forces. The United States not only shaped Panamanian history but actually carved the country from Colombia, making it almost impossible to separate U.S. foreign policy from domestic political forces in any account of Panama's evolution. Indeed, one might argue that the U.S. military intervention was not external but simply an outgrowth of the relationship the United States created when it pressed to create the Canal Zone and took a piece of Panama as its sovereign territory.

Our definition of external pressures for democratization, however, does not include the use of force to create a fertile field where free expression can sprout. Instead, our model includes in this category programs, such as those advanced by NGOs, foundations, and even the U.S. State Department, to build civil society or market support for free expression. Compared to the invasion, these programs have done little to create an atmosphere for democracy in Panama. Indeed, in that respect the invasion should be seen as part of the political schema that created the current media atmosphere in Panama and thus reinforces our foundational principle that such developments are more important than current global forces or other external forces in shaping the country's media system.

The examples cited also support our contention that media systems in nations that lack strong democratic roots tend to support and reflect oligarchic tendencies. In Panama many of the current media leaders belong to the nation's oligarchy. Even in the postinvasion era, presidents have either belonged to the oligarchy (Perez Ballardares) or had strong links to it (Moscoso).

Panama also reinforces our conjecture that apparent competition inside a media system may reflect nothing more than interelite battles in a changing oligarchic system. Panama's history of conflict among political and economic elites, exemplified in *El Panamá América* and *La Estrella*'s pitched ideological battles over the candidacy of Arnulfo Arias in the predictatorship years, clearly shows that polarization and division existed and continues to exist within the Panamanian oligarchy. The political opening forced by the Carter administration during Panama Canal Treaty renegotiations renewed those divisions, this time between *La Prensa*, the voice of the opposition, and *La Estrella*, the newspaper that speaks for the sector of the oligarchy backing conservatism and militarism.

Although we advocate multiple voices and differing viewpoints reflected through media competition, the battles of Panama's media civil war bring so much intensity into the political system that this debate is often a destructive and polarizing force. As we note later in our discussion of corruption in the Panamanian media system, only once these media systems begin to replace their partisan ways with a stronger professional demeanor will the media be able to move away from the country's divisive political culture.

Already raging for decades, this seesaw battle between different elite factions in Panama has yet to be resolved. *La Prensa* not only carried this ideological media battle into the present but also spread it more widely by serving as a counterweight to the conservative elements that controlled Panama's electronic media. The paper remains the leading critic of some electronic media owners who were allied with conservative elements in the nation's oligarchy and the PRD.

During the years of dictatorship, one of the nation's top television stations, Canal 4 (founded in 1961), and the leading radio news station, RPC Radio, were owned by the Eleta family, which supported the military regime. Various members of the Eleta clan also served as leading politicians and bureaucrats in Panama and usually were part of the anti-Arias coalition. The story is typical, for the nation's broadcasting system was shaped largely by families, such as the Eletas, that supported authoritarianism. Other political opponents of the Arias clan included the Chiari family, which controlled Canal 2 (founded in 1964), the country's other main television outlet. The Chiaris, too, numbered among Panama's leading politicians. Although neither family was considered part of the Twenty Families oligarchy, they supported the Duque faction of the elite.

In 1983, during the Noriega era, a third prodictatorship television network began broadcasting. This network, Canal 13, was owned by Nicolás González Revilla, who had been Panama's ambassador to the United States during the Torrijos regime.[26] González Revilla was a powerful businessman and politician with direct ties to the nation's oligarchy. These historical ties to the oligarchy and the support of authoritarian governments continue to inform the editorial content of Panama's television system.

In the postinvasion years González Revilla merged his operations with the Eleta family's media holdings to create the media conglomerate known as MEDCOM. MEDCOM not only controlled the most popular television stations and the top radio news station in Panama; it also owned a monopoly on the country's cable television system through its subsidiary, Cable Onda 90.[27] González Revilla became MEDCOM's president.

In Panamanian media circles MEDCOM's powerful grip on broadcasting was referred to simply as "the monopoly," and with good reason. MEDCOM's two national television channels control, on average, 72 percent of the viewing audience.[28] As in El Salvador and many other parts of the isthmus, a single dominant broadcasting entity had evolved, and predictably that entity would use its power to guard its position in the market.

During the Perez Balladares administration, a U.S. cable television firm attempting to open a division known as Cellular Vision de Panama (CVP) accused González Revilla of colluding with the president to block it from doing business in Panama.[29] Perhaps they had reason to suspect collusion: not only is the Perez family a member of the powerful Twenty Families oligarchy, but Perez Balladares and González Revilla are cousins—in fact, Perez Balladares was an investor in his cousin's television operations during the 1980s.[30]

La Prensa derided and criticized the moves by González Revilla and the Eletas to consolidate their media power. Investigative editor Gustavo Gorriti wrote critically about the media mergers and subsequent government decisions favorable to MEDCOM's powerful position. (See chapter 8 for more details on Gorriti's views and the fallout from his criticisms.) "Vertical integration of the media is much more dangerous here than in the States," Gorriti said. "The effect of the acquisition of independent media by one source runs at counterpurposes with the quality of journalism. How can a journalist report when they are controlled by those who represent the most powerful political sectors?"[31]

La Prensa passed up several opportunities to expand into electronic journalism. In the postinvasion years, when the Chiaris sold Canal 2 to a consortium (TVN—that is, Televisora Nacional) aligned with the PRD's opposition, the newspaper's board chose not to invest in the national network. The paper's general manager, Correa Esquivel, said the board declined to move in that direction because it believed that a multiplicity of media voices bolsters a democracy.[32]

Control of Panamanian television has grown in importance with the medium's increasing influence. Television penetration of the market is more than 70 percent (González Revilla estimated it closer to 80 percent), with 60 percent of the nation's poor able to afford a television set.[33] A population's ability to afford a television and electricity is, of course, important to the medium's reach. In addition, Panama's underprivileged population has been smaller than its neighbors': official government figures posted the poverty rate at 37 percent, with 21 percent living in extreme poverty with few resources.[34]

The importance of television in Panama, one of the richest markets in Central America, is also directly related to its power to draw advertising revenue. In the years immediately following the invasion, television billed $30 million in advertising annually and was expanding rapidly. In fact, it controlled 53 percent of the nation's advertising revenue.[35]

MEDCOM controls the lion's share of advertising revenue and is free to set its own price because it enjoys a near monopoly and because, as in the print arena, there is no independent ratings arbiter for television. Advertising rates for TVN, the nearest competitor, which averages 18 percent of the viewing audience, are keyed to MEDCOM's rates. MEDCOM thus has uncommon economic leverage in the market. The remaining two stations, the Catholic church's FETV and the educational station of the University of Panama, are not part of the advertising equation because they operate as nonprofit businesses.

At one time the U.S. military provided some competition by broadcasting English-language programming in the Canal Zone. Those frequencies were returned to the Panamanian government at the end of 1999, however, when the canal reverted to Panamanian control. González Revilla said the main reason for the merger to create MEDCOM was anticipation of additional competition once those frequencies were redistributed. Although González Revilla has signed programming and news cooperative agreements with Mexico's Televisa, this was one of the outside investors that he feared entering the market. Mexico's upstart TV Azteca network was also viewed as a possible competitor. González Revilla cited still other international broadcasters as potential rivals: the powerful Venezuelan TV programming and broadcasting entity Grupo Cisneros; Angel González González, the Mexican media baron with monopoly control of television in Guatemala and holdings throughout Central America; and the Miami-based Spanish-language network Univision (which is also partially owned by Mexico's Televisa). Other broadcasters from the United States are also potential competitors. AOL/Time-Warner (with its HBO franchise and CNN), Disney (with ESPN), and Viacom (CBS) all have small footholds in the region with Spanish-language versions of their services on cable television. As it does elsewhere in Central America, cable television penetration remains limited in Panama—only 3 or 4 percent of the market—but any of those concerns would provide formidable competition were they to acquire one of the nation's open television frequencies.

Despite criticism from his domestic critics, González Revilla cited all these potential broadcasting adversaries as the reason for creating MEDCOM. "We have very complex reasons for our business plan. We must perfect our joint operations before someone from the outside can come into Panama and take advantage," he said. Correa Esquivel scoffed at that explanation. He said listing all the potential investors for the country's open frequencies was a convenient cover for a strategy that calls for buying up more broadcast properties, manipulating ad rates to MEDCOM's advantage, and filtering more of the political views abhorrent to the nation's oligarchy from the airwaves.

The concerns about MEDCOM's alignment with the PRD government have lessened with the end of the Perez Balladares administration. Although González Revilla's familial connections to the party and the former government are more obvious than similar connections of powerful media owners in other parts of the region, MEDCOM's stations slant their content far more subtly than do stations elsewhere in Central America where dominant broadcasters have aligned themselves with conservative elites.

Panama offers some of the region's best programming; its television is far more advanced than that of neighboring countries such as Honduras or Guatemala. Panamanian television news usually avoids the tabloid sensationalism that often characterizes television news in the region. Most of the news and information programs are serious and issue oriented. "We don't have to be negative to cover what is important," González Revilla noted. Despite the criticism from his political opponents, MEDCOM stations do attempt to provide balanced coverage, at least on the surface. Unlike other networks in Central America, where the voices of dissent are never heard, the MEDCOM stations feature comments from the full range of Panama's political spectrum.

Seasoned media observers are nevertheless able to pick up the occasional subtle shading in news and information programming on MEDCOM's broadcasting outlets. Supporters of the PRD said that the bias has appeared in the decisions MEDCOM reporters have made when choosing whom to interview for stories. The reporters often interviewed people who backed the PRD or the oligarchy even though they had no special expertise and were never identified as PRD supporters. When given a choice between interviewing PRD supporters or others, MEDCOM's outlets usually picked the PRD supporters. Members of the PRD were often thrown easier questions than those addressed to members of other parties. During the Perez Balladares administration, the MEDCOM stations were often accused of ignoring news that would reflect badly on the PRD government.

"When we don't criticize and dwell on the negative," González Revilla responded, "we are hit for being linked to the government. There is always a political perception here. Most of the media here is antigovernment, so if you provide a balanced product you are seen as being progovernment."

Many critics worried that MEDCOM has not sated its appetite for additional media properties inside Panama. González Revilla said the company did have expansion plans that included adding at least one station to give it a bigger stake in radio entertainment programming.

With RPC Radio MEDCOM has Panama's top news and information station, a position it has held since it was founded in 1949. The station averages about a six rating, around 165,000 listeners daily. Panama's top-rated station, Super Q, averages a ten rating, attracting 275,000 listeners daily.[36] Super Q specializes in pop music from the United States and uses the popular Top 40 format. This entertainment success is what has drawn González Revilla's interest.

Radio is still the most important medium in Panama, with a 92 percent penetration of the market. As they are in much of Central America, however, the radio airwaves are oversaturated, and the total share of radio advertising has been consistently shrinking in the 1990s. Panama has 110 radio stations, shrinking from 206 stations in 1992. The capital, Panama City—a city of about a million people in a country of three million—supports 63 separate stations. Panama is a small country about the size of South Carolina, and many stations are simply repeaters that give these capital-based stations a nationwide reach. All these stations split an advertising pie of only $5 million annually. This total has proven too small to support all the country's stations, which accounts for the decline in the 1990s.

RPC Radio's main competition for the news and information audience is Radio KW Continente, which averages a three rating, attracting 82,000 listeners daily.[37] Like *La Prensa* and *El Panamá América*, Radio KW Continente traces much of its popularity to its stand against the country's dictators in the preinvasion period. The station was bombed by the Panamanian military and subsequently closed during the Noriega era. Today it represents those ideologically aligned against the PRD and counterbalances Radio RPC, although both radio networks provide generally straightforward and objective news broadcasts. As in the realms of newspapers and television, however, both these stations, through their information and talk-show programming, manifest the polarization in Panamanian society.

MEDCOM's intentions to expand its holdings in the radio spectrum, its actions to exclude other cablecasters, and its formation to consolidate ownership of Panama's major broadcasting and cable entities are somewhat predictable given our theoretical model. We have noted that owners of media systems will protect their market interest in a nation, usually thus supporting an institutionalized hierarchy or oligarchy. Because MEDCOM is headed by González Revilla, a member of that oligarchy, its formation seems to support that premise.

Furthermore, we have noted that globalization and the international trend toward media concentration and consolidation lead media owners to erect walls to protect their interests in these small markets. González Revilla cited fears about larger global competition as his reason for pushing for the MEDCOM merger, but as his critics have noted, the merger reduced internal competition, gave MEDCOM a monopolistic hold on broadcast advertising and cable, and provoked fears of vertical integration of the Panamanian media. These powerful media holdings also gave rise to general fears that the electronic media system was tilting toward the conservative PRD.

We have also noted that fears of globalization actually undercut democracy and the multiplicity of voices in media systems by forcing oligarchic small market systems to create barriers to new owners, thus reducing competition in these nations. Panama certainly offers an excellent example of this model in action.

Panama, like many nations in the region, has created its own unique media system. It differs from both the almost-complete media oligarchy of Honduras and the media system of El Salvador, which operates mainly to serve the oligarchy. In fact, it combines elements of both examples: many of the major media leaders are members of the oligarchy, while the other key players are families or individuals who support one of the sectors of the nation's oligarchy. The media system avoids uniformity through the polarization that has been evident in Panama's oligarchy for generations.

Perhaps the greatest threat to free expression in Panama, as in other nations in the region, is that a handful of powerful businesspeople or families controls the most powerful instruments of communication. A democracy uses the media to redistribute power by leveraging the powerful through the dissemination of information; leaving the gatekeeping role in the hands of a few with designs on that power can be dangerous.

Aside from *La Prensa,* seven individuals or families control five of the six newspapers in the country, the top two television stations, and the top radio information stations in the country. The Panamanian electronic media king, MEDCOM, commands three-fourths of the nation's television audience and an important slice of the nation's radio audience.

Despite the support of MEDCOM, *La Estrella,* and the Duque faction of the oligarchy, however, the Perez Balladares administration lost its bid to change Panama's constitution and win the right to have the president run for reelection. Gorriti, *La Prensa's* investigative editor, noted that this outcome was an important indicator of democratic development. In his view, many Latin American nations lack developed institutions, such as independent legislatures or judiciaries, that could provide the necessary checks on the all-too-frequent authoritarian use of central executive power from the chief administrative position. In these countries the media provide the only possible check on the powers of the central government. Giving that central government the opportunity to renew its contract with the populace instead of working within prescribed limits, in Gorriti's view, would only allow more centralized power in a system with few checks on the presidency. Gorriti and *La Prensa* thus worked hard to provide a critical function during the Perez Balladares administration. The Perez Balladares government struck back with its own media campaign to discredit *La Prensa,* the raid on Correa Esquivel's home and car being just one of the tactics. With his administration beset by charges of corruption and connections to Colombian drug lords, however, Perez Balladares was unable to deliver the presidency to his successor in the PRD's leadership.

Ironically, Mireya Moscoso de Gruber, the leader of the Arnulfista Party, won the 1999 elections. Moscoso, the widow of Arnulfo Arias—the namesake of her political party who was forty-five years her senior when they wed—defeated Martin Torrijos of the PRD, the son of the man who had unseated her former husband in the coup of 1968. With Moscoso's success Panamanian politics seems to have closed a cataclysmic thirty-year cycle. Through it all, however, the nation remained divided along the same fault lines so evident in the Panamanian media.

In an attempt to erase some of the state powers that allowed the seizure and closure of media outlets under the nation's dictators, one of President Moscoso's first major acts was to remove two of Panama's restrictive gag laws from the books.[38] In the past those laws had allowed the government to threaten journalists, to close critical newspapers, and to seize the property of powerful political opponents. Without those powers, perhaps the wounds that the state inflicted on the media in the internecine war for ideological control of the nation's oligarchy will finally begin to heal.

4　The Return of the Conservatives in Nicaragua

The story of the media and political power in Nicaragua is yet again one of important families: this time, the Chamorros and the Sacasas. Both families have controlled the nation's presidency, and both families enjoy tremendous influence inside the nation's media. Both families rode the wild turns of Nicaragua's history in the past century: guerrilla war, dictatorship, revolution, and counterrevolution, all in a land where even nature conspires to make death a constant companion. For to know Nicaragua, a land of lush mountainscapes and picturesque lakes, is also to know its history of devastating earthquakes and hurricanes.

During the nineteenth century Nicaragua was the leading candidate for a interoceanic canal, although that undertaking went to Panama. In addition, Nicaragua was once called the granary of Central America. Nevertheless, decades of looting by the Somoza family, the ravages of wars, and economic mismanagement by the communist Sandinistas and their successors have left the country with the hemisphere's second worst economy; only Haiti is poorer. A rising crime rate indicates the rampant misery and frustration in this nation of 4.5 million people, where 80 percent of the population are underemployed or unemployed and at least 70 percent live under the poverty line.[1] To make conditions worse, Hurricane Mitch destroyed much of the nation's infrastructure in 1998, leaving behind at least $1 billion in damage and claiming thousands of lives in a country about the size of New York State.

The twists and turns of Nicaragua's history and politics are complex and sometimes difficult to navigate. Nevertheless, they are important in explaining the nation's media and power equation. For as we have stated, political developments matter more than current global forces or external pressures for democratization in shaping a country's media system.

Many important substrata of Nicaragua's historical development were forged in nineteenth-century domestic political battles and through U.S. foreign policy designs for the region. Discussions about using Nicaragua as a canal site have made the country a focus of interest for the United States since the 1840s.[2]

During the nineteenth century much of the isthmus was embroiled in political conflicts and occasional small wars between competing camps, the liberals and conservatives. Liberals wanted Central America to play a more integrated role in the world economy and to institute secular governments. Conservatives pressed for protectionist economic policies and favored social policies and politics that included the views of the Roman Catholic church and bolstered traditional Spanish culture. Both camps often created strong, authoritarian central governments and attempted to retain power through corrupt means, including fraudulent elections. This pattern continued during the next 150 years throughout the region.

Our story begins with the United States' plans for a canal between the Atlantic and Pacific Oceans. Nicaragua's Jose Santos Zelaya, a dictator aligned with the Liberal Party, had consistently resisted U.S. overtures to secure a canal zone in Nicaragua. The United States eventually moved on to support the Panamanian secessionist movement in Colombia, solving its problem of fixing a site for the canal by helping to create Panama and the Canal Zone. Zelaya remained in disfavor with Washington, however. In 1909 the United States broke relations with his government and helped spark a revolt to have him overthrown, partially because he was negotiating with the Japanese to dig a competing canal.[3]

In 1912 the United States sent marines to help prop up the Conservative Adolfo Díaz as Nicaragua's president, and the country became a protectorate of the United States. The marines stayed for two decades. Augusto Sandino, a general who was also an activist in the Liberal Party, launched a guerrilla war against the marines and their Nicaraguan supporters. Sandino, who wore a jaunty cowboy hat, became legendary for his ability to elude his pursuers. In order to fight Sandino with local troops, the United States trained, equipped, and advised the Nicaraguan National Guard in the 1930s. When the marines were withdrawn from Nicaragua in 1933, Anastasio ("Tacho") Somoza Garcia was appointed as the general in charge of the National Guard. In 1934, after a meeting in the presidential palace to arrange a peace treaty with the Liberal government of President Juan Sacasa, Sandino was seized by members of the National Guard and executed.[4] The orders for the execution came directly from General Somoza.

Although Somoza was aligned with the Liberal Party and related to President Sacasa through marriage—the president was the uncle of Somoza's wife—Somoza seized power for himself in 1937.[5] Backed by the United States, he ruled Nicaragua for almost two decades, until he was assassinated by Conservative activists. He was succeeded by his son Luis Somoza Debayle, a member of the Nicaraguan Assembly. Health problems led Luis to give way to his brother Anastasio ("Tachito") Somoza Debayle, who, like his father, had been the head of the ruthless National Guard.

The National Guard's role was to harass political opposition to the Somoza dictatorships and to maintain a firm anticommunist presence in the region during the cold war. To silence the voice of the opposition, the National Guard was not above firebombing or closing opposition newspapers. In addition, in 1948 Tacho Somoza signed a restrictive media law giving his Interior Ministry wide powers to regulate expression.

The opposition to the Somozas coalesced around the newspaper *La Prensa*. Like all Nicaraguan newspapers, its birth resulted from politics during a time of struggle. In 1925 the United States had brokered an election in an attempt to end the violent feuding among Nicaragua's political parties. The Conservative Carlos Solórzano was appointed president, but Liberals were given key cabinet posts, and Juan Sacasa became the vice-president. This deal upset many Conservatives, who felt the nation's executive office should be theirs alone, and Gen. Emiliano Chamorro led a coup. The U.S. Marine Corps was brought in to settle the matter and restored President Díaz to office until elections could be held in 1932.[6] Looking for a new base for his political activities, General Chamorro invested in the new Conservative paper *La Prensa* in 1926.

The Chamorro family had been prominent in Nicaraguan history even before the founding of *La Prensa*. Four Chamorros, including Emiliano Chamorro, had served the nation as president and as leader of the Conservative Party.[7] In the nineteenth century the Chamorros' economic might began with their land and cattle holdings, but the family diversified into coffee, sugar, and other holdings. They continued to expand their interests, becoming one of Nicaragua's leading merchant and banking families before moving into the media, where they maintained a strident voice for the Conservative cause.[8] Once the Somozas installed themselves as Nicaragua's leaders and top representatives of the Liberal Party, the mission of *La Prensa* was clear: it would serve to counterbalance authoritarian power and work to unseat the dictators. *La Prensa* was thus pitted against the now-defunct *Novedades,* the voice of the Liberal Party and generally the mouthpiece of the Somoza regimes.

General Chamorro's nephew, Pedro Joaquín Chamorro Zelaya, a prominent Conservative senator, became the principal owner of *La Prensa* in 1932, the year of Sacasa's victory.[9] Chamorro Zelaya's son, Pedro Joaquín Chamorro Cardenal, would later devote his life to opposing the Somozas in the columns of *La Prensa.*

Before that, however, Pedro Chamorro Cardenal was a fervent follower of the Conservative cause who was linked to the assassination of Tacho Somoza in 1956. He was jailed and exiled on a number of charges, including smuggling guns.[10] In the 1960s Pedro Chamorro Cardenal took control of the family newspaper, working to become the journalistic nuisance of the Somoza regimes. He particularly enraged Tachito Somoza, who responded by ordering that *La Prensa* submit to government censors. Whenever international human rights groups and media organizations, such as the Inter-American Press Association (IAPA), managed to pressure Somoza into relenting and sending the censors home, Chamorro would respond with a fresh series of broadsides. Somoza would then impose a new round of censorship. This cycle continued for years, and Chamorro received wide international recognition for his role as the opposition critic of the thin-skinned dictator. Chamorro's role as director of the IAPA and as a key member of the organization's top committees also gave him an international forum to criticize the regime's crackdowns on free expression.

While Chamorro was carrying on the Conservative opposition in the columns of *La Prensa,* a leftist guerrilla movement was forming in the hillsides of Nicaragua. Inspired by the Cuban Revolution of Fidel Castro and the image of Sandino as a national liberator, various revolutionary groups came together as the Sandinista National Liberation Front (Spanish acronym, FSLN) in 1961. For much of the next eighteen years the National Guard would fight a low-intensity war against them. With this pressure from the left, the old political divisions between Liberal and Conservative began to fade in importance, replaced by a new type of polarization.

Several key events in the 1970s built public support for the FSLN and the overthrow of the last Somoza. First, during the devastating earthquake of 1972, which destroyed downtown Managua, National Guard troops ran rampant through the city, looting instead of trying to create order. Tachito Somoza funneled off millions of dollars meant to help victims and to rebuild Managua.[11] The ruins of old Managua stood for almost thirty years after the earthquake, a testament to his greed.

In 1978 the crusading newspaper publisher Pedro Chamorro Cardenal was gunned down on a Managua street by a Cuban businessman,
supposedly angered by an article in *La Prensa*. Although some disagree,
many believe that Tachito Somoza ordered and paid for the assassination.[12] Before his death Chamorro had tried to unite disparate groups to
oppose the dictatorship by carrying out national strikes and protests. His
assassination did just that, drawing together opposition politicians, the
Catholic church, the middle class, and the nation's business community. More than 120,000 people marched in his funeral procession, which
became an anti-Somoza rally.

Finally, the rise of the so-called *Terceristas*, a wing of the FSLN not
tied to communism, opened the door for many to join the revolution.
The *Terceristas* were led by the bold and dashing Edén Pastora, who used
the *nomme de guerre* "Commander Zero." Pastora's daring raid on the
National Palace just eight months after Chamorro's murder showed the
vulnerability of the Somoza regime. Pastora captured 500 members of
the government and then exchanged them for the Sandinista leader
Tomás Borge and 82 other FSLN prisoners, as well as $5 million and free
passage to Panama.[13]

A year later the Somoza dynasty would be smoldering in ashes. It died
a painfully slow death, however, and not without further casualties. The
National Guard raided and ransacked *La Prensa*'s headquarters and then
set it on fire. The only legal paper in the country became *Novedades*,
although the nation's revolutionaries printed various underground newspapers, such as *Catacumbas* in León and *El Pueblo* in Managua.[14]

When Tachito Somoza fled to Miami and the National Guard surrendered in Managua in July 1979, the revolution was over. The Sandinistas heralded their triumph in the party's official newspaper, *Barricada*,
published for the first time four days after their victory. Carlos Fernando Chamorro Barrios, Pedro Chamorro's youngest son, had become a
Sandinista after his father's murder. He helped create the paper, and served
as its editor for the next fourteen years.

The remainder of the Chamorro family was left to decide how to
resurrect *La Prensa*. Jaime Chamorro Cardenal (Pedro's brother) and Pedro
Joaquín Chamorro Barrios (Pedro's son and namesake) wanted the paper
to back its traditional constituencies, the Catholic church and the country's Conservative business elite. These forces were shaping up as the
main opposition groups to the country's new rulers, the left-wing Sandinistas. Xavier Chamorro Cardenal (another of Pedro's brothers), who had
succeeded the legendary publisher as the top editorial force at *La Pren-*

sa, saw the situation quite differently. He thought the Sandinistas deserved the family's support.

Rather than work for his nephew at *Barricada*, Xavier fought for control of the family's flagship paper. The solution was a split. Xavier was given 25 percent of *La Prensa*'s operating capital, and he took the majority of the newspaper's staff. He went on to found the popular newspaper *El Nuevo Diario* in 1980. The paper supported the new government but also became the most sensational newspaper in the country. Pro-Sandinista rhetoric found its place next to stories of religious miracles, space aliens, and bloody crimes. The paper aimed to reach the country's working class, and because most working people favored the Sandinistas, the publication adopted that editorial line, which persists to the present. Meanwhile, *La Prensa* resumed publishing a month after the Sandinista victory and soon found itself back in its usual mode as hypercritical opposition to the government. For the next fourteen years a prominent member of the Chamorro family would be at the helm of each of Nicaragua's newspapers.

The Sandinista directorate that ran the country was uncomfortable with *La Prensa*'s criticisms, however, and by September 1980 the government had issued tougher decrees giving itself stronger powers of censorship and the right to close publications and radio stations. During the next four years the Sandinistas closed the newspaper seven times, and heavy censorship or staff protests to it stopped publication twenty-four other times.[15] The Sandinistas also organized *turbas divinas*, politically motivated mobs, to vandalize the newspaper and the homes of the Chamorros, along with harassing the newspaper's staff. The Sandinistas accused the newspaper of being a tool for the Reagan administration, which had organized a counterrevolutionary army (the Contras). The counterrevolution had begun, and the United States was financing and directing it from neighboring Honduras. The Sandinistas finally closed *La Prensa* altogether in 1986, and Pedro Chamorro Barrios went into exile in Costa Rica.[16]

In a nod to open elections and pluralism, however, the Sandinista leader Daniel Ortega, who had become the nation's president, allowed *La Prensa* to resume printing again before the 1990 elections. At this point Cristiana Chamorro, the daughter of Pedro Chamorro Cardenal, was running the newspaper; her mother, Violeta Barrios de Chamorro, was heading the coalition of political parties united against the Sandinistas. In an upset victory, she won the election and became Nicaragua's president.

Quickly assessing the political terrain and not admitting total defeat, the Ortega government repealed many of the nation's restrictive media laws. This allowed them to establish a voice in the media as a legitimate opposition while they waited for the next election cycle. With their loss at the polls, the Sandinistas also declared a unilateral cease-fire in their war against the Contra armies. The Contra War formally came to a close on 27 June 1990, although sporadic flare-ups with Contra supporters continued through 1994.

Most experts agreed that the end of the cold war and with it the Soviet Union contributed to the Sandinistas' demise. After thirty years of war, facing a U.S.-sponsored embargo and having lost its patrons in Russia and Cuba, Nicaragua saw its economy crumble. Angry voters reacted by giving Violeta Chamorro the reins of power. The publisher's wife was left to clean up the mess.

Cristiana Chamorro was left to guide *La Prensa,* but not for long, as a battle for control of the newspaper and its editorial direction ensued shortly thereafter when her brother Pedro returned from exile. Cristiana felt the paper should support her mother's administration. Pedro saw it differently. He argued that *La Prensa* had always been an opposition voice; he wanted the paper to take a more objective tack and become one of the region's better publications, which meant that it could not be his mother's lapdog.[17] Complicating matters, Cristiana is married to Antonio Lacayo, who served as Violeta's top aide and has political ambitions of his own. Eventually, after much internal struggle, both Cristiana and Pedro Chamorro Barrios were removed from leadership positions at the newspaper, and Pedro Chamorro Cardenal's brother, Jaime, returned as the newspaper's president. Pablo Antonio Cuadra, Jaime's cousin and a famous poet and novelist, became the newspaper's editor.[18]

In 1996 *La Prensa* found itself in the untraditional position of backing Arnoldo Alemán Lacayo, the mayor of Managua, against Daniel Ortega of the FSLN. Alemán led the Liberal Alliance, the modern-day successor of the nation's Liberal Party, but in the strange deviations of Nicaraguan politics, the Liberal Alliance occupies the far right of the Nicaraguan political spectrum. This development stems from the policies of *Somocismo* and the dictators' hijacking of the Liberal Party label for their anticommunist politics. The Liberals became the strongest backers of the Contras, just as the Conservative Party found its greatest support among moderate factions of the country's business elite. In essence, the Liberals leapfrogged the Conservatives to represent the country's most conservative political forces. When Violeta Chamorro became president, she represented moderate, centrist political ideals. With the Chamorro family paper supporting a Liberal candidate for the first time, Violeta

Chamorro became the first Nicaraguan president in more than a century to peaceably hand over power to a member of an opposing political party.

Violeta Chamorro had wanted to regain a position on *La Prensa*'s board after leaving office. The newspaper's executive board, however, now controlled by the siblings of her martyred husband, wanted her to resign her position with the Conservative Party. The board viewed her connections with the Conservative Party as a conflict of interest for the modernizing newspaper. Cristiana Chamorro, Violeta's daughter and at one time the publisher of *La Prensa*, still retains a position at the paper. She acknowledged her mother's dismay at losing control of *La Prensa:* "My mom said that it was the second worst hurt after losing her husband."[19]

La Prensa's board is now run by Jaime Chamorro Cardenal, the brother of the martyred Pedro Joaquin. The paper's publisher is Hugo Holmann Chamorro, the son of Pedro Joaquin's sister, Ana Maria Chamorro de Holmann. Holmann said that market concerns drove the paper's move to depoliticize. "We actually were going bankrupt," Holmann said, "because the newspaper tilted to become a government-oriented newspaper" under Violeta Chamorro. "The paper didn't say anything," he added. "It wasn't independent. And so the readers recognized that and circulation went as low as 16,000."[20] During the newspaper's heyday in the Somoza era, daily circulation had been as high as 55,000. Holmann and the paper's board thus decided the paper needed a new design and a new editorial direction.

In 1999 Holmann hired David Hume to head the newspaper's redesign project. Hume, a respected Argentine journalist who is now a U.S. citizen and formerly with the *Miami Herald*, decided to include some of the old *La Prensa* formula and something new, too. In one of the biggest breaks with the past, he decided to drop support for the Conservative Party. Hume recruited editors and reporters of all political stripes as he fashioned his team. The editors immediately below Hume in this new hierarchy came from markedly different political backgrounds: Eduardo Enriquez had been a key editor at *La Tribuna*, at one time a media bastion of the Liberal Party, and Roberto Fonseca was a mainstay at the Sandinista's *Barricada*. Along with bringing a modern, full-color design to *La Prensa*, Hume is also credited with reviving the newspaper's investigative tradition.

"The paper will also have less ties to the positions and rulings of the church," Hume said. A decade ago there would have been little if any criticism of the Catholic church in *La Prensa*. "Not anymore," Hume said firmly.[21] Hume is responsible for eliminating a weekly column by the church and replacing it with regular coverage of religion from a beat reporter.

The IAPA awarded the remodeled paper a prestigious investigative reporting prize in 2001, which gave something of an international seal of approval for the changes. The paper has also reclaimed its position as the most popular in Nicaragua after two decades of being eclipsed by *El Nuevo Diario*. *La Prensa* is the only newspaper in Nicaragua with an independently audited circulation. The audit of 2001 showed the paper was selling almost 38,000 copies daily, a 46 percent increase over its circulation in 1998, before Hume was brought in to revamp the publication.[22]

"I have no complaints about the modernization of the newspaper," Cristiana Chamorro said about the revamped *La Prensa*, adding, "I just want people to remember we are the ones who fought the dictators. We stood up to the Sandinistas." She also praised her mother, noting that the former president "fought for free expression, and now she can't have a place in her newspaper."

With the end of the Sandinista era, Chamorros other than Violeta faced new and daunting challenges. At *Barricada* Carlos Chamorro looked at ways to transform the party daily from the voice of the government into an opposition publication. A year after the Sandinista defeat in the elections, he submitted a redesign plan to the party leaders. The paper's emblem changed from a guerrilla with a rifle to an outline of Sandino's cowboy hat; the editorial line changed, too. The paper became the most objective news outlet in Nicaragua and ran investigative stories instead of pieces meant to parrot the party line. The paper not only carefully documented the presidency of Violeta Chamorro, Carlos's mother, but also analyzed how the Sandinistas started to splinter. Sergio Ramirez, the leader of the *Tercerista* faction of the FSLN, began moving to unseat the former president Ortega as the party's leader.

Sandinista hard-liners, the so-called orthodox wing of the FSLN, began to have second thoughts about the new direction of *Barricada*. In 1993 the newspaper published an investigative report linking a cache of arms to passports discovered in Managua. The weapons and papers belonged to members of the FMLN, the Salvadoran allies of the Sandinistas who had signed a peace treaty to end their own civil war less than two years earlier. The scandal cast doubt on the sincerity of the Salvadoran left in supporting peace; in addition, the story embarrassed the Sandinista leadership because of its source.[23]

Ramirez, who had served as Ortega's vice-president, was ousted from presidential contention from within the party and went on to form the Sandinista Renovation Movement, after which the hard-line Sandinistas moved against Carlos Chamorro. In 1994 Tomás Borge and group of bodyguards burst into the editorial offices of *Barricada* and seized control of the paper. Carlos Chamorro was dismissed, and 80 percent of the staff were either fired or resigned. Despite street protests by some Sandinistas, Borge, the only surviving member of the original FSLN founding directorate and the chief censor during the Sandinista regime, began remaking the paper in its original image. Borge sought to return the paper to the point where it could help promote Ortega's candidacy in the 1996 presidential election. It would operate mainly as a propaganda tool instead of a news source. Ortega's subsequent failed candidacy, however, the paper's editorial shifts, and the party's lack of funds combined to doom *Barricada*. Its daily circulation sank below 7,000 copies, and it folded in January 1998.[24] An advertising boycott, organized by the Alemán administration (see chapter 7) also contributed to the paper's demise.

During the summer of 2000 Borge resurrected *Barricada*, but this time it appeared as a weekly. With a five-person staff (less than a fifth of the staff when the paper folded) and distribution solely through party channels instead of street sales, the publication was a ghost of its former self. The paper tried competing with more popular weeklies, such as *El Semanario*, the publication of Ramirez and his Sandinista Renovation Movement. *El Semanario* is known for its mix of investigative reporting, crisp writing, and coverage of literary issues. The party was unable to sustain even this scaled-back version of *Barricada*, however, and it too soon collapsed.[25]

The important 1990 elections may have provided the pretext for the ideological shift at *Barricada*, but they also gave political aspirants inspiration to start new publications. Haroldo Montealegre saw his chance and returned from exile to start *La Tribuna* in 1993. The Montealegres had been large landowners and bankers before they shifted their operations to Miami in the Sandinista era. As a member of the nation's upper crust, Montealegre intended his newspaper to appeal to the business class of post-Sandinista Nicaragua. He also used it to compete for the candidacy of the Liberal Alliance in the 1996 presidential election.

Although Montealegre's ambitions were thwarted by Arnoldo Alemán, who eventually carried the Liberal banner into the presidential palace, *La Tribuna* benefited from Alemán's victory, because it was able to attract more government advertising, at least at the beginning of the Alemán administration. The paper was known for some of the nation's most sober and objective reporting during the administration's early years. Media critics complained that it constantly shifted its editorial stances, however, confusing readers with its different positions. Although the paper employed some of the most modern equipment in Nicaragua to produce a visually appealing product, it circulated to only about 8,500 readers daily. Seeking to prop up *La Tribuna*'s finances, in 1988 Montealegre began publishing *El Mercurio*, a daily tabloid aimed at taking readers from the popular *El Nuevo Diario*, which still thrives on scandal and sensation.

Montealegre's banking concerns fell on hard times, however, and the Alemán administration stopped buying advertising from the paper, causing *La Tribuna* to collapse in 1999.[26] *El Mercurio* was spun off as a successful weekly publication but under different management. *El Mercurio* now competes with *Sucesos*, both of which are weekly publications that specialize in salacious pictures and gory stories, attracting a weekly readership of about 50,000 each.

Of all the nation's newspapers, *El Nuevo Diario* appears to be from an older era, printing only in black and white on thin paper. The publication does not just specialize in police-blotter news; it often scores with important investigative reports and scoops. Xavier Chamorro, the paper's publisher, still uses the old formula that made *La Prensa* popular: cover topics that generate conversation and remember that facts sometimes get in the way of an entertaining story.

Francisco Chamorro, the managing editor, claims the newspaper circulates 40,000 copies daily,[27] but estimates of its circulation based on audits of its competitor, *La Prensa*, put the figure around 28,000.[28] In 1998 it was the leading Nicaraguan daily, with a circulation of 30,000. Whichever figures seem most credible, the paper has declined in popularity since the Sandinista era, when circulation was about 55,000 daily.

The decline in readership relates to the country's poor economic conditions. Some media managers estimate newspaper circulation has declined at least 30 percent in the post-Sandinista era. Also, although the Sandinistas launched a literacy program in the 1980s, 33 percent remain illiterate.[29] The press nevertheless continues to be influential in Nicaragua, as it is elsewhere in the region, because it sets the agenda by deciding which stories to cover. In addition, these publications reflect the viewpoints of the nation's opinion leaders.

This analysis of Nicaragua's newspaper industry reveals the continued dominance of some of the nation's leading families in the media. Although the Sandinista Revolution temporarily adjusted the media scene, not even this polarizing and violent convulsion of the nation's social and political system could change old patterns. Like some of the Twenty Families in Panama and the *turcos* of Honduras, the media leaders of Nicaragua are the country's oligarchy. The Chamorros are the best example, having produced presidents, publishers, revolutionaries, and martyrs. This family dominated Nicaragua's newspaper scene for a generation, and Violeta Chamorro provided the unifying force to move the country into the post-Sandinista era. The return of the Montealegres and their entry into the media competition only underscore that the publishing business is reserved for elites and the aristocracy—although, as *La Tribuna* demonstrates, even elite families can fail in the harsh economic climate of Nicaragua.

The political bases and origins of all Nicaragua's newspapers seem to justify our belief that media systems generally support and reflect oligarchic tendencies in nations without strong democratic roots. Control in post-Sandinista Nicaragua has returned to oligarchic forces, the country's right wing or moderates with links to the middle class. The left—the Sandinistas—are sniping against one another like children after their team has lost an athletic contest, indulging in the typical finger-pointing of those who have tumbled out of power unexpectedly. Even their publications have been marginalized or have dropped from sight altogether. The nation's conservative oligarchy (despite the Liberal Party labels) has returned to power.

The Sandinista Revolution's legacy for Nicaragua's media comprised little beyond a sad history of censorship and government control and a splintering of viewpoints as the nation attempted to regroup after the Somoza era. This splintering was reflected in the three directions the Chamorro family took. *El Nuevo Diario* is arguably still aligned with the Sandinista cause, but politics appear to be an afterthought, with sensationalism being its chief tactic to sell newspapers. Xavier Chamorro has clearly placed entertainment ahead of ideology. This is a twist on the old family formula. The Chamorros had earlier printed sensational news as bait to get readers to consume their opposition views. Allowing the paper to survive, the allure has become the publication's raison d'être. Also, like most institutions in Nicaragua, the Chamorro family is far from monolithic. In the end, the family has fought to make its ideas the country's guiding light for almost two hundred years.

All this substantiates our view that political developments matter more than current global forces or external pressures for democratization in shaping a country's media system. Nicaragua is still dominated by the Chamorros and Lacayos, families with rich histories in the nation's politics, media, and economic development. The Lacayos, members of the nation's elite merchant class who had large cotton holdings and have played key roles in Nicaraguan broadcasting, have been economic and political allies of the Chamorros for generations. The historical record shows that the media are an important force in the nation's politics and so deeply intertwined in political and economic functions that it is difficult for them to ever achieve an objective stance.

The shattering of the Chamorro family's unity during the Sandinista era also seems to support our point that apparent competition may only reflect inter-elite battles in a changing oligarchic system. This time, the competition among publications—*Barricada*, the party mouthpiece turned objective investigative vehicle; *El Nuevo Diario*, a tabloid appealing to the base instincts of the proletariat; and *La Prensa*, the longtime opposition paper shifting to accommodation—and these inter-elite battles became uniquely intrafamily battles for control of the country's message. These intrafamily divisions accurately reflect the divisions inside Nicaraguan society. The left-wing Sandinistas' transformation from controlling force to opposition dictated a transformation at *Barricada*. As the core of the Chamorro family shifted from opposition to presidential power, so too the editorial line at *La Prensa* changed. Even *El Nuevo Diario* followed more of the *Tercerista* line of *Sandinismo*, reflecting the views not only of Xavier Chamorro but also of the publication's minority investors, such as Danilo Aguirre.

This shifting ideology can be seen in the Nicaraguan electronic media as well, but the shifts there reflected more the end of the Sandinista era than the divisions of Nicaraguan society. Because television consumes at least 70 percent of the nation's $25 million annual advertising pie, and because it reaches at least 70 percent of the population, far more than the nation's paltry newspaper readership, it is quickly becoming the principal medium in Nicaragua.[30]

The history of television dates back to 1955 and the first Somoza regime. At that time the government ran the only television outlet, Canal 6, which programmed mainly English-language soap operas and series from the United States. By 1957 the government had begun importing programs from Mexico, supplementing those with live local programming. For the first time the country's only television channel carried mainly Spanish programs.

In 1962 Luis Somoza gave the rights to Nicaragua's first commercial station to Octavio Sacasa Sarria. The Sacasas were the political enemies of the Chamorros. In the disputed 1925 elections Gen. Emiliano Chamorro had led a coup against the government because it had named the Liberal Juan Sacasa as vice-president. Afterward Sacasa took to the hills with Liberal Party generals and their followers to fight the Conservatives. Sacasa led this guerrilla campaign until the United States brokered a cease-fire at Tipitapa in 1927. Although the guerrilla war and his strength at the negotiation table gave Sacasa impetus to win the next election, they also unleashed Sandino, who with four hundred followers continued to wage guerrilla war. Sandino disliked the cease-fire agreement because it guaranteed the United States a say in Nicaragua's domestic affairs. Eventually Sandino's guerrilla war weakened Sacasa's administration and opened the door for Tacho Somoza.

Twenty-five years after his father had pushed Sacasa aside, however, Luis Somoza handed Octavio Sacasa the keys to media power. Despite competition from four other commercial VHF stations and three UHF stations, the Sacasa family's Canal 2 now commands 75 percent of the nation's viewing audience and, likewise, a large chunk of the available advertising revenues.[31]

Because of his support for the Somozas, Octavio Sacasa fled to Miami as the rebels rolled into Managua. The Sandinistas promptly seized Canal 2 and turned it into an arm of their propaganda apparatus for the next decade. Still in Miami, Sacasa raised funds for the Contras and, by some accounts, transferred CIA funds to Contra leaders.[32] When Violeta Chamorro became president, she restored Canal 2 to Sacasa as part of her reconciliation plan.[33] Considering the history of enmity between the two families, this was an important gesture exemplifying how the country could begin to move beyond the political polarization of its past. It was also a personal gesture for the president, because her mother was part of the Sacasa clan, and President Chamorro had distanced herself from many of these relatives because of their links to the previous dictatorships.[34]

When the Liberals obtained the presidency, powerful Canal 2 at first returned to its old role as a progovernment, far-right cheerleader, echoing its stance of the Somoza era. Nevertheless, the Sacasas invested significant sums to upgrade Canal 2 after the Sandinista takeover. Even their competitors acknowledge that they have built the most professional television network in Nicaragua, with the country's best news and entertainment programming. Their station also carries programming from various international sources, including CNN. This professional reformatting led the network to evolve toward more objective reporting, which has some wondering whether it has left its partisan role behind. At the same time, some observers claim that the Sacasas have benefited from their access to the Liberal government built through years of friendships, political favors, and obligations.[35]

When he was at Canal 2, Danilo Lacayo, the former host of the top-rated information and news program on television, "Buenas Dias Nicaragua," saw it differently. A former press secretary for Pres. Violeta Chamorro, Lacayo acknowledged that people initially thought he would carry a certain bias. (Many people in Managua's media circles believe that Chamorro interceded with Sacasa to win her aide the position.) In response, Lacayo asserted that his program would not be so popular if viewers saw it as anything other than independent. "We criticize government actions every day," Lacayo said, despite the fact that he is related to the president. "As a medium, we are not affiliated or linked or close to the government."[36] Lacayo noted that this remained true even with the shift to a Liberal government, which is important given the long history of Sacasa support for the Liberal cause.

Indeed, the network was instrumental in revealing corruption in the Alemán administration, which testifies to Canal 2's increasing independence. President Alemán retaliated by ordering tax audits of Canal 2. The Sacasas were eventually fined 5 million cordobas (about $400,000).

In an odd twist, Lacayo also showed his own anti-Alemán viewpoints when he was caught in a corruption scandal involving Comptroller General Agustin Jarquin Anaya in 1999. Jarquin, a prominent Sandinista, had needled the Alemán administration with his own attack on corruption. Lacayo (known for his contacts and sources inside the Liberal Party) agreed to feed Jarquin politically sensitive information for the latter's investigations.[37] In turn, the comptroller's office secretly paid Lacayo to publicize its various investigations on a regular basis. When the arrangement came to light, Jarquin lost his job and went to jail briefly. His attacks on Liberal Party corruption had made the former comptroller so popular, however, that he was named the Sandinistas' vice-presidential candidate in 2001. Lacayo did not rebound so well. He lost his position at Canal 2. In 2001 he was anchoring a news program on Managua's UHF station Canal 23, which is known for its low ratings, usually about 1 percent of the viewing audience.

The evolution of Canal 2 also appears in its prominent on-air personalities. The former managing editor of *La Tribuna* and former editor of *El Nuevo Herald* in Miami, Joel Gutiérrez, came aboard as the popular morning news anchor and interviewer. Carlos Chamorro, the former publisher of the Sandinistas' *Barricada,* now hosts the popular political talk show "Esta Semana." Like many independent producers in Nicaragua and elsewhere in Central America, Chamorro buys the time for his program and then resells blocks to advertisers, thus retaining some independence from Canal 2.[38]

The Sarcasas' resurgence also opened the door to one of their rightwing business partners from Miami, Angel González González. A former executive for Mexico's Televisa, González has often served as a broker of television programming in Latin America.[39] González built a media empire in Guatemala (see chapter 5) and invested in both El Salvador and Nicaragua in the postwar era.

González initially acquired Canales 10 and 12, but he added Canal 4 in 1998. Canal 4 had been the FSLN's network, but without government revenue to support operations and with shrinking party resources, the Sandinistas were forced to sell. Although the station has not completely abandoned its pro-Sandinista line, its editorial message has softened. The forced sale of the station may be yet another example of capitalism's revenge on the Sandinistas. González has not fired the staff, made up mainly of Sandinistas, but he has pledged to support the policies of the Liberal government. As a group González's Nicaraguan stations are the second most powerful force on the television dial, commanding 17 percent of the audience.

The only other important television network is TeleNica 8, which appeals to 4 percent of the Nicaraguan audience (Managua's UHF stations fight over the remaining three percent) and is owned by Carlos Briceño. Briceño returned from his Sandinista-era exile to handle publicity, along with Danilo Lacayo, for Violeta Chamorro's 1990 presidential campaign. While in exile Briceño had worked for *The Miami Herald*, CBS News, and Univision. After persuading the government to compensate him for properties seized from his family during the revolution, Briceño parlayed his capital and various loans into the startup cash needed to begin his network. Soon after he opened the network, Briceño developed a poor reputation because, as did Nodarse in Honduras, he illegally rebroadcast films from the United States.[40] He has since stopped that practice.

Like Canal 2, Briceño's station has taken a pro-Liberal stance with its news and information programming. Besides running his station, Briceño hosts two programs, "Porque Nos Importa" and "A Fondo." He also handled much of President Alemán's public relations.[41] The obvious conflict of interest does not seem to matter much in a television system weighted heavily with owners friendly to the Liberal Party and right-wing political causes.

To further keep the left from the nation's airwaves, President Alemán shut down the government's Canal 6 soon after he came into power. The network was staffed mainly by Sandinistas who were placed there after the revolution. During the Chamorro era the president had used a censor to monitor their activities and broadcasts, but Alemán took his dislike for the Sandinistas a step farther, shutting down the network and firing its 150 employees. Canal 6, the nation's oldest network, eventually reopened, but it is seen as the propaganda arm of the Liberal Party and draws very low ratings.

These changes in television all show the resurgence of the right wing and Nicaragua's oligarchy. Sacasa, Briceño, and Lacayo all represent the old family-based elite of Nicaragua's past. Although competition is more prevalent now than it was in the Somoza or Sandinista eras, the Liberal Party viewpoint still dominates the airwaves, a situation that harks back to the 1960s and 1970s. Moderate voices and the remnants of the Sandinistas find their views limited to González's stations, and given the Mexican broadcaster's history in neighboring nations, that too may change.

Again, Nicaraguan television seems to reinforce the nation's oligarchic tendencies. The system may enjoy more freedom now than in the controlled eras of the Somozas or the Sandinistas, but the media-owning families' political bases nevertheless limit expression. This suggests, again, that media owners will protect their market interests by supporting institutionalized hierarchies or oligarchies rather than open the airwaves to the true marketplace of ideas. Furthermore, González's history of aligning his stations with far-right political elements in Guatemala and for a time in El Salvador, along with his business relationship with Sacasa, reveals him to be a broadcast entrepreneur predisposed to ultraconservative points of view. He is the classic example of the nonthreatening interloper from outside the system. As we have noted, media owners from outside these nations need to appear nonthreatening to authoritarian or oligarchic forces before they can affect the ownership structure of the broadcast system. With his pledge to support the Liberal government and his friendship with the Sacasa family, González fits that model.

To find the left-wing viewpoint in Nicaragua's broadcast media, one must turn to the radio. The Sandinistas guaranteed themselves a radio presence by redistributing radio frequencies to key Sandinista loyalists before the Chamorro administration took control of the broadcast system. The Sandinistas created the People's Radio Broadcasting Corporation from stations they had seized from the Somozas and their followers. Ironically, the Sandinistas first nationalized the stations and then privatized most of them for their own benefit.

La Prensa dubbed this redistribution and privatization the *piñata*,[42] because the Sandinistas looked like children elbowing for the spoils of the state they once controlled. The Sandinistas found legal means for the transfer, and some argued that they were justified since they had been underpaid during the previous decade, but once *La Prensa* christened this unethical behavior, it stuck in the craws of many Nicaraguans. In a nation with massive unemployment and poverty, the *piñata* was a political scandal from which the Sandinistas still have not fully recovered. When the Sandinistas began their land redistribution program in the 1980s, they seized the Somoza estates—more than 2 million acres, including 40 percent of the nation's best farmland. Some of this land was also redistributed, as part of the *piñata,* to Sandinistas, who thus became large private land holders.

Even Commandante Borge, the ardent communist, made off with vacation homes, aquaculture farms, and ranches. He sold one of his vacation homes in 2000, using the proceeds to retire *Barricada's* debt.[43] Before leaving the government, Borge also took the concession for newsprint distribution from the Mexican national paper enterprise PIPSA, so that he not only guaranteed the Sandinistas a cheap supply of paper but also ensured himself a profit from all the newspapers in the country.

During the *piñata* Carlos Jose Guadamuz, a Sandinista broadcaster, was given control of Radio Ya, the nation's top station. Guadamuz made his mark as a broadcaster and program manager at the Sandinista station Voz de Nicaragua in the 1980s. Radio Ya may reach as many as 100,000 listeners daily and still follows FSLN orthodoxy, with loyal support for former president Ortega.[44] The station is also known for its coverage of sports, especially baseball, which is Nicaragua's national pastime. The station's popular news, information, talk, and sports programs have made it a commercial success.

The Sandinistas wrested control of Radio Ya from Guadamuz in 2000 however, transferring ownership to a consortium of owners friendly to the Sandinista cause. Guadamuz had run afoul of the Sandinista leadership by criticizing Ortega and by preparing to launch a bid to become the mayor of Managua.[45] In preparation for the 2001 presidential election, the Sandinistas and Liberals had agreed to a political pact that in effect eliminated minor parties such as the Sandinista Renovation Movement from contention. The political pact also divided the capital into political districts that diminished the efforts of Guadamuz to organize his supporters. By removing Guadamuz from the popular network, the Sandinistas effectively undercut his base of support and dashed his immediate political plans. After losing in the rough and tumble of Nicaraguan politics, Guadamuz found a refuge of sorts in a low-rated midday television talk show at the government's Canal 6.

Dennis Schwartz Galo, the new general manager of Radio Ya, says the image of the popular station has softened since the Sandinista era. "Five years ago our style offended people," he said. "But not now. Now we want to be friends with everyone, except of course, the ultraright wing."[46]

The Sandinistas also hold sway at the nation's fourth most popular radio network, appropriately named Radio Sandino. Before the Chamorro transition the station was given to the Sandinista hard-liner Commandante Bayardo Arce, who had worked at *La Prensa* during the Somoza era before becoming a member of the party command structure. Arce is among the FSLN's leaders in the National Assembly.

The main competition for these Sandinista stations is Radio Corporación and its unabashedly pro-Liberal programming, which ranks second with listeners. Milo Gadea Pantoja, who co-owns the network with his father, Fabio Gadea Mantilla, speaks proudly about the history of the station his father started in 1965. Gadea Pantoja likes to point out that the network was bombed by the National Guard during the revolution because it remained independent from the Somozas. "We defend democracy," he said. Gadea Pantoja noted that the network remained true to its history by taking a strong stand against the Sandinistas, too. Radio Corporación was heavily censored when the Sandinistas were in power, and the Gadea family was stripped of one of its radio properties by the FSLN. "They are wolves. We have not advanced because of them," Gadea Pantoja added.[47] Sandinista activists bombed the network's headquarters and transmitter in 1990. During the Chamorro era pro-Sandinista mobs stormed the network's broadcast facilities three times, destroying offices and broadcast equipment.

Radio Catolica, the official voice of the Catholic church, remains influential, although the AM station ranks sixth in a country that increasingly prefers FM radio. During the Sandinista era the government often censored and closed Radio Catolica and harassed its staff. Like *La Prensa*, it counterbalanced the Sandinista government. Because 80 percent of the population is Catholic, the station retains impact, although its political influence has waned because it no longer serves as one of the few principal critics of the government.

Radio is still the country's most pervasive medium, enjoying a 94 percent penetration rate.[48] As they are in many Central American nations, however, the airwaves are crowded in Nicaragua: 137 AM and FM stations broadcast in various parts of the country. Some of these are repeater stations. Managua's most popular stations, including Radio Ya, Radio Sandino, and Radio Corporación, all have repeater transmitters that extend their networks nationwide. Radio broadcasting exploded in popularity during the presidency of Violeta Chamorro, when the government removed almost all oversight for obtaining a license. The number of stations more than tripled, although the nation's poor economy has since driven many out of business. These stations must compete for a shrinking advertising market, estimated at only $2.5 million annually. Their problems resemble those facing the radio industry throughout the region, especially Panama. Nonetheless, Panama's radio advertising revenues are twice as great as Nicaragua's, even though Panama has only 65 percent of Nicaragua's population.

Profit seems to be a secondary motive for running a popular radio network in Nicaragua, however, at least for the leading broadcasters. As they do in the newspaper business there, political positioning and the ability to use a medium for organizing, assembling supporters, and disseminating ideas for a political agenda appear to be the main purpose driving most of the nation's popular stations. The ethical ideal of serving the public by providing information seems to have been lost in this equation, ranking somewhere below making profits. Like most of the media in Nicaragua, radio has followed the pattern of polarization instead of being shaped mainly by capitalist or democratic forces.

As we have noted, the historical political composition of these Central American nations matters most when considering the landscape of their media systems. In the case of Nicaraguan radio, all the major political players of the past century are present in force: the Sandinistas, hoping for another run at government; the far-right Liberals, supporting the current president; and even Radio Catolica, upholding the banner of the old Conservative alliance.

By using their ability to redistribute some of the nation's economic power, the Sandinistas have established themselves as a force on the radio dial, although their influence elsewhere in the media system has receded significantly. Since profit is not their primary objective, they will likely be able to withstand the competition in Nicaragua's weak radio market. Ironically, since they control key popular stations, they may be among the few radio owners making profits from the medium. The political power the Sandinistas used to leverage their current position has made them part of the nation's hierarchy, at least where radio is considered. Ortega, Borge, and Arce may not have been able to redistribute wealth to the proletariat, but they have managed to do a good job for themselves. In so doing, they have become part of the country's hierarchy. Perhaps they have also learned that success in a capitalist system demands more than rhetoric and ideological arguments; wealth and resources are just as important. The Sandinistas have always recognized the importance of controlling the messages transmitted through the media. Now they are running their enterprises for profit and political gain, much as does the oligarchy against which they have so long fought.

Nevertheless, Sandinista radio and, to a lesser extent, *El Nuevo Diario* seem to provide the sole voices counterbalancing the views of the extreme right in Nicaraguan politics. Like the opposition in Panama, the

Sandinistas have learned that they must create space for their message in the media before launching a counteroffensive to retake the government. Understanding this dynamic relationship between the media and state in these one-dimensional democracies helps one to understand the strategy employed by President Vladimir Putin of Russia, who concentrated on eliminating his major competitors in the media while consolidating power. By keeping at least some hold on media properties, the Sandinistas have demonstrated that they understand this lesson all too well. With television increasingly in the hands of ultraconservative right-wing supporters of the government, and most of the newspapers benefiting from the Alemán government, the media outlets that broadcast left-wing views offer the only hope for some semblance of pluralism in this country.

The current problems of the media and democracy in Nicaragua are evident to the international community. In 2000 the United Nations Human Development Program released its ratings of sustainable democracy in Latin America. Nicaragua ranked near the bottom; only Guatemala and Haiti were rated lower.[49] The United Nations' concern for sustainable and inclusive democracy related to impartial information available from the media and to the separation of the media from state power. Our analysis also calls these issues into question.

With no real history of democracy in Nicaragua, politicians and journalists alike fall back into the old patterns of using the media as a megaphone for warmed-over political rhetoric instead of trying to approach the country's long list of problems in some unified and objective way. Although the Sandinistas and the Alemán administration did cut a political deal to restructure the nation's electoral system—the third major change in the past thirteen years—which shows that these political camps can compromise, the forces of right and left seem prepared to continue their battle to control the messages emanating from the nation's media for some time to come. This system only reinforces Nicaragua's politics of polarization, which accentuates the pain in a weary country looking for peace.

5 *Guatemala's Struggle with Manipulation*

A new media era in Guatemala makes itself heard each day at 4 A.M., but ironically the sound echoes an ancient time in this part of Central America. The distinctive clicks and diphthongs of one of Guatemala's Mayan dialects float across the country, transported on the signal of Radio Nuevo Mundo. This is the call of the *campesino.* Prime-time listening for this group of farm laborers begins before dawn, since they are usually toiling in the fields as the capital's office workers begin to rise.

Although Mayan programming has expanded on Radio Nuevo Mundo and other radio outlets since Guatemala's 1996 peace accords, its beginnings (like those of many media trends) can be traced beyond the events that may have created more opportunities and notice for this increasingly popular format. In 1991, during Guatemala's long-running guerrilla war, Florencio Simòn Chuy (who is known in the Mayan community by the name Jolom B'alam) approached the owners of Radio Nuevo Mundo about offering fifteen minutes of programming in the Mayan dialect K'icheé.[1] He was given the 4 A.M. slot, one day a week, for the transmission of his program, which has grown in popularity ever since.[2]

The increased popularity prompted the management at Radio Nuevo Mundo to expand the Mayan programs. And why not? That popularity was boosting the station's overall ratings, and management was selling advertising briskly in the Mayan timeslots without having to pay for the programming. The Mayan-language programs helped build Radio Nuevo Mundo into the third most popular radio outlet in the country.

Marketers soon identified Mayan-language programming as offering advertisers the most growth potential, despite the low income level of the audience. By 1998 Simòn served as executive producer for fifteen hours of programming each week, with the shows carried throughout the country on Radio Nuevo Mundo's network of repeater stations. Mayan programming in several dialects could be heard on the network for ninety minutes six days a week and for six hours on Sunday morning.

In other countries expansion of programming for indigenous groups may seem like a commendable advancement, but in Guatemala such a development is almost revolutionary. Peace accords signed in 1996 finally ended the longest guerrilla war in the region, a thirty-six-year conflict with 200,000 casualties.[3] Written by the Guatemalan Truth Commission, a UN-mandated report about the conflict accused Guatemalan military leaders of genocide aimed at the country's Mayan community. More than four hundred Indian villages were destroyed. This violence against Guatemala's indigenous groups stems from centuries of prejudice and oppression by a powerful Spanish criollo minority in the capital. For the most part, that powerful group had also managed to stymie efforts at nationwide indigenous radio programming at least until 1991, when peace negotiations began.[4]

During the 1980s Simòn was a driving force behind a Mayan cultural program produced for the most popular radio network during that period, Emisoras Unidas, but the network dropped the program after only a few months. Simòn maintained his program was cut because the network's owners were pressured to drop it. He tried to distribute the program via an independent network of stations as a *radio periódico*, a popular means of self-syndication in the Latin American system of radio and, sometimes, television. He failed to achieve national coverage, however, because not enough owners were willing to broadcast the program. Until Radio Nuevo Mundo, no one was willing to take a chance on the program in any permanent way, even though it was offered for free.

Simòn used the peace negotiations to interest Radio Nuevo Mundo's management in starting indigenous programming, because the rights of indigenous groups were at the heart of many of the guerrillas' demands. But Simòn's efforts came with a price. Almost as soon as the program began, Simòn received anonymous threats from people who opposed any sort of indigenous voice on the airwaves. This racist attitude percolated to the surface despite his efforts to limit the program to uncontroversial, apolitical topics. After the threats came the attacks. Between 1991 and 1996 Simòn was attacked four times. During one assault he was stabbed repeatedly. On another occasion he was kidnapped and beaten; eventually his attackers dumped him along a roadside. The attacks stopped following the peace accords, but he still receives occasional threats. Simòn believes that the management of Radio Nuevo Mundo was willing to continue with the programs, despite the attacks and threats, because they had been targets of government-sanctioned violence during the guerrilla war, when paramilitary groups carried out extrajudicial killings and other acts of terror without fear of reprisal from the government.

"We were always interested in peace," Simòn said. "Many Mayan groups are leftist and political, but not us." Simòn sought to provide programs for communities and *campesinos* whose interests seemed to have been left out of the peace negotiations. That focus on education, culture, music, religion, and the preservation of Mayan languages seems more in tune with the mood of Guatemala today. Simòn's strategy to stay on safe editorial ground created a format that remained relatively consistent despite the political changes that characterized the latter part of the 1990s in Guatemala. This consistency contributed to the program's growing popularity.

The development of Mayan programming on Radio Nuevo Mundo marks an important postwar development in the Guatemalan media scene, yet it runs counter to the major trend characterizing the media in the postwar years. Perhaps the greatest threat to Guatemala's uneasy peace and the further development of this nascent democracy lies in a broadcast spectrum increasingly closed to alternative voices and the growing dominance of media chains. These chains either reinforce the power of the country's longtime business families or represent outside forces in collusion with the Guatemalan government and the military. Before the media could mature and find some measure of independence to counterbalance the postwar political administration, the forces of globalization and media ownership trends sweeping the isthmus conspired to prevent the media from providing voice to political factions that have always been disfranchised in Guatemala. Radio Nuevo Mundo's Mayan programming shows the greater trend has not smothered all growth of alternative voices in the system. But our main focus concerns that greater trend, namely, the use of the media to provide control in systems striving to appear democratic.

While alternative indigenous-language programming constitutes a new frontier of hope showing the democratic possibilities inherent in Guatemala's postwar system, the acquisition of radio properties by the media baron Angel González González represents both the older, closed authoritarian system of the past and the dark side of media globalization. In a future where the means of communication are owned by a select and privileged few, how can communities and grass-roots organizations access and participate in the communication system as they attempt to build democracy? In his work on the threat that globalization and integration of media structures pose to democracy, Robert McChesney writes: "In non-democratic societies those in power invariably dominate the communication systems to maintain their rule."[5] This supports our belief that owners of media systems will protect their market interests by supporting an institutionalized hierarchy rather than open the media system to democratic forces or the true marketplace of ideas.

González's corporate designs illustrate these concepts. In Guatemala González has become the agent of those in power as a way of furthering his corporate goals. By showing he is a friend to the power structure, he maintains dominance in the media sphere, where he can exert the power delegated from Guatemala's elite factions. Some of the region's other media barons, such as Esersky in El Salvador, may wield more power than González does in Guatemala, but his grip on key broadcast holdings makes him a major force, and his regional holdings throughout Latin America add to his clout.

González has a virtual monopoly on Guatemala's commercial television, and in the 1990s he began acquiring considerable radio holdings. Beyond branching into radio González started investing in other broadcast systems throughout the isthmus (see chapters 2, 4, and 6) during the latter portion of the decade. By the end of the century he had acquired a stake in the broadcast operations of all Central American countries except Panama and Honduras.

People in media circles throughout the region call González "the Mexican" not only because of his country of origin but because of his connections with Mexico's giant Televisa, one of the top content providers for Latin American television. González avoids Guatemalan laws preventing foreign ownership of media because he is married to a Guatemalan woman, and the majority interests in his media holdings are listed in her name.[6] Using these means he controls the four main Guatemalan commercial television outlets; the only VHF television network outside his control is the nation's public television outlet. Control of the public station is moving from the army to the state as part of the country's postwar transition. In 1998 González's stations attracted 96 percent of Guatemala's television audience. (Other owners control four UHF stations based in Guatemala City, which along with the government's station compete for the remaining 4 percent of the audience.) Since 1998 González has also doubled his radio holdings in Guatemala, where he now owns twenty-one stations.[7] In addition, he owns most of the country's cinemas, which provide him a source of films for his television channels.[8]

(His cinemas also generate advertising revenue, but ad revenue from Guatemalan cinemas stands at less than 1 percent of the country's total.)[9]

González has worked for almost two decades to acquire this level of dominance in the Guatemalan system. Before he owned media, he represented Televisa, selling programs to broadcasters in the region; he also sold advertising for one Guatemalan station. In 1981, with Televisa as a partner, he took over his first Guatemalan television station. Televisa still holds minority ownership of two of Guatemala's television outlets, Canales 3 and 7. González also partners with Televisa in Mexico, where he owns six affiliates of the Mexican network in southern regions bordering Guatemala.[10] In the 1990s González teamed with Mexico's new commercial broadcast company, TV Azteca, to buy Guatemala's Canal 13.[11]

González bases his Guatemalan operations on cooperation with the government. His stations' news and information programs carry bland items that either pose no challenge to the president or favor whichever party holds power. The amateurish local news programs are some of the worst in Central America. These low-cost efforts at information programming often appear designed to keep the Guatemalan audience uninterested in politics.

The quality of many domestic programs produced on González's monopoly stations suggests someone taking the idea of maximizing profits and reducing expenditures to absurd levels. The Mexican media mogul is not scrimping because he lacks income, however; his television monopoly alone gives him the largest share of advertising revenue of any media owner in Guatemala. His radio investments and television holdings throughout Mexico and Central America bring in additional money. In 1996 television took in 28 percent of Guatemala's advertising revenue, and the medium's share of the advertising market continues to grow.[12] Because González controls 96 percent of the Guatemalan viewing audience, he gets almost all the television advertising revenue. Advertising figures from 1998 show that slightly more than 60 percent of Guatemalans owned a television, mostly clustered in the capital, where the medium reaches almost 98 percent of the city's population. González's commercial and thus political clout is strongest in Guatemala City, the largest city in Central America, with a population of three million.

As a way to extend his reach nationwide, González began buying radio properties in the mid-1990s. In the course of buying his twenty-one stations, he acquired Radio Sonora, a longtime leader in news. Radio Sonora's general programming, however, was generally regarded as inferior to Guatemala's radio ratings champion, Emisoras Unidas. After González took control of Radio Sonora, the station adopted a tabloid style and developed a quick-hitting format more common to news radio in the United States. Radio Sonora also began simulcasting television news programs such as "Notisiete," the country's most popular, which runs on González's Canal 7. By 1998 the changes had resulted in a major ratings upset for Radio Sonora, which averaged a 9.2 rating, meaning slightly more than 9 percent of Guatemala's population listened to this station on an average day.[13] Radio Sonora's closest competitor, Emisoras Unidas, registered a 6.9 rating during the same ratings period. Most stations registered less than 1.0 in Guatemala's crowded radio market.

This incursion into radio allowed González to gain control of more than 30 percent of the Guatemalan listening audience in a relatively short period. His management strategies also increased his stations' audiences. Most important for our purposes, this transfer of media power to the owner with the largest ad revenues not only strengthened González's position as a broker of the information flow but also enhanced the conservative elements in Guatemala's power structure.

González and two other ownership groups share control of roughly 65 percent of the country's radio audience. Until González entered the radio competition, Guatemala's Archila family carried the most clout on the radio dial. The family's Emisoras Unidas, which Radio Sonora dethroned as the country's top radio network in 1998, is still considered by many media observers to be the best radio outlet for news and information. Emisoras Unidas traditionally had the most access to government sources, presenting a mix of news and information that represented conservative and centrist portions of Guatemalan society and politics.[14] Besides owning Emisoras Unidas, the Archila family has a dozen other stations, all based at their modern, computer-driven radio production center in the capital.

The largest radio chain in the country does not compete in the areas of news, information, or music. Radio Grupo Alius, a thirty-station group, broadcasts Christian religious programs exclusively. The stations steer clear of Guatemala's religious divisions and devote their broadcasts to nondenominational evangelical programs that appeal to Catholic and Protestant audiences alike. (Guatemala has been the scene of intense competition among various Protestant groups to convert members of Guatemala's large Catholic population. Guatemala's state television channel still shows evangelical programs, a holdover from the 1980s, when Gen. Efrain Rios-Montt, one of the country's dictators, urged massive conversions to evangelical sects.) This group of religious stations is owned by Alfonso Liu, the head of a successful family of Chinese Guatemalan entrepreneurs.[15]

In a system dominated by these chains, how can stations with alternative programming compete? Stations such as Radio Nuevo Mundo, the home of the most popular Mayan programs, fight hard to carve out a special niche. Although Radio Nuevo Mundo is the third most popular station in the country, it reaches only between 3 to 4 percent of the nation's listeners on a daily basis. One problem facing owners of smaller media concerns is the oversaturation of the Guatemalan radio market. Partly because the government has adopted a laissez-faire approach and partly because entrepreneurs clamor for licenses, the Guatemalan radio spectrum has splintered into tiny portions. The country has 296 radio stations covering an area about the size of Tennessee, with 80 stations based in the capital. Many of the stations outside the capital, however, are merely repeaters for stations originating in Guatemala City. Furthermore, many popular stations are simulcast on AM and FM, which artificially inflates the number. Nevertheless, Guatemala's radio spectrum is oversaturated, reducing the impact of individual stations. Whether by design or accident, this licensing policy has rendered the country's most popular communications medium an ineffectual means to motivate mass audiences.

Radio's impotence in Guatemala comes at a time when television's influence is ascending, as it is throughout the region. Although radio remains the most popular medium, television attracts an increasingly large audience and slice of the nation's advertising pie. Advertising survey information from 1996 showed at least half the population owned a radio (while just 12 percent owned a phone), and ratings from June 1998 indicated that radio had a 98 percent penetration.[16] According to estimates from 1996, by contrast, 43 percent of the population owned a television, and 60 percent could view television on a regular basis in 1998.

Radio's popularity may stem from Guatemala's low Spanish literacy rate. Advertising experts note that only 65 percent of Guatemalans can read Spanish. Guatemalans speak at least twenty-four other languages, mostly Mayan dialects, although Garifuna and Xinka minorities also exist. Some of the Mayan dialects spoken in the country, although similar to one another, share only a few words. This diverse linguistic landscape makes mass communication difficult, but most Guatemalans understand spoken Spanish and have access to a radio, which makes that medium the most appealing. It is also the easiest to receive, given the country's rugged terrain of mountains and rain forest.

Despite the fractured nature of the country's geography, linguistic terrain, and radio licensing, the study of media power in Guatemala shows a broadcast system dominated by three families. The Archilas, the Lius, and González control most of Guatemala's radio audience of more than 11 million people. In a country where just 12 percent earn enough to exceed the official poverty level, and 60 percent fall in the category of extreme poverty,[17] these media barons control powerful communication instruments with the potential to sway Guatemala's masses.

Nevertheless, the media have traditionally been a weak, disorganized, and fractious group, far from an effective counterweight to those in power. As we have noted, the media's historical role and their relationship to the nation's politics are important factors when evaluating a nation's media dynamics. As might be expected given the fractured nature of radio broadcasting in the country, both television and print surpassed it as instigators of reform during the only period when the Guatemalan media managed to provoke change and mass demonstrations.

In 1993, before González had driven other competitors out of the television market, President Jorge Serrano Elias ordered Guatemala's security forces to seize control of Canales 11 and 13. The channels had run interviews of the Nobel Peace Prize laureate Rigoberta Menchú and other representatives of human rights groups.[18] This was just the beginning of Serrano's media crackdown. During his bid to throw out the constitution in what has been called an *autogolpe* (many in Latin America refer to this concept as a self-coup), Serrano installed censors at all the major media outlets except those owned by González.

Newspapers and magazines led the way against Serrano in 1993, perhaps the first time in the country's history that the media collectively flexed their muscles. During Serrano's attempt to grab extraconstitutional power, newspapers rallied to oppose censorship and eventually catalyzed street protests against Serrano. At the country's only news magazine, *Crónica*, censors attempted to stop its distribution after they found articles criticizing Serrano in the text. The censors ordered all copies of the weekly magazine be impounded. Editors and reporters responded by smuggling out copies in their underwear or tucked inside their pants before giving them away on the streets of Guatemala City.[19]

Censors were also trying to stop the flow of information in the country's oldest daily newspaper, *La Hora*. Oscar Marroquín Rojas, the paper's publisher, remembers ordering reporters to smuggle newspapers to a nearby bus stop so they could be given away to people on the buses.[20]

Across town, at the relatively new *Siglo Veintiuno* (Twenty-first century), editors changed the paper's masthead to read *Siglo Catorce* (Fourteenth century) to signal the presence of government censors. Whenever censors touched a story, the editors replaced it with blank space rather than run the altered version. Other papers followed suit. Only *Prensa Libre,* the capital's most-respected paper, failed to protest the censors.

Less than a week after Serrano began his media crackdown, reporters from most of the nation's major media outlets rallied in downtown Guatemala City to protest the censorship. Hundreds of citizens joined the protest. After days of similar protests sparked by the recalcitrant print media, Serrano left the country for exile in Panama.

"We brought down one president," Estuardo Zapeta, a prominent columnist at *Siglo Veintiuno,* remembered years later. "We can do it again."[21] As Zapeta recalled it, the Serrano era created a new sense of vitality for the Guatemalan media. Some members of the press began to believe that the media could play a balancing role with the central government in the evolving system, much as it does elsewhere in Central America.

Nevertheless, the belief that these newspapers could provide the same sort of balance that other papers bring to more entrenched democratic systems, such as those in the United States and Europe, inflates the role of newspapers in the Guatemalan system. The country's poor literacy rate constrains the papers' impact. Fewer than 65 percent of the population can read Spanish. The country's mountainous terrain also limits the distribution of the major newspapers, which are based in the capital. Of course, newspaper columnists and some of the country's better reporters set the media agenda for the nation, much as newspapers do in more developed systems. In addition, as do their counterparts elsewhere in Central America, many of Guatemala's radio stations use the newspapers as their main source of news, and some of their talk and public affairs programs also draw from newspaper reports. Still, newspapers have little impact beyond the stories or opinions radio stations pick up and amplify. Moreover, many radio news directors, who usually have no economic connection to the major papers, edit the messages they take from the print media, further filtering the product before it reaches listeners. This unreliable system gives newspapers their only way to sway or even connect with large segments of the population.

In such a system a galvanizing event such as overt state censorship was the only context in which newspaper messages (or lack of them, in the case of *Siglo Veintiuno*) could offer significant resistance to the central government's attempts to seize more control. Indeed, only the synergy of all the media—newspapers, television, and to a lesser extent, radio—simultaneously focused on censorship and extraconstitutional presidential powers proved to be a catalyst for demonstrations. In today's system, with broadcasting increasingly in the grip of those who favor institutional power and readily bow to censorship, the media may have less power to invoke antigovernment sentiments and see them explode into palpable political change. In the 1990s, however, the aggressiveness demonstrated by editors and columnists such as Zapeta stood in marked contrast to the historically weak role of the Guatemalan press.

In Guatemala newspapers seem to appeal almost solely to government, media, and business elites. Fewer than 3 percent of the population read the papers on a daily basis, although the readership's elite status let print media take in 40 percent of the nation's advertising revenues in the mid 1990s.[22]

Prensa Libre is the most popular of Guatemala City's seven daily papers and the only paper that regularly distributes outside the capital. *Siglo Veintiuno* can sometimes be found outside Guatemala City, but distribution remains inconsistent. *Prensa Libre* distributes 120,000 copies daily and sells a column-inch of space to advertisers for $13.40.

A conglomerate of five successful families opened *Prensa Libre* in 1951; the same five families—including the Zarcos, Garcias, and the Contreras clan—have owned the paper and its spin-off publications ever since. These owners were generally sympathetic to the probusiness party of Guatemala's president Alvaro Arzú Irigoyen, the National Advancement Party (Spanish acronym, PAN). During the Arzú administration, however, the government openly split with this group of media owners. First the government pressured advertising away from the paper (see chapter 7), and then members of the Arzú administration began an organized public relations campaign to demean the group's members.[23] At the close of the 1990s these developments had left *Prensa Libre* searching for its editorial place in the Guatemalan system; the paper with a history of taking moderate to conservative stances in support of the government began to represent some of the more liberal voices in the business community.

Nevertheless, fellow journalists have treated the paper and its owners to a milder form of the criticism they leveled at broadcaster González: some cannot forgive them for submitting meekly to censorship during the Serrano era, the only major newspaper group to do so. The owners of *Prensa Libre* adopted an attitude in keeping with the typical approach of the Guatemalan media until the 1990s, taking limited and isolated stands against the government while usually acceding to those in power.

This traditional role of Guatemalan newspapers was established during the nineteenth century under the dictator Manuel Estrada Cabrera. Estrada kept a tight system of censorship in place for most of his rule. His power unraveled in 1920, however, when the first paper of note started publishing and immediately took a concerted stand against the dictatorship and censorship. The paper, *La Hora*, belonged to Clemente Marroquín Rojas, who in founding the paper initiated a Guatemalan publishing dynasty. Marroquín's paper was the first to adopt social reform as a platform. It challenged the central government by publishing stories about army massacres of peasants and covered union battles against government forces and the nation's business elite.[24] Clemente Marroquín eventually served as vice-president under Julio Mendez Montenegro in the 1960s while other members of the Marroquín family guided the paper, which remained critical of the government.[25]

La Hora, the country's oldest newspaper, continues to run stories from a socially progressive position, along with investigative work, but it may be fighting a losing battle. The nation's only afternoon daily, its circulation has steadily declined for years, and as of 1998 it was publishing only 3,000 copies daily. Oscar Marroquín, who heads the family ownership group, is in his seventies and often speaks of retiring and closing the paper. In addition, an advertising boycott of the paper orchestrated by the Arzú government has been slowly choking the Marroquín family's enterprise.

La Hora has faced government pressure before, however. The dictator Gen. Jorge Ubico Casteñeda ordered the paper closed and forced the Marroquín family into exile. Ubico sought to eliminate press freedoms entirely. He also used troops to break up labor meetings and student protests. He said he believed Guatemalans "needed a strong hand" to keep order and quell dissent.[26] With the downfall of Ubico in 1944, the Marroquíns returned and reopened the paper, reestablishing it as a voice of the country's opposition. The family's political line has maintained a steady drumbeat for liberal and progressive social change since that time, even during the protracted guerrilla war that began in the 1960s.

Although *La Hora*'s direct power in the Guatemalan system may be waning, the Marroquín family's influence on the quality of the nation's journalistic enterprises remains as strong as ever. As do the Chamorros in Nicaragua, the Marroquíns powerfully influence the media scene in Guatemala. Gonzalo Marroquín is the editor of *Prensa Libre*. His cousin, José Rubén Zamora Marroquín, founded *elPeriodico*, a publication that was eventually bought out by the *Prensa Libre* group.

Zamora Marroquín started *elPeriodico* in 1996. Like many papers in Central America, *elPeriodico* was born of protest. Zamora Marroquín had been the editor of *Siglo Veintiuno*. After a dispute with *Siglo Veintiuno*'s ownership group, he broke away to found his own newspaper. In doing so, he took many of the older paper's better reporters and staffers, a group that had been battle-tested during the heady days of protest against Serrano's censorship campaign. After founding *elPeriodico*, the iconoclastic editor went about recruiting some of Guatemala's best journalists. The resulting publication connects directly with the Guatemalan intelligentsia and upper crust, even though it occasionally stoops to the tabloidism rampant in the country's papers. Coverage of sensational topics did not boost the newspaper's circulation, however. One reason Zamora Marroquín sold the paper to the *Prensa Libre* group in 1998 was declining circulation: only 30,000 copies are sold daily.[27]

The *Prensa Libre* group also owns one of the country's most notorious tabloids, *Nuestro Diario*. This paper began during the Ubico dictatorship in the 1930s as a progovernment publication—the paper's owners traded favorable coverage for seats in that era's rubber-stamp legislature. In the mid-1940s the Guatemalan government under Pres. Juan José Arévalo purchased *Nuestro Diario* and ran it as a state corporation. When that paper was sold in a privatization effort in 1950, the five-family group that bought it relaunched it as *Prensa Libre*. In 1997 the *Prensa Libre* group brought out a newer version of *Nuestro Diario* in response to a successful entertainment-oriented publication started by their competition. The paper is filled with entertainment gossip and the type of stories common in U.S. supermarket tabloids.

With these three publications, the owners of the *Prensa Libre* group control a little more than half the newspapers circulating in the country. They have revamped their publications' designs, and their modern looks and approaches appeal to different market segments. Intellectuals and the elite class constitute the main audience for *elPeriodico*, while blue-collar and pink-collar workers are attracted to *Nuestro Diario*. *Prensa Libre*, the traditional newspaper of record, represents business interests—increasingly, liberal business interests that might oppose the central government.

The *Prensa Libre* group finds its main competition in the owners of *Siglo Veintiuno*. *Siglo Veintiuno*'s ownership group founded its flagship paper in 1990 and expanded its enterprises through the next decade. The group comprises major investors under the name Corporación de Noticias. Four families representing some of Guatemala's largest corporate interests are the main investors in the group. *Siglo Veintiuno* is distributed to 55,000 readers daily and is the only paper to compete with *Prensa Libre* outside the capital.[28] Although the newspaper and its spin-offs may not be as profitable as some of its investors' other businesses (including Guatemala's major brewer, liquor distributor, and supermarket chain), *Siglo Veintiuno* has garnered acclaim from outside the country. In 1999 the paper was called one of the five best in Latin America at the Second Annual Congress on Latin American Journalism.[29]

Nevertheless, although non-Guatemalan critics have praised *Siglo Veintiuno*'s independent voice, the paper seemed in tune with the Arzú administration during the latter portion of the 1990s. Significantly, the paper was one of the few unscathed by a nationwide advertising boycott aimed at journalists whom President Arzú viewed as enemies. Media and political observers in Guatemala said the publication expressed the views of the president's faction of the PAN.[30] Although Arzú still faced criticism from the paper, it generally represented moderate to right-wing viewpoints in the country's business community. Moreover, Arzú was often allowed to air his controversial views in the paper, especially his views on the media.

The paper may have expressed this bias because its owners were aligned with Arzú's political and economic policies. Indeed, they represented some of the most successful business and oligarchic families in Guatemala: the Castillo, Botrán, Gutiérrez, and Paiz families.

In the 1980s the Castillos were considered to be the richest family in Guatemala.[31] In 1985 the family's assets were estimated at $67 million, equivalent to almost a third of the country's national budget at the time. The Castillos started their empire as brewers with the Cerveceria Centroamericana in 1886. Since 1929 the Castillos have been the only brewers in Guatemala, producing the two national brands, Gallo and Monte Carlo. In the 1940s the family branched into soft drink production and distilled water and acquired a Canada Dry distributing license. In the 1950s the family diversified into marketing to help distribute its various beverages, a move that brought further expansion into advertising firms in the 1960s.

As might befit a company with a base in beverage production, the Castillos were early investors in bottling firms, investing in one bottling company, La Mariposa, in 1893. La Mariposa is now responsible for distributing Pepsi in Guatemala, along with mineral water and fruit drinks. The Castillos also have interests in other bottling firms and the glass company CAVISA, the tenth-largest firm in Guatemala.

The various wings of the Castillo family have extended the family's core businesses to include dairy farming, cattle ranching, and banking. Despite Guatemalan business's record of poor labor relations, the Castillos have for decades paid workers above-average salaries. Workers at the family's breweries have also received substantial benefits, including health care, education, and even housing.

The Castillos' partners in *Siglo Veintiuno*, the Botráns, also boast a history of success. The Botráns immigrated from Spain to Guatemala at the beginning of the twentieth century. They started a small distillery and are known today for their production of rum and vodka. The family participated in Guatemala's sugar-cane boom in the 1960s, and it now operates the third-largest sugar mill in the country. The family also diversified into banking, transportation firms, and cement factories.[32]

Another key partner in the *Siglo Veintiuno* group, the Paiz family, owns the top supermarket chain in Guatemala. The family was prominent in the Christian Democratic Party when it was active in the 1980s.[33]

The *Siglo Veintiuno* group's latest venture, the tabloid publication *Al Día*, has become a publishing sensation in Guatemala. Begun in 1996, it is now the second most popular paper there.[34] The paper's success has led many observers to blame *Al Día* for shifting Guatemalan news squarely into the tabloid zone. The paper distributes 60,000 copies daily. Its stories focus on sensational police raids, disasters, rat infestations, and other tabloid fare.

Although many parts of Central America haven't developed the sophisticated niche marketing necessary for a large magazine industry, Guatemala had one of the best glossy news magazines in the region. The weekly *Crónica* (whose style owes as much to *Time* as it does to Mexico's renowned investigative magazine *Proceso*) had an intellectual and editorial impact on the country and was respected in the journalistic community, which gave the magazine a presence beyond its 10,000 weekly circulation rate. In 1998, however, the magazine's owners lost a year-long battle with the Arzú administration. Using the advertising boycott President Arzú had employed against other publications, the government began pressuring the magazine for change. Eventually the owners buckled, and *Crónica* was sold to new owners aligned with the Arzú administration.[35]

This panorama of the Guatemalan media landscape shows a system facing backlash from a strong central government after the media finally asserted themselves early in the 1990s. It also shows that traditional methods of appeasing the central government are just as important in the current system, perhaps because of the large foreign ownership bloc in the broadcast industry. The dominance of the broadcast media—due in large part to poor distribution practices of Guatemalan dailies and low literacy rates—coupled with their tendency to acquiesce to government demands, may be further retarding the development of democracy and delaying the maturation of the media's role in Guatemalan society.

In describing the development of the Latin American press, Silvio Waisbord, a specialist on Latin American media, notes that most media systems began in what he calls the "oligarchic period."[36] The end to Guatemala's protracted guerrilla struggle did not wipe away the oligarchy, and the ensuing uneasy peace in some ways bolsters the nation's longtime ruling forces. The low circulation figures for the nation's newspapers certainly suggest that the press addresses only the elite. Except for the tabloids, most of the newspapers directly address the oligarchy or members of the business class who seek to open the system and diffuse the oligarchic power structure. Unlike other portions of Latin America that evolved away from the oligarchic period before the electronic media made a major impact, however, Guatemala (and many other parts of Central America) saw the electronic media capture most of the mass audience before that evolutionary process could begin. The system cannot move forward, for broadcasters are trapped in a stasis they helped create to retain lucrative broadcast licenses. Newspapers are blocked from acquiring the mass audience necessary to counter a strong centralized government and thus advance the nation's media evolution. The anti-Serrano movement saw newspapers and parts of the television industry combining to create an antigovernment media synergy that eventually transferred itself into mass protests. With the television spectrum now in the hands of a Mexican investor beholden to the government and the radio spectrum divided and diffused—owners friendly to the nation's oligarchy control 95 percent of the listening audience, while the remaining portions of the spectrum are divided into tiny fractions for a wide list of owners—the Guatemalan system has actually moved backward from the Serrano period and seems locked into its current state for the near term.

These developments among the media are in keeping with the evolution of large business interests in Guatemala. The agro-export sector of the Guatemalan economy shows a similar type of elitist structure. The history of Guatemala's elite class and oligarchy stretches back to the 1840s and the beginning of coffee farming.[37] Coffee remains the country's most important export crop, and Guatemala is the world's fifth-largest coffee producer. Although the country's oligarchy began forming around the coffee elite, it avoided the monoculture of its neighbors Honduras and El Salvador, where one crop dominated, and other export crops, especially cotton and sugar, also developed their own elite factions. Much as their counterparts did in El Salvador, the coffee elite expanded their plantations in the nineteenth century by using the state to expropriate land from indigenous groups. In the 1880s, during the dictatorship of Justo Rufino Barrios, Guatemala's coffee elite pressured the government to deal with a labor shortage that was stalling further expansion of the coffee crop. The state obliged with a set of laws and cruel enforcement that impressed indigenous workers into service and left them nearly slaves to the plantation owners.[38] This policy stayed in effect for more than fifty years.

During the civil war some members of the agricultural oligarchy were linked to death squads and Mario Sandoval Alarcón's fascist National Liberation Movement (MLN).[39] The MLN had been part of the ultraconservative political scene in Guatemala for a generation, from the 1960s through the 1980s. The MLN also helped finance and organize El Salvador's reactionary ARENA party. Through the MLN and its secret operations, members of the oligarchy were able to coordinate domestic coercion with the country's military and also support clandestine paramilitary groups.

By the 1980s, after almost 150 years of catering to the agricultural elite, the Guatemalan land tenure system reflected the vast discrepancies in power and wealth built up over time. For instance, during that period just 1 percent of the country's coffee growers produced 70 percent of the crop because they controlled the vast majority of land. Currently, an elite group constituting just 2.5 percent of the country's agricultural businesses controls 65 percent of all agricultural land in the country.[40] Discrepancies are also apparent in the sugar and cotton industries. Forty-seven families controlled 75 percent of all cotton production, and 7 percent of the sugar farms controlled 95 percent of the harvest.[41]

The Guatemalan media reflect this oligarchic system. A dozen families dominate the electronic media, controlling all the television stations and almost all the radio stations, and two business groups made up of nine families control all but one of the nation's newspapers and 99 percent of the newspapers in circulation. Many of these media owners also own major businesses or industries in Guatemala. Some are part of the agricultural oligarchy. Indeed, outside of the *Prensa Libre* group and the radio and television holdings of González, economies of scale mean that most of Guatemala's media properties are unprofitable and may be owned strictly for the political or social clout they yield.

Again, Guatemala provides an apt example for our conjecture that lacking strong democratic roots, media systems will tend to support and reflect a country's oligarchic tendencies. In such a system, radio programs such as Radio Nuevo Mundo's popular Mayan-language and cultural fare represent a strong break with the past. Such programs point the way toward a possible pluralistic future for the media and thus society in Guatemala. It is unclear, however, whether such programs will find fertile ground in the postwar era or whether they will eventually face new authoritarian challenges through backlash from a traditionally strong central government and its paramilitary allies, the protectors of the nation's oligarchy.

Current debates about the media are not centered on access for a wider public and thus cannot provide a road toward democracy. Instead, the media squabbles seem to involve little more than elites fighting, with the government and among themselves, over shades of difference. The nation's poor and developing populace matter only as consumers, listeners, and ratings points.

6 Costa Rica, the Exception That Proves the Rule

As the twenty-first century begins, Costa Rica faces a new challenge from outside the nation's media system. Known for years as "the Switzerland of Central America," Costa Rica has developed as an enclave of peace surrounded by tumult. The country's advanced social welfare and educational systems, along with its long-standing democracy, have proved to be buffers against the wars raging elsewhere. They have also provided strong foundations for the country's journalists. The country's prosperity and educated population of 3.5 million have become highly attractive to media investors in the information age.

In a pattern atypical for Central America, international investors, including those from outside the region, have descended on Costa Rica not just to serve this populace but also to profit. This influx has spawned debate about their long-term effects on the country's media system and politics. Costa Ricans themselves are wary. They are unaccustomed to such concentrated attention from outside commercial forces.

When looking at democratization in Central America through the prism of media systems, we have noted that these systems cannot support democracy without the proper historical foundations and support from elites. But what can be gleaned from Costa Rica, a nation with deep roots in a democratic tradition? This is not one of the isthmus's protodemocracies we analyzed previously. Costa Rica's democratic tradition began in 1889 and is regarded as the most stable and enduring not just in Central America but in all of Latin America.[1] Our theories about media development seem to have less application here, for not only do the country's democratic roots reach back to the nineteenth century, but its agriculturally based oligarchy has faded in importance. Costa Rica's unique situation, however, allows us to look at a potential future for media systems throughout Central America as we analyze how this enclave developed.

Like its political and social welfare systems, Costa Rica's media system is the most advanced and specialized in Central America. Until the 1990s and the arrival of international investors, that system developed internally. As our previously stated principles suggest, Costa Rica's political history will reveal important clues explaining why the nation's media system has developed and supported democracy while the media in neighboring countries have sometimes limited the full range of debate necessary in a democratic system.

Costa Rica's singular attributes go back to the nation's founding. Several elements combined to creating an atmosphere that allowed this unique nation to develop. Many Costa Ricans believe that the seeds of democracy were planted because their nation developed around small land holdings and had fewer ties to conquistadors with large *haciendas.* This largely mythic view has some basis in fact. Although Columbus mistakenly named the country "rich coast," it would not yield its true bounty for centuries. Columbus thought Costa Rica would be filled with gold mines, but the country lacks significant mineral resources. Spanish settlers in Costa Rica suffered trying to maintain the colonial era's traditional *haciendas* and labor-intensive crops because they were unable to depend on large numbers of indigenous laborers, as could their counterparts elsewhere in Central America and in Mexico. The indigenous population was sparse, having been drastically reduced through diseases the Spaniards brought with them. Partly as a result of this, Costa Rica did not develop a large mestizo population, as did its neighbors. Forced to farm their own lands, many Spanish nobles chose other parts of the region to colonize. According to the myth, a homogeneous nation of small land holders eventually became today's democracy.

The process was much more involved, however, as has been pointed out by Lowell Gudmundson, an expert on Costa Rican history. Because Costa Rica evolved far from Guatemala City, the region's colonial capital, it developed different customs and commercial hierarchies. Costa Rica was the southernmost point in what was the Kingdom of Guatemala under Spanish rule. (Panama was not considered part of Central America and until 1903 was part of Colombia.) Gudmundson has noted that the region's sparser population and hence fewer laborers meant that Costa Rica's elites, unlike those elsewhere in Central America, did not develop solely as holders of large agricultural properties before diversifying into a merchant class.[2] Costa Rican elites meshed these roles in the early phases of colonialism while establishing ways to work with a larger group of small land holders. This relationship between elites and so-called smallholders, uncommon in Central America, affected class relations in Costa Rica for centuries. The elites discovered that they needed to respect the smallholders' social and political views if they were to lead the area's economic progress. By 1821, when it gained independence, Costa Rica was more open to dialogue among its classes and to a more equitable division of land and property than was any other place in Central America.[3]

In the nineteenth century Costa Rica's rugged land participated in the region's coffee boom, and the country developed its first major export crop. Although large coffee plantations did develop, and new elites who focused on coffee processing emerged, the business structures already in place allowed smallholders to profit from the boom as well. Costa Rica thus developed a critical number of middle-class entrepreneurs.

Costa Rica also benefited from its reputation as a Central American backwater. Its reputation as a poor territory kept the nation outside many of the region's geopolitical struggles during the colonial era. With the United States' designs for an interoceanic canal focused on Nicaragua and then Panama, Costa Rica escaped Washington's early imperialist policies as well. Costa Rica is notable for repulsing the invasion of the freebooter William Walker and his U.S.-based mercenary army in 1857, the last time Walker would threaten Central America after his disastrous rule over Nicaragua.

Although the United Fruit Company had its beginnings in Costa Rica, and the nation ceded territory to the company to develop a railroad along the Caribbean coast, its political influence fell far short of that in Guatemala, where United Fruit helped foment the infamous 1954 coup that led to nearly half a century of instability. Nor would the company have the same political influence and dominance as in Honduras. When United Fruit began operations in Costa Rica in the latter part of the nineteenth century, the society was already blending in complex ways, and the nation's elite, formed around the coffee industry, was moving toward democratic forms of governance. In all these ways Costa Rica managed to insulate itself from the political and economic shocks that radically affected the development of its neighbors.

By rejecting the politics of class differences that have characterized many of the problems of neighboring states, Costa Ricans developed a political system known for compromise and open discussion of competing ideas. In turn, the Costa Rican media have earned a reputation throughout Latin America as a cornerstone of these political traditions. The nation had already drafted a law guaranteeing press freedom by 1835.[4]

In 1889, the year generally regarded as the beginning of the nation's democracy, *La Prensa Libre,* Costa Rica's oldest newspaper, began publishing in San José, the capital. This newspaper, which still exists, has survived in part because of the nation's high literacy rate—listed at 95 percent, the highest in Central America—and the populace's interest in current events, business, and government.[5] Currently run by Andrés Borrasé Sanou and his son Carlos, *La Prensa Libre* circulates 50,000 copies daily. Since its inception the paper has tried to reflect centrist to moderate-right views and remain independent from political parties. This alone sets it off from the partisan press of the era when it began—and from some contemporary newspapers. "*La Prensa Libre* hails the president one day and criticizes him the next," noted Rolando Angulo Zeledón, one of Costa Rica's longtime radio *noticieros.*[6] This early move toward professional objectivity and the nation's high literacy rates also helped diminish class differences in Costa Rica.

The Borrasé family acquired the newspaper in the 1920s. After being educated in New York at Columbia University's prestigious journalism school, Andrés Borrasé became the newspaper's director in 1949. This was a heady time in Costa Rican politics, the beginning of what is called the second phase of the nation's democracy, which began with a new constitution following the Costa Rican civil war. Andrés Borrasé remembers the decade's previous years as a very different time for journalists, a time when presidents and politicians were inclined to pressure journalists to print stories with a particular spin.[7]

Most political analysts peg the 1940s as a watershed era for Costa Rica's democracy. The worldwide depression had hit Costa Rica's economy hard, accentuating class differences. Economic difficulties then combined with the country's controversial entry into World War II supporting the Allies to spark unrest. Unions and the communist party organized against the nation's elite. Pres. Rafael Angel Calderón Guardia stood at the center of the storm. A leader of the National Republican Party, Calderón represented the nation's agricultural elite when first elected, but at heart he was a reformer. He began the move toward a safety net for the poor and elderly by creating a social security system. Unlike elite groups in neighboring countries, Costa Rican elites have often shown a willingness to share wealth with other classes. Nevertheless, Calderón's push toward a social welfare democracy was too much for most of the elites, who abandoned his cause. To support his new programs, Calderón cobbled together an alliance with the communists and the Catholic church.

Opposition to the president began to coalesce around Otilio Ulate Blanco, who published the now-defunct *Diario de Costa Rica*, but it could not prevent the election of Calderón's handpicked successor and vice-president, Teodoro Picado Michalski, in 1944.[8] Ulate claimed election fraud because, he said, unions and the communists harassed voters.

Tensions were mounting as the country's middle class and merchants with anticommunist fears aligned with the nation's agricultural elites. Many of the nation's newspapers were filled with invective and polemics during this period; many were founded just to represent a particular viewpoint. *La Nación* was thus born in 1946 to rail against the redistributive social policies of the Picado-Calderón alliance. Even more conservative than *Diario de Costa Rica*, *La Nación* was started by the Jimenez de la Guardia family to represent the views of the nation's agricultural elite, who had dominated the political scene during the first phase of Costa Rica's democracy. The Jimenez de la Guardia family included prominent landholders with diversified interests in coffee, cattle, rice, and sugar production. It also owns the nation's largest brewery, the Costa Rican Brewery Company. The family would later open the nation's first McDonald's franchise, the first to be based outside the United States.[9]

In 1948 Calderón, backed by Picado, made another run for the presidency. This time he faced publisher Ulate, who won easily. Calderón's supporters were unwilling to hand over power to Ulate, however, and a forty-day civil war ensued. José Figueres Ferrer led the forces opposing Calderón. His forces triumphed and established an anticommunist junta before restoring Ulate to the presidency in 1949.

By the time the publisher had become president, however, Figueres had moved to reshape the nation's democracy. A new constitution established a powerful electoral tribunal, among other reforms. While banning the communists (the Popular Vanguard Party, or PVP), Figueres's junta decided to broaden and expand social welfare and educational programs meant to include the nation's lower classes and to redistribute some of the nation's wealth. Figueres and his National Liberation Party (Spanish acronym, PLN) went on to triumph in the 1952 elections. He further expanded Costa Rica's social welfare programs during his administration while continuing to fight communism. As sociologist Jeffery Paige reported, "Communists were imprisoned, exiled and murdered."[10] The party did not return to the Costa Rican political scene until 1972. By reshaping Calderón's social welfare programs while working to diversify the Costa Rican economy from its agricultural base, Figueres diminished the power of the traditional elites while rallying populist support for his policies.

Figueres and the PLN are credited with not only restoring democracy in Costa Rica but deepening it beyond the type of superficial, fledgling democracy run strictly by elite forces now common throughout Central America. Importantly, Figueres, the first Costa Rican president not descended from Spanish conquerors, came from the country's middle class. He also pushed to abolish the Costa Rican armed forces after the civil war. Because of Figueres's rabid anticommunist policies, the United States saw no reason to interfere with his policies, which included a tough renegotiation with the United Fruit Company over proceeds for the state.

The Figueres era also changed the way the media reacted to politics. "In the 1940s we left journalism in the hands of political parties," said radio journalist Angulo. "*El Diario de Costa Rica* was controlled by one political party. *La Tribuna* was in the hands of another. Today, not a single medium is controlled by political parties. That is the greatest success we have achieved." Significantly, the newspapers Angulo mentioned have disappeared in the modern landscape, where the media do not stake their existence on the political fortunes of one party. Although tendencies to support political policies or parties sometimes appear in the Costa Rican system, they are much more subtle than the polarized media slants of Costa Rica's neighbors.

"In some countries in Central America," said Shirley Saborío, the editor of Costa Rica's glossy business magazine *Actualidad Economica*, "at publications like *Siglo Veintiuno* in Guatemala, *El Diario de Hoy* in El Salvador, or *La Prensa Grafica* there, it is easy to predict how they will handle information, and their focus is clearly in the interests of the owners of the publishing group. In Costa Rica, it's not that way. I think the people demand each day more objectivity and analysis and more precision in the news."[11]

Although still regarded as a conservative paper, *La Nación* has emerged as Costa Rica's most popular publication, and it is often mentioned as one of the best newspapers in Latin America. The Jimenez de la Guardia family loosened its grip on the paper by selling shares in its enterprise, and at times they have claimed as many as 2,000 individuals own a stake in the company. *La Nación* and Panama's *La Prensa* are the only two newspapers in Central America controlled by large numbers of shareholders. Nonetheless, the Jimenez de la Guardia family in various forms still controls most of the shares in the company that publishes *La Nación*, which circulates 113,000 copies daily. "*La Nación* is a corporation in which some families and family members are majority holders," explained Eduardo Ulibarri, the paper's editor. "No one person controls the company. I would say that the owners' influence over content is very limited. The newspaper has a philosophy that all upper management shares. Based on that, each individual has a high degree of independence, which is extended down to all levels. Because of the structure of this media outlet, the power of the owners is very limited and diluted."[12]

Ulibarri sees the media as playing an essential and important role in the nation's democracy, although they have become depoliticized since the 1940s. "The media construct a national identity through their selection, the type of realities they portray and personalities they give play to," he said. "They are essential ingredients of the national fiber. Without them there would be no common frame of reference within which to discuss issues."

La Nación is the most profitable publication in the country, attracting 70 to 80 percent of all print media advertising. This is an important and influential position, because the Costa Rican advertising market is the richest in Central America, drawing about $185 million annually, more than double the total of the neighboring Panamanian market, which is estimated at $78 million. By some estimates, the newspaper was on track to draw $56 million in advertising revenue in 2000.[13] To put this in perspective, *La Nación*'s revenues were more than double those of the entire media market in neighboring Nicaragua and were equal to the entire market in nearby El Salvador, which is estimated at nearly $50 million in revenues.

The size of the advertising pie reflects Costa Rica's relative wealth. Its economy is more diversified than those elsewhere in Central America, with only about a quarter of the nation's jobs devoted to the agricultural sector. Costa Rica's industrial sector is more advanced than those of its neighbors and employs about a quarter of the nation's workers. About half the population works in the service sector and tourism industry, a principal mechanism for attracting foreign exchange. Although the economy is relatively strong, about 13 percent of the work force is either unemployed or underemployed, and estimates place the poverty rate at 7 to 25 percent. Many of the poor, however, receive benefits from the state's various social welfare agencies. Costa Rica thus ranks thirty-first on the UN's Human Development Index, on par with industrial nations, whereas none of its neighbors ranks higher than 112.[14]

To further diversify and attract more readers, *La Nación* launched a second publication, *Al Día*, in 1992. Unlike *La Nación*, which is a colorful yet serious newspaper of record, *Al Día* uses a tabloid style, light features, and a focus on entertainment news and sports to attract a younger audience. *Al Día* circulates to about 35,000 readers daily and in 2000 was estimated to bring in an additional $3.5 million in advertising revenue for the corporation that owns *La Nación.*

A variety of magazines also flourish in Costa Rica's sophisticated media market. Although the publishing group behind *La Nación* discontinued its impressive review of politics and economic news in the magazine *Rumbo,* it retains the country's top magazine with *Perfil,* a classic glossy women's magazine. *Perfil* pulls in an additional $1.5 million in advertising revenue for the group.

In addition, the *La Nación* group has controlling interest in the nation's most profitable weekly publication, *El Financiero,* although several other investors also have a stake in it. Like the group's other publications, *El Financiero* does well at attracting advertising, taking in $1.3 million in 2000. Although it began in the mid-1990s, a time of economic downturn for the nation, the timing proved effective, as the business community was hungry for more analysis of the Costa Rican market.

The Jimenez family publications face their main competition for circulation in *Diario Extra,* a flashy tabloid with a reputation for hard-hitting investigative reporting that sometimes matches the work of *La Nación.* Ulibarri, *La Nación's* editor, has quite a bit of respect for the material in the feisty competitor, which is published by William Gómez: "Gómez represents the typical model of a person who is a visionary: active and a great risk-taker. Courageous." Ulibarri added that "*Extra* is very successful and is still at a stage in which Gómez is not only the owner but also the director, the driving force" behind the publication. The paper, which began publishing in 1978, circulates to 100,000 readers daily, and in 2000 it drew an estimated $3 million in advertising revenue. (Gómez has since branched out, buying a radio station, Radio America, and a UHF television operation named Extra TV that runs on channel 42 in San José.)

In 1995, during difficult economic times, Gómez acquired a minority stake in *La Prensa Libre.* The Borrasé family had been struggling to keep the operation profitable, and the newspaper's staff failed in an attempt to buy control of the paper. *La Prensa Libre* was estimated to have brought in only $1.5 million in advertising revenue during 2000, performing far below its competitors. "The market is too small for so many media outlets," noted Gómez. "It is impossible for us to have six newspapers and our population is 3.5 million!"[15]

Costa Rica's newest daily publication, *El Heraldo,* seems to be struggling with the realities of this limited market. Founded as a corporation headed by Manuel Polini Nietzen in 1994, just before an economic downturn hit the country, *El Heraldo's* daily circulation has fluctuated from 10,000 to 25,000 copies. In 2000 the publication's advertising share was the lowest among the daily papers, and it seemed to be shrinking. *El Heraldo*'s advertising revenues were estimated at about $800,000 annually, a tiny sliver of the market when compared to the colossus of *La Nación*.

On the business front, *La Nación*'s major competitor for advertising is *La Republica*. Begun in 1950 as a voice for social welfare programs, *La Republica* generally supports the social policies of the PLN, although that tendency is less noticeable now than when the paper was founded. Costa Rica's Una Co-op, an investment cooperative, sold its control of the publication to Hollinger, Inc., an international publishing chain based in Canada, when the Costa Rican market opened to international media investors in the mid-1990s.

Given the sophisticated nature of the Costa Rican media market, its reputation for freedom, and its revenues and revenue potential, it was only a matter of time before global forces entered the market in a major way. Hollinger, a Toronto-based company with newspapers in Canada, owns publications in several countries, including the *Chicago Sun-Times*, London's *Daily Telegraph*, and the *Jerusalem Post*. In the Costa Rican market Hollinger's *La Republica* circulates 60,000 copies daily and brought in an estimated $4.8 million in advertising revenue in 2000.

The Costa Rican market also supports a number of important weekly publications, among them an English-language newspaper originally intended for the country's large expatriate community, the *Tico Times*, which is known for strong reporting and breaking stories. The *Tico Times* circulates 12,000 copies weekly and brought in about $750,000 in advertising revenue in 2000.

The glossy bimonthly magazine *Actualidad Economica* focuses on marketing and business analysis. This magazine, founded in 1986 by the Trejos family, attracts about $800,000 annually in advertising revenue and circulates 6,000 copies every two weeks. *Actualidad Economica* also distributes three issues annually throughout Central America.

These examples show why Ulibarri, the editor of *La Nación*, characterizes the media of his country as "very dynamic" and influential with the population, which in turn, because of its need to interact with the nation's democratic government and the open business climate, demands deeper analysis and a richer media environment than do consumers elsewhere in the region. It is also evident that although Costa Rica's elites control a large slice of the country's print media, the market has opened itself to diverse voices and even ownership from international chains. This development makes Costa Rica importantly different from many of its neighbors and underscores the diversity in policy debates that characterizes the nation's democratic traditions.

Diversity of ownership is reflected on the nation's radio dial as well. Although its various outlets allow for a multiplicity of viewpoints, however, the radio spectrum is not as oversaturated here as elsewhere in the region: Costa Rica has the smallest number of radio stations of all Central American nations, with about one hundred stations on the AM and FM bands (and as elsewhere, some of those stations are retransmitters that give stations based in the capital a nationwide reach). Of course, Costa Rica is also the second-smallest nation in the region, about the size of West Virginia. Here as elsewhere in Central America, radio is the medium with the most market penetration, with 98 percent of the population exposed to radio on a daily basis. The nation's various stations split an advertising market of about $19 million annually, again the richest in the region. As do their counterparts throughout the region, however, Costa Rica's radio owners must still compete for a small slice of their country's total advertising market that remains disproportionate to the medium's reach.

Radio Monumental, founded in 1929, remains the top station. In 2000 the station was estimated to garner $2.8 million in advertising revenue. The station's mix of news and entertainment, along with its longtime presence as an established leader, contributed to its performance.

Radio Columbia and Radio Reloj are other important stations. *Noticiero* Angulo operates popular independent *radio periódicos* on both stations. Angulo's news program on Radio Reloj has been one of the top-rated news and information programs in Costa Rica for decades. Radio Columbia is rated second in its ability to attract advertising revenue, drawing about $1.8 million in 2000. Radio Reloj also posts respectable advertising numbers, listed at $1.5 million in 2000.

The top-rated news and information programs belong to Radio Omega, which runs them in the afternoon.[16] Radio Omega is generally rated as the country's third most popular station, with advertising revenues of $1.7 million in 2000.

Nevertheless, television is the dominant electronic medium here, as Costa Rican television has a 90 percent penetration of the market and the lion's share of advertising revenue, with almost $93 million in 2000.

The Picado Cozza family, longtime representatives of the nation's conservative elite, owns the nation's top network, Teletica Canal 7. Teletica commands 50 percent of the morning audience and more than a third of the afternoon and evening audiences. This reflects in the station's advertising revenue, about $34 million in 2000.

The Picado Cozza family's holdings in cable television, Cable Tica and Cable Color, form a near-monopoly in Costa Rica. Although the family has not used that power to exclude competing stations, as Esersky has in El Salvador, the lack of strong competition in cable has raised concerns among some media critics.[17] In 1996 TelePlus, a subsidiary of the Florida wireless cable operator Tel-Com Wireless Cable TV Corporation, spent $4 million to enter the Costa Rican market and began constructing a broadcast tower on Mount Irazu, the nation's second-highest point, with 750,000 homes in its radius.[18] So far TelePlus has not challenged the Picado Cozza family's dominance, but the market is still relatively new, with cable penetration at less than 20 percent.

Since the mid-1990s many of the Picado Cozza family's domestic competitors in broadcast television have abandoned the market, selling out to a firm known as Repretel, a holding company for the Mexican media baron Angel González González's operations in Costa Rica. Until the mid-1990s foreign ownership of Costa Rica's television media was barred, but González's control of Repretel was masked by his Costa Rican partners.[19] Currently Canales 4, 6, 9, and 11 belong to Repretel, and ownership of Canal 2 was expected to shift to González's group by 2001. Although Canal 9 is now merely a retransmission channel for Canal 4, this would give González control of four VHF networks and the ability to control a fifth if he were to devote the necessary infrastructure investment. The combined advertising revenue from the Repretel group was about $56 million in 2000.

González's advertising, programming, and information clout in the Costa Rican market has raised concerns among domestic owners. The Repretel group makes González's market influence equal to that of *La Nación*'s publishing group and exceeds that of Teletica and the powerful Picado Cozza family. González personifies the forces of globalization, since he controls at least twenty-two stations in Latin America, including properties in Mexico, Peru, Ecuador, Chile, and the Dominican Republic, besides those he controls in Central America.[20] For Costa Ricans, González represents global television programmers' hunger for new and profitable markets where they can gobble up stations to transmit their wares. With its alluring demographics, stable climate for economic development, and peaceful democracy, Costa Rica is a lucrative target for expansion among global media investors.

"The danger is that they could create a monopoly that would stay in the hands of a foreign corporation," warned Borrasé, the publisher of *La Prensa Libre*. González's monopoly hold on Guatemala's television system substantiates that concern for Costa Ricans. "They don't know our idiosyncrasies," the publisher said of the Repretel group, which González programs from his headquarters in Miami. "They could end up being harmful to our culture."

"A monopoly can function in Guatemala because they have a dictatorial base there," said Juan Carlos Gamboa, the executive director of the National Chamber of Television (Spanish acronym, CANATEL), a group representing the Costa Rican television industry. "But in the case of Costa Rica, the concentration of power is different. It is not in the hands of one person."[21]

Others have mixed emotions about González's entry into the Costa Rican media system. Gómez, the publisher of *Extra* and an owner of an UHF television station, was concerned that Repretel's economic might will enable González to obtain higher-quality and cheaper television programming than his Costa Rican competition can. "His monopoly is having an effect on advertising, because he is obtaining the exclusive international broadcast rights, and smaller channels have no way to counter his predominance," said Gómez, who owns one of those small channels. "We have to be careful not to sell him all of the on-air frequencies."

On the positive side, however, Gómez said Repretel has forced Canal 7, which once was the only economic powerhouse in television, to improve its programming and news. "The arrival of Angel González to the TV market has caused a positive evolution of our television. With his investments he has pushed the competition, Canal 7, to disburse money to improve coverage, buy new equipment, transmit events live within minutes, and offer varied programming."

According to Saborío of *Actualidad Economica*, Repretel's "arrival was good because of the injection of modern equipment," which forced the Picado Cozza family to upgrade its broadcast programming and news. As for González's market strategy, she said the Repretel incursion into the market "had no real effect on information in terms of content but appears to be more in the interest of financial principal." In her opinion, González improved the quality of news and information programming in Costa Rica while creating "a clear and distinct" choice in news products for viewers.

Nevertheless, other journalists, including Ana Cristina Rojas, who has reported extensively on the Repretel mergers, believe that the concentration of ownership in an international media conglomerate raises concerns about the quality of information coming from their media outlets. Rojas said that the situation opened the door to "the manipulation of information" in the Costa Rican media scene.[22]

Repretel's staff resists these charges. Roxana Zúñiga, the news director and anchor for Repretel's news operation, has a long history of experience in the Costa Rican market at such established news operations as *La Nación* and Radio Reloj. She noted that her news operation has a strict code of ethical behavior, and she wants her news programs to shun sensationalism.[23] In addition, Fernando Contreras, Repretel's president, responded to these criticisms by saying that some members of the media "want to exaggerate the relevance" of his group's acquisitions. He explained that modern broadcasters look less to program a channel to meet the needs of everyone and instead seek different outlets to program for a market's various demographic groups: one channel for children, one for young adults, one for women, and so on. He said one strategy for opposing the historical dominance of the Picado Cozza family in Costa Rican television was to set up a flexible bloc of stations that would allow advertisers more choices, much as a theatergoer has more choices at a multiplex theater.[24]

Owners of smaller media outlets, such as Borrasé of *La Prensa Libre*, nevertheless expressed concern that this new high-level competition for advertising would further threaten the profitability of niche outlets such as his own. Borrasé said that a multiplicity of voices could exist in the current democratic system only if owners were "required to have a conscience." Otherwise, the large media's monopoly over advertising would pose "a danger" to the diversity that now exists in the Costa Rican media scene. Contreras, however, argued that Repretel's strategy simply seeks "more efficiency" for his stations, letting those stations compete with dominant Canal 7 by combining their strengths to appeal to advertisers.[25]

Elbert Durán Hidalgo, the news director of "Radio Periodicos Reloj," one of the most popular news programs in the country, noted that concerns about concentrated power in the advertising market should not be focused solely on the incursion of González and Repretel. He pointed at the concentrated power of *La Nación*'s publishing group as a domestic form of the same problem. "That's too much power concentrated in one company in a small society," he said.[26]

In the mid-1990s Jon Vanden Heuvel and Everette Dennis analyzed the Costa Rican media for the Freedom Forum and noted the dominance of the Picado Cozza family's television properties, *La Nación*, and Radio Monumental. They found that the nation's media system exhibited a "healthy pluralism," but their report predated González's major incursion into the market and the Repretel mergers.[27]

Three media groups appear to be the key players in the Costa Rican system. Their influence can be measured by looking at their market influence in this sophisticated system, where more advertising information is available than elsewhere in the region. The Picado Cozza television properties control about 18 percent of the country's advertising; González's Repretel controls about 30 percent. The champion remains the Jimenez family's *La Nación* publishing group, with 34 percent of the market. The Jimenez group's nearest print competitor for advertising, Hollinger's *La Republica*, accounts for barely 3 percent.

Undoubtedly this competitive discrepancy explains why Hollinger's entry into the market—another incursion by an international media chain—escaped the controversy González's incursion provoked. By taking only a small taste of the Costa Rican market, Hollinger proved to be a nonthreatening competitor, although the company owns hundreds of newspapers internationally.

What is more striking about this concentration of media power in the hands of three distinct groups is their political similarities. As noted in earlier chapters, González is an outspoken supporter of right-wing and conservative causes, and his stations have tended to back those types of governments in Guatemala, El Salvador, and to a lesser extent, Nicaragua. The Picado family has deep roots in the conservative politics of Costa Rica, and the family's members are part of the country's elite. Even though they have sold shares in their media enterprises, the Jimenez family retains a strong and influential conservative presence.

Indeed, we have already mentioned Durán's concerns that the Jimenez family has too much media power in the country. Considering the family's total economic clout—with its brewery and agricultural enterprises—the use of the media to promote the family's economic interests raises concerns about vertical integration in the Costa Rican marketplace. Such concerns echo those over similar vertical integration of media structures in some of Costa Rica's neighbors.

This dominance of conservative elements seems to cast González's entrance into the market in a somewhat different light as well. On first blush, González's ultraconservative political stance and his tendency to buy out his competition seem antithetical to Costa Rica's diversity of voices and democracy. As it turns out, however, the political slant of domestic media forces such as the Picado Cozza and Jimenez families and their own push for market dominance seem to show that the Mexican investor is not so unlike other media powers in San José.

So far this preponderance of conservative media seems not to have undercut Costa Rica's democracy, which mirrors the situation in Europe and the United States. Their market dominance leaves little space, however—only 18 percent of the available advertising dollars—for all the other voices in the system. By taking so much of the advertising, these three key media groups can not only set rates and manipulate the cost of advertising but also choke off small competitors.

Perhaps because of Costa Rica's very different historical development and deeply rooted democratic system, its free markets have welcomed foreign investment. So far these global investment forces have produced mixed reactions. We have not seen this unfettered entrance of foreign investment elsewhere in Central America except when investors such as González have aligned politically with the central powers of the state. Such alliances have not been an important consideration in the Costa Rican context. Although we have noted that elsewhere in Central America outside ownership must appear nonthreatening before it can gain a toehold in the market, Costa Rica shows that a democratic system obviates this concern. Media investors who threaten to change the equilibrium of the Costa Rican market are allowed into it, as are nonthreatening owners such as Hollinger. Such investors may meet different levels of welcome, and obviously those that threaten a market's equilibrium, as González has, will likely spark controversy, but this is all part of the rough and tumble of the marketplace.

Nevertheless, our analysis suggests that Costa Rica is following a similar trend toward concentrating media power in the hands of elite elements, often former oligarchs. The Jimenez and Picado families became key media holders partly because they wanted to counter social welfare policies promoted by the PLN and the state. Since they lacked influence with the Costa Rican government during the PLN's generation-long dominance, these families developed media power as a counterbalance. This resembles patterns of media development elsewhere in the region. The obvious ideological nature of these investments receded over time, however, and these conservative families did not challenge the state for control or use their media outlets to gain new political power. Although these media outlets have certainly had some impact on the political system, and the political viewpoints of these families are sometimes obvious to media observers, their ownership and control has meant less in Costa Rica's democratic system, with its multiplicity of viewpoints, than has media ownership in states with a history of centralized, authoritarian governments and few, if any, opposition voices in the media.

Because of Costa Rica's democratic traditions, so far the state has resisted erecting barriers to new global investors. This outcome contrasts with our findings as to the pattern of media owners' reactions in small markets. Nevertheless, it allows us to further define our claim that such trends are typically confined to small markets with oligarchic media systems. As noted, Costa Rica's history produced a diverse media marketplace, and thus our concerns about limits to diversification seem not to apply. Although the Costa Rican system seems to be heading toward a more oligarchic system of conservative control, it has so far remained sufficiently diverse to not undercut democracy or stop outside investors from entering the market. There are legitimate concerns about the future, however.

One might also argue that the concentration of media power in the conservative elite, as represented by the Jimenez and Picado families, reflects the development of the Costa Rican political and social systems. Although to some extent the second phase of Costa Rica's democracy represents a break with that tradition, elite forces are still the primary players in the nation's politics. As Jeffery Paige noted, Costa Rica has "the most aristocratic political elite in Central America."[28] Since Costa Rica's independence in 1821, about 75 percent of the nation's presidents have been able to trace their lineage to at least one of three elite families.

Nonetheless, those families have not tried to rein in thought and speech that run counter to their viewpoints. Perhaps this openness was encouraged in the free exchange between classes that developed during the nation's colonial and predemocratic eras. Whenever this open dialogue first developed in Costa Rica, it marks the nation as part of the vanguard in democratic movements. Democracy continues to deepen and strengthen in Costa Rica, putting it further up the evolutionary ladder compared to the fledgling movements toward democracy elsewhere in the region and in other parts of Latin America. The nation's communication system, which allows this free exchange of thought, has only bolstered the nation's democracy, and vice versa.

"Because it is a country with an imperfect but very dynamic democracy, there is room for discussion and the participation of citizens in the decision-making process, the expression of opinions about those decisions, and about public matters," Ulibarri said. "All of this helps the freedom of the press."

The continued evolution of Costa Rica in its second phase of democracy has further helped this media system. Instead of being preoccupied with class warfare, the battle against poverty, and other inequities apparent in Latin America, Costa Rica has moved to strengthen governmental and social institutions while building a strong civil society, so that it appears on par with industrialized nations. When the nation's elites agreed to a new constitution in the post–civil war era, they made a compact with the nation: to exchange political office peacefully, to share the nation's resources with all classes through a social safety net and educational programs, and to allow the free exchange of ideas. The nation's communication system has also advanced in this second phase by dropping the heated rhetoric of the past and moving toward a rarity in Latin America—an attempt at an objective media stance.

With this advancement, however, Costa Rica's concerns have become similar to the problems confronting the rest of the industrialized world: media concentration and its effect on pluralism.

Some political analysts have already warned about cracks in Costa Rica's system. The 1998 presidential election, which brought in the administration of Miguel Angel Rodríguez of the Social Christian Unity Party (Spanish acronym, PUSC), raised concerns about voter attitudes to the political system as a whole. Besides the two dominant parties, the PUSC and the PLN, minor parties placed eleven other candidates on the ballot, a record. Although this speaks to the nation's openness and diversity, it also indicates that some political leaders are dissatisfied with the major parties. Voter participation also declined. An incredible 80 percent of eligible voters usually cast ballots, but that total dropped to 70 percent in the 1998 elections. This is still an enviable percentage by most standards, but some analysts believe it showed further disappointment with the main political parties. Voters complained that the PUSC and PLN have both become more centrist, making it harder to distinguish significant differences between them once a voter discards the spin and rhetoric of the political season. Voters also seemed dissatisfied with the way politicians made extravagant campaign promises that they were often unable to keep.[29] The parties' inability to respond to these voter demands relates in part to Costa Rica's international debt, which grew during the last generation because of expenditures on social welfare programs. Although the country has worked diligently to reduce the debt, it had to curtail some of these programs as it weathered intermittent economic storms in the 1990s.

This voter dissatisfaction and the move toward smaller government programs have obvious parallels in the rest of the industrialized world, especially the United States. And as it has been in the United States, some voter disaffection has been directed at an increasingly commercial and concentrated media system. When media power concentrates in increasingly fewer companies, as has been the case in the United States, journalists tend to abandon public service and civil society and turn toward entertainment. The bottom line supplants the ballot. The media come to view the public not as voters but instead as consumers. As the president of Costa Rica's public broadcasting system, Oscar Aguilar Bulgarelli, aptly capsulized concerns for the Repretel mergers: "The problem is the idiotizing of the population with 525 hours of soap operas every month."[30]

This focus on entertainment creates superficial and flaccid coverage of politics and government, while in-depth analysis, which is an essential component of democracy, is forgotten. When the media system consistently attempts to distract citizens from daily realities instead of engaging them at key moments in important policy and social debates, it undermines democracy. Although this issue concerning the relationship between the media and democracy arises only in a democratic system far more entrenched than is common in other parts of Central America, it is no less important for the sustainability of democracy in Costa Rica and elsewhere.

7   *State Power,*
the Static in the System

In Central America journalists are often portrayed as romantic heroes because they accept the Quixotic challenge of tilting against the all-powerful mechanisms of the state. From Guatemala's insightful columnist Estuardo Zapeta to Panama's crusading editor Gustavo Gorriti, leaders in journalism believe that the media must represent society by providing some balance in systems where strong centralized governments prevail. Latin America's political history shows a predisposition to autocratic and militaristic governments that have often sought to repress free expression. Fearful that competing ideas would threaten their regimes, many Central American governments have turned to censorship, political manipulation, or economic pressure to silence journalists, ruin their careers, or damage the media outlets where they ply their trade.

In the preceding chapters we discussed some of the censorship, state-sponsored violence, and other antimedia tactics various Central American governments have used to control information and thought inside their nation's borders. In this chapter we will examine these tactics in more depth. As noted in these pages and by many other sources, the media are inextricably intertwined with the ruling oligarchies of most Central American nations. Media systems have not only served as a hothouse to germinate new policies for government; they have also bred the leaders of nations. President Flores of Honduras and former president Chamorro of Nicaragua offer two recent examples of the way the media hold real power in the region. Where systems are accustomed to autocratic ways and oligarchic rule, it is not hard to imagine that the state might deploy its considerable powers to thwart those who would use the media as a crucible to forge new systems of government or at the very least pressure the government for change.

In fact, the media in Central America possess little if any independence from the state. As Waisbord notes: "All news organizations are shaped, constrained, informed, [and] subjected to diverse interests. . . . the press is, above all, a political institution" that cannot be separated from the larger political sphere surrounding it.[1]

The history of Central American (and Latin American) media provides countless examples of the media's intimate relationships with the state in the form of legitimate subsidies and advertising. Often these economic relationships have grown out of the political realities tying elite media owners to government officials. Sometimes the government has used these relationships either to change the media landscape or to pressure the media for the government's gain. Such events support the claim, attractive to many experts on political communication, that the state largely controls the breadth of public debate and the outlines of society's mediated spaces, despite the effects of transnational communications firms and other supranational forces in our globalized world.[2]

As we have noted, many of the media outlets examined in earlier chapters are not maintained solely for their profitability. The owners often use them to advance their political careers or to disseminate the political ideology of important subsets of a nation's oligarchy. Sometimes a media outlet constitutes both a political tool and an advertising voice for its owners' other holdings. The media outlet may not be profitable in itself, but its communication function amplifies the profits of other properties.

As these developing nations grope for some sense of democracy, however, their media take on different roles and different responsibilities. If the media in oligarchic societies are to play the idealized role most liberal theories would give them, providing voice to the voiceless—breaking down the barriers of power so that the middle class, at the very least, finds a place at the table—then they must somehow find independent power in the marketplace. Whether this power stems from newsstand sales, subscriptions, ratings, or other means, unless the media grab the economic resources available to them, they inevitably stay shackled to the government, party, or oligarchic force that subsidizes their existence.

As we noted earlier, a media organ that seeks to promote democracy within an oligarchy must withdraw itself from state support and subsidies, existing as an independent force in the marketplace and drawing true mass support; *only then* will it have the ability to make some change in the overall media system of its country. Again, the small size of Central American media markets makes this task all the more difficult. Systems in states where most individual media organs need state support will tend to support authoritarian or oligarchic systems.

As media systems in Central America seek to become more market oriented and break ties to the state, struggles have inevitably resulted. This chapter is devoted to exploring some of those struggles.

Honduras

During much of the 1980s and 1990s, José Rolando Sarmiento was one of the most influential journalists in Honduras. He covered the Contra War along his country's border with Nicaragua. He climbed the ranks as a radio reporter to become the nation's top radio anchor and eventually news director of HRN, the top-rated network in the country. All that changed in 1997, after President Flores was elected.

Sarmiento said that HRN's powerful owner, José Rafael Ferrari, asked him to support various development projects and policies of the new Flores administration on the station's news programs.[3] Ferrari, a Liberal Party ally of the new president and, like him, a member of the *turco* media oligarchy, wanted HRN's news to reflect positively on Flores's agenda. Although Sarmiento believes that news coverage should balance positive and negative elements and often criticized Honduran media for being overtly negative, he declined to accept this change, which he viewed as state pressure to sanitize the news. He resigned from his position at HRN.

Raul Valladares, the news director who supplanted Sarmiento at HRN, characterized Sarmiento's departure differently. He said he respected Sarmiento's style but felt that it was anachronistic and "less agile than necessary."[4] Valladares said that journalists should offer "aggressive," attention-grabbing items. He viewed the style of Rodrigo Wong Arévalo, the guiding force of television's popular "Abriendo Brecha" as more in keeping with the way HRN should shape its news. Wong Arévalo commonly mixed opinions and facts on his program, which tended to reflect his personal outlook on the day's news and information.

Sarmiento, who went on to become a popular *noticiero* on Tegucigalpa's Radio X, denied that his departure rested on presentation style, the mixing of opinion with news, or his popularity as an anchorman. Rather, he felt forced to resign because of what he viewed as the state's direct intervention through Honduras's Liberal Party politics. Many other journalists felt similarly, and with reason: President Flores was rewarding some journalists with key government appointments and ambassadorships (see chapter 1) while pressuring media owners and editors to dismiss or demote others who had fallen out of favor with the administration. Around the time that Sarmiento left HRN, several reporters at newspapers in Tegucigalpa also complained about demotions or dismissals based on the president's whim. Unlike Sarmiento, however, few were willing to tell their stories publicly because they feared they would never work in the profession again.

International journalism groups such as the CPJ criticized President Flores's actions and noted the pressure he put on his country's media outlets. The CPJ also noted discrepancies in coverage of Hurricane Mitch. Although the Honduran media generally gave the government high marks for its response to the disaster, the international media were filled with reports of government incompetence.[5]

Sarmiento left HRN because he wanted to avoid just such discrepancies in the reporting of basic conditions. Although his departure from the nation's most important radio network—indeed, one of its most important media outlets overall—did not stop his reporting, it did diminish the impact of his voice. His program on Radio X slowly gained popularity, but Sarmiento no longer had a nationwide audience: he could be heard only in the vicinity of Tegucigalpa, the capital. In addition, Radio X was a relatively new and unknown station, and as an independent *noticiero*, Sarmiento lacked the resources to promote his change of venue, all of which further reduced his ability to reach an audience. He felt that his career had been altered irrevocably because he was caught in a political riptide.

Sarmiento noted that his experience and the pressures put on other Honduran journalists perpetrated a system of self-censorship where journalists must understand the boundaries the state has placed on discourse. Although negative views and coverage are allowed in such a system, they are confined to particular topics. According to Sarmiento, journalists who did not push for "real change" and acquiesced to the government's neoliberal views (which U.S. influence has made fashionable in the region) succeeded without penalty in the Honduran system. The topics that seemed to be off-limits included government corruption, environmental stories that threatened to expose problems in development plans of the government or powerful business interests, overcrowding in the nation's prisons, and most human rights abuses by the police and military.

Sarmiento's case clearly shows the results of the merger among Honduras's political, economic, and media elites. Other parts of the region, such as Nicaragua and (to a slightly lesser extent) Panama, have seen similar mergers, but the results have not always been the same. In Nicaragua the Chamorro administration, although aware of its powers to shape the commercial media, generally acted as a positive influence. In Panama the media powers behind the administrations of the 1990s—the Duque family with the Perez Balladares administration and Eisenmann of *La Prensa* with the Moscoso administration—sometimes tried to shape the media system, but they were often restrained by a political split within the nation's ruling class.

Interestingly, these developments presaged the rise of Italy's Silvio Berlusconi, who also fuses the might of the media, business, and politics within his administration. Although some media scholars have recently written of an Italian model for the media in the twenty-first century, a more accurate harbinger may be the Central American media of the 1990s. The scholar Brian McNair has commented on the political evolution of both Italy and Russia to show how a merger of media, political, and business elites into a new form of oligarchy can produce negative results. McNair has predicted that Russia's harsh, bare-knuckle capitalism, with its media mafias, may exemplify not political primitivism at work in a transitional postcommunist society but rather the shape of political systems to come, what he calls a "media-ocracy."[6] Such a system seems to be at work in Honduras, where the state has been slowly merging with the media system in the transition away from militarism.

Like any evolutionary transition, the changes in Honduras did not come quickly or smoothly. Although in the mid-1990s the Honduran media seemed emboldened to report on past abuses by the country's military, journalists elsewhere would have considered the stories to be historical, not current affairs. These revelations were significant because they were part of the process of change as elite control shifted from the military to civilian hands; stories of the military's human rights abuses were a necessary part of that evolving climate. In 1996 Serapio Umanzor of *La Prensa* won an international reporting prize for his series on the secret war that the Honduran military had waged against dissidents in the 1980s—which means that many of the human rights violations he covered had been committed almost fifteen years earlier. Umanzor's stories broke a terrible silence about abuses by the nation's military, but they were not the first stories about these abuses.

In fact, the *Baltimore Sun* broke stories about the torture and execution of members of Honduran left-wing groups in 1995, and that newspaper was continuing to search for answers about the roles that the CIA and U.S. military played in those events.[7] The *Sun*'s search for answers was propelled by the need to find out what had happened to Father James Francis Carney, an American who had served as a chaplain for antigovernment guerrillas in the early 1980s. Carney was likely questioned, tortured and executed by Battalion 316, a Honduran anti-insurgent military force trained by the United States that became, in effect, a government-directed death squad. In 1999 the Honduran government said it would excavate a site at El Aguacate Air Force Base and analyze the bodies it had found to see whether Carney and others executed in extrajudicial fashion by the military were secretly buried there.[8] The United States had built the base in the early 1980s, and it was used as a training center for Contra forces.

While he was head of the COSUFFAA and the nation's military, General Hung Pacheco defiantly protected thirteen fugitive military officers linked to political killings during the 1980s. Not only were the fugitives allowed to draw military pay, and given other benefits (such as health coverage, free cars and gas, life insurance, and bodyguards for their families), but the military actively shielded them from prosecution.[9] Others were allowed to flee the country and escape justice. Although the civilian government pressed the military to arrest these officers and bring them before the nation's courts, it was rather slow to admit its own culpability in allowing death squads to function. The Inter-American Court of Human Rights of the Organization of American States (OAS) ordered the Honduran government to pay compensation to some of the families of political activists kidnapped, tortured, or murdered by the military in 1986. The Honduran government finally complied with that ruling fourteen years later, when it paid $1.6 million to families of seventeen people. The government explained the delay by noting it needed time to investigate each case adequately.[10] This outcome, however, did not address the concerns and questions of others who claimed that (echoing events in Chile and Argentina during the same era) their family members had been attacked or disappeared during what Umanzor characterized as a "dirty war." The Honduran government has acknowledged that as many as 184 political activists may have suffered from the military's terror campaign in the 1980s.

Given this slow process of revelation and investigation, it is not unusual for journalists to note the timidity of the country's media. Rossana Guevara, the former news director at VICA television in San Pedro Sula, has written about the "fear created by the military in civil society," although the wars that raged on the isthmus are long over.[11] In Guevara's view, these fears and other pressures routinely cause self-censorship in Honduras, and journalists often acquiesce to a system "for deforming the truth."

Some leading journalists, such as Sarmiento of Radio X, see the state's power over the media in such a system as akin to something out of the

Middle Ages. Journalists would like to help change systems such as that in Honduras, but they are restrained by fear—a reasonable emotion, considering their circumstances. Sarmiento dreams of a media system that can support a variety of alternative voices, gathering alternative opinions, news stories, and viewpoints from around the region. Such publications, programs, or broadcast outlets would draw strength from their diversity in the sea of conservative thought currently submerging the region. Sarmiento pointed to National Public Radio (NPR) in the United States as a model of the way a state can give support to an influential media outlet that airs a wide range of viewpoints. In his view, this provides a model for media outlets everywhere: a system in which journalists actively report and discuss government policy and action without fear of intimidation. According to Sarmiento, the media in Honduras have reported merely for the nation's bureaucrats, business interests, and intelligentsia, not for the population at large.

El Salvador

While the state sometimes used fear to control journalists' messages in Honduras, more sophisticated devices for media control evolved in El Salvador and elsewhere. For example, as we have already explored (see chapter 2), the nation's conservative forces and ARENA compromised the integrity of some of the most powerful radio stations by purchasing *campos pagados* that masqueraded as news and information programming during the 1999 elections.

The state's use of economic means to control the media constitutes a tradition throughout Latin America. In their Freedom Forum analysis of the region, Vanden Heuvel and Dennis compare the relationship of the media and the state to semifeudal structures, the media oligarchies of the region being "semi-independent vassals" that support government policies while occasionally having minor differences.[12] These comparisons echo the analysis Sarmiento offered of Honduras. This relationship has existed for more than a century as dominant media structures arose in the region. The Salvadoran government was not the first in Latin America to use advertising and subsidies to prod the media into line, but such economic penalties have proved effective in El Salvador, as they have throughout Central America (and Mexico as well). They are one method for maintaining the semifeudal relationship with the state.

The tradition of using state advertising to control editorial content may actually stretch back to 1665, when the British state initiated the practice to control the *London Gazette*. Significantly, the British government remained a major advertiser for centuries and was listed as the second-largest advertiser in the United Kingdom through the early 1990s.[13] As Straubhaar has noted, excepting the United States and Canada, governments are often leading advertisers supporting commercial media.[14] The state thus not only plays the role of primary advertiser but also sets and enforces advertising rules.

As is true of others in Latin America, the Salvadoran government remains its nation's largest advertiser. In 1989 President Alfredo Cristiani, an ARENA member, led the retrenchment of free expression during the final years of the civil war. Helped by the media owner Boris Esersky and other key members of the oligarchy, President Cristiani sought to squeeze media outlets willing to air opposition opinions. These outlets had either sprung up during the Duarte era or managed to survive the violent repression of the media in the early 1980s. Cristiani turned off the advertising tap for all media outlets that diverged from the government line or failed to support ARENA's conservative agenda. This boycott was magnified by Esersky's hold on the nation's advertising agencies, which joined the economic blockade. Key members of the oligarchy, as the nation's influential business elite, followed the course mapped out by Cristiani and Esersky by canceling their advertising.

The boycott was aimed primarily at Canal 12, the maverick television network started by Jorge Zedan only three years earlier. The boycott cost Zedan's network most of its advertising. Esersky also yanked Canal 12 off the nation's cable television system. Instead of quietly folding his hand, however, Zedan fought back creatively. To protest the government's actions, Mauricio Funes, the most popular anchor on Salvadoran television, temporarily pulled his program from Canal 12. Besides attracting public attention to the boycott, Zedan and his sales staff began drumming up alternative sources of advertising. Canal 12 began catering to groups such as trade unions and professional organizations that could not get advertising space elsewhere because they were considered part of the government's opposition. By focusing on small businesses and grass-roots organizations for support, Zedan managed to make ends meet, but his network was never extremely profitable.

Esersky applied further economic pressure to businesses that dared run the advertising blockade he had set up. Esersky barred advertisers who decided to do business with Canal 12 from advertising with his profitable station group, TCS.[15] Businesses or other advertisers were forced to choose between having access to almost all the Salvadoran television viewing audience or supporting Canal 12. There was no middle ground. Not surprisingly, those who stayed with Zedan were viewed as making a political choice. Many advertisers simply could not afford TCS's advertising rates, however, and Zedan's need to find a large group of small business-es to supplant the advertisers who had left during the boycott lowered the price of advertising at his network.

Canal 12 continued to suffer from the advertising blockade even af-ter the war, because Esersky refused to relent. After a decade of endur-ance, Zedan cut some of his losses by selling controlling interest of the network to Mexico's TV Azteca. With Zedan out of the driver's seat, the advertising blockade was lifted at Canal 12, although it continued for other media outlets judged to be in the anti-ARENA camp.

The Calderón Sol administration, which followed Cristiani's, for all intents and purposes kept up the politically motivated boycott, and Zedan's Canal 12 was not the only target. *Co-Latino*, the nation's only daily willing to publish left-wing viewpoints, suffered from the boycott through the Calderón Sol era in the late 1990s and beyond. Of course, *Co-Latino* had been part of the original blacklist of media outlets when Cris-tiani launched the boycott.

At the beginning of the Calderón Sol administration, Francisco Va-lencia, the director of *Co-Latino*, had correctly predicted "mediating the economic boycott or impeding our development is one practice that will not disappear until far in the future." In Valencia's opinion, "the direct dependency of the periodical businesses on publicity and the complicity with the circles of power" would remain the worst problem confronting journalism in El Salvador, a seemingly unwashable stain left from the years of military control and civil war.[16]

This opinion aligns with Robert McChesney's theories concerning the media's dependence on corporate advertising in the United States and in other capitalist systems. As McChesney has noted, increased depen-dence on corporate sponsors has warped many media outlets, making them antidemocratic forces rather than outlets for public service and a balance against powerful government elites.[17]

Until El Salvador's peace accords were signed, even the more conser-vative or moderate media outlets often avoided items that might run afoul of the government. Many journalists admit to having censored them-selves in the war years, especially during the Cristiani era, so that their media outlet would not be put on the advertising blacklist. Statements from the country's full spectrum of political thought—the opposition as well as the far-right ARENA—were often censored not by the government but by journalists afraid to anger the government.[18]

At Esersky's TCS control of the airwaves in the government's favor is even more absolute. Some journalists refer derisively to TCS, the multichannel Salvadoran television network that controls 90 percent of the nation's audience, as *TeleCensura* (Telecensorship). David Rivas, of the Salvadoran Press Association (Spanish acronym, APES), complained that government officials and party officials from ARENA need only to call TCS to have stories spiked.[19] Such direct political influence parallels the situation when the dominant broadcaster in Mexico, Televisa, collaborated with the PRI at the height of its domination.

Like Mexico's Azcarraga Milmo, the media tycoon who built Televisa into a Latin American broadcasting empire, Esersky is something more than a media owner; he is a media *caudillo* in the term's true political sense. The parallels between Esersky and Mexico's "El Tigre," who underwrote the PRI's campaigns and seven decades of rule, are manifest. Esersky finances the campaigns of ARENA candidates, gives free advertising to the party and his political patrons, and consults with the president of the country. In effect, his stations are ARENA's propaganda arm. As some media experts have noted, Televisa became the apparatus of ideological control for Mexico's ruling party, the PRI;[20] TCS plays the same role in El Salvador.

The rise of Esersky and TCS in El Salvador is predicted in some ways by the analyses of media scholars such as Straubhaar, who examined the Brazilian media landscape. As Straubhaar has noted, authoritarian systems such as those in Brazil and El Salvador often breed one dominant television force, which in turn determines the shape and character of other broadcasting outlets and the niches they will fill in a country's media system.[21]

Esersky's control of advertising and information goes beyond internal censorship. Journalists who have worked in them report that his news operations maintain a list of sources and interview subjects who are politically cleared to appear on TCS stations.[22] Esersky's system of control thus includes censorship (both internal and directed by government and party officials), source blacklists, and collaboration with the government to pressure his competitors.

Not satisfied solely with the advertising blacklist, the state also rewards those who it decides support ARENA. In effect, the Salvadoran government's advertising budget has become a system to reward media outlets for offering supportive coverage and for filtering out offending stories and information.

"The attitude in the public sphere is that government activities should be removed from citizens," explained Funes of Canal 12.[23] Under the present system, the public is not allowed to see how the government runs the ship of state, he added, which is the point—so much for the openness necessary if the public is to see the functions of a true democracy. Three years after Funes expressed that opinion, he saw the state's repressive policies return, with Canal 12 again the target. When a series of earthquakes ravaged the country in 2001, Funes's program "Hechos" began pointing fingers at authorities who were slow to deal with those left homeless. "Hechos" claimed that communities where ARENA lacked support were skipped in some of the initial relief efforts. This was an important development because of the magnitude of the disaster, which left about 1 million people homeless.[24]

President Flores was upset by these critical reports. During a phone call to coordinate disaster relief efforts, Flores complained about the reports to Mexico's new president, Vicente Fox. Because Mexico's TV Azteca now controlled Canal 12, Flores asked Fox to intervene.[25] Soon the owner of TV Azteca, Ricardo Salinas Pliego, was calling Funes in San Salvador. After three years, the Mexican network was about to end its hands-off policy toward its new Salvadoran affiliate. The message from Mexico City was clear to Funes: back off.

The day after the call, a vice-president from TV Azteca flew to San Salvador for a series of meetings. First, the representative of the Mexican network met with President Flores to assuage his feelings. He next held a terse meeting with Zedan, the founder of Canal 12 and still the network's general manager. Zedan holds a minority share in Canal 12, but TV Azteca holds the majority interest. Zedan was told that Canal 12's Mexican owners had no desire to stir up trouble in El Salvador. He was also told that his network's news programs should take a lighter approach toward the Salvadoran government's relief efforts; otherwise they would be replaced with Mexican soap operas.[26]

To make its point more forcefully, the Flores administration reinstated the wartime advertising boycott against Canal 12. As they had in the first boycott against the station, many private firms sympathetic to the ARENA cause canceled their advertising accounts. "We're losing about $125,000 a month," Zedan told reporters.

In a reconciliation of sorts, Enrique Altamirano, the publisher of *El Diario de Hoy*, defended President Flores. *El Diario de Hoy* ran a series of editorials attacking Funes, "Hechos," and Canal 12 for their reports surrounding the earthquake. The editorials dredged up much of the civil war era's ideological animosity and assaulted Funes's credibility because he had interviewed guerrilla groups during the war and opened his program to viewpoints from the left. The editorials also accused the network of staging interviews for political gain and instigating antigovernment protests by earthquake victims.

During the media flap generated by the earthquakes, President Flores denied he had gone on the offensive against the television network. Although the network documented its claims, the president denied that the government had reinstated its advertising boycott. "We don't interfere with private enterprise," he said dismissively at a news conference.

El Salvador's human rights ombudsman, Marcos Alfredo Valladares Melgar, nevertheless launched a review of various government practices connected to the Canal 12 case.[27] Part of Valladares's investigation revolved around whether victims' phone calls to Funes's program had been intentionally jammed. Many of the callers had complaints about the government, but their comments were sometimes drowned out by static. This was not the first time Canal 12 had experienced problems with the state-operated phone system. In 2000 Zedan had filed a complaint about phone tapping through the state-run company.[28]

The human rights ombudsman also reviewed the treatment of the Canal 12 reporter Milagro Vallecillas, who broke some of the stories about the treatment of earthquake victims. Vallecillas claimed she had been denied access to government news conferences about disaster relief and that government officials had broken off interviews when she asked questions about the way aid was being handled. Vallecillas eventually left the country after receiving threats related to her earthquake-victim reports and after *El Diario de Hoy*'s criticism of Canal 12.

Although TV Azteca eventually ceased threatening to cancel Canal 12's news programs, the Mexican owners decided to shop the troublesome Salvadoran network to potential buyers.

Both the earthquake incident and the civil war boycott demonstrate how various media outlets cooperate with the state to curb criticism of the government. Powerful media owners such as Altamirano and Esersky resumed a familiar pattern: oligopolistic media defending the state. The Salvadoran media outlets that cooperated with the government-organized boycotts and thus practiced varying degrees of self-censorship in effect became extensions of the state. By lashing out on behalf of the ARENA government, the conservative media played their part in the symbiotic relationship they have built up with government elites over decades of sharing power. The media were thus no different from a ministry of propaganda or, at the very least, a public relations firm with the central government's account. The Salvadoran media shirked their duty to counter the state's power by reporting governmental malfeasance, making them not a watchdog for the public but a lapdog for the government.

As the communications scholar John Keane has written, most states strive to subordinate the media system. Keane has listed five methods governments use to control the media: (1) emergency powers acts, (2) police and military secrecy, (3) officially disseminated lies, (4) corporate arms of the state that escape public accountability rules, and (5) the manipulation of state advertising.[29] In El Salvador the state employed most of those devices in its mission to control the media, turning them to propaganda and self-censorship. Keane's point, however, is that these devices appear not just in weak transitional states such as El Salvador but also in the major powers, such as the United States and the United Kingdom.

Nevertheless, there are differences. Although the media everywhere must rely on the state as the principal source of information, especially quotations, soundbites, and photo opportunities, in Latin America the key difference may be the role the state plays with advertising. As the Salvadoran example demonstrates, when the state is the major advertiser, it can manipulate advertising accounts to exert financial pressure on its critics in the media. In a small market such as El Salvador's, the state can easily coax other key advertisers to boycott its opposition. Since such governments are supported by an oligarchy or key elites who are also primary advertisers, such elite pressure on opposition media outlets becomes a handy lever to press when media criticism builds to a level the central government finds threatening. The Salvadoran model of government manipulation through advertising would be put to the test in other countries throughout the isthmus during the 1990s.

Guatemala

The administration of President Arzú moved quickly to deal with the media when he entered office in 1996. Besides canceling state subsidies to the media—both legitimate and illicit—Arzú also personally organized an antimedia campaign and advertising boycott with great parallels to the Salvadoran example.

Given the media's growing liberty, strength, and independence, as evidenced through their efforts to catalyze society in the struggle to overcome state power during the Serrano era (see chapter 5), some of Arzú's early moves seem to indicate a carefully calculated design at least to neutralize the media. Indeed, considering the aftermath of the Arzú era, this deliberate manipulation to keep the media off balance appears to have been the president's plan from the beginning of his term.

After Arzú's PAN lost elections in 1999, the media began to scrutinize his administration's finances. Of course, this was easier with an opposition party in power. Early word of the financial scandals to come had begun to leak out in the waning days of Arzú's administration and did not help the PAN's standing at the polls. When the scandals finally broke after Arzú left office, they implicated many former advisers and key party officials. Less than six months after the transfer of power, the scandals led fifteen members of the PAN's delegation in the Guatemalan legislature to resign their party affiliations because they were embarrassed by the corruption scandals. Even before the scandals, the PAN held only thirty-seven legislative seats and were far outnumbered by the far-right governing party, the Guatemalan Republican Front (Spanish acronym, FRG), which had sixty-seven seats.[30] The party seemed to be a fractured, hollow version of what it had been when Arzú was president.

By employing an aggressive policy with the media, Arzú had been able to keep them from the watchdog role essential to democracy, namely, attempting to oversee the workings of the government. The media were unable to unearth the corruption hidden behind the president's smoke screen of antimedia tactics.

The antimedia campaign looked very much like the ideological campaign employed in El Salvador, except this Guatemalan version was more personal. For example, the government's efforts often centered on its problems with the news magazine *Crónica*, which fought Arzú's advertising boycott by taking its problems to international press groups, such as the CPJ. During the advertising boycott, editors said, the magazine lost up to 90 percent of its regular advertisers and was forced to cut its size in half.[31] Nevertheless, Luis Flores Asturias, Arzú's vice-president, maintained a regular column in the magazine throughout the entire boycott. The magazine's principal investor, Francisco Perez de Antón, the wealthy owner of a popular Guatemalan restaurant chain, was also often identified as a supporter of the PAN. Perez de Antón often told the media that the boycott was based on personal feelings that the president and others in his faction of the PAN bore toward *Crónica* and had nothing to do with ideology.[32] However, in a country fresh from a civil war where death squads had often hunted journalists because of their points of view, the idea that a personal vendetta could be settled bloodlessly with an economic blockade was often lost in the discussions of Arzú's political motivations for erecting this economic wall.

Another of Arzú's motivations may have been to tamp down any resurgence of Guatemala's National Union Center Party (Spanish acronym, UCN). At one time the UCN was one of Guatemala's major parties and had been the base of support for Arzú's predecessor in the presidency, Ramiro de León Carpio. During the Arzú administration the UCN still had the most officially registered voters in the country, although by the 1999 elections this moderate party was no longer a major competitor for power. The newspaper *El Gráfico* was the UCN's mouthpiece, and it was near the top of Arzú's hit list.

Started in 1963 as a sports broadsheet, *El Gráfico* eventually became a political vehicle for its founder, Jorge Carpio Nicolle, as well as the rest of the Carpio family and the family's political allies. In the wake of Serrano's fall and exile in 1993, Carpio announced that he would run for the presidency, but he was assassinated soon afterward. In his stead, his cousin Ramiro de León Carpio went on to become president. The IAPA is still prodding the Guatemalan government to seek justice for the prominent publisher's murder. In the late-1990s *El Gráfico* was circulating 30,000 copies daily, but by 1998 the economic blockade had drastically reduced the paper's advertising. The boycott eventually snuffed out its existence.

The boycott also squeezed *La Hora*, the country's oldest newspaper, until there was almost nothing left. Run by Oscar Marroquín Rojas, the don of the country's dominant journalism family, *La Hora* is a sharply written paper filled with political analysis, and it has long been a base for brave journalists to wade into the swamp of the nation's divisive and dirty politics. The boycott and other economic factors, however, helped shrink the paper's circulation to 3,000 copies. The Marroquín family was clearly a target of the boycott, for it extended to *elPeriodico*, the brainchild of José Rubén Zamora Marroquín, Oscar Marroquín's nephew. The Arzú administration had battled with *elPeriodico* from its inception; the boycott eventually forced Zamora to sell control of the newspaper to the *Prensa Libre* group of publications, where Zamora had a key ally in his cousin Gonzalo Marroquín, the editor of *Prensa Libre*.

The Arzú administration tried to cover up its involvement with the boycott. It would not take responsibility for its role in the closure of *El Gráfico*, the forced sale of *elPeriodico*, or the financial problems at *La Hora* and *Crónica*. Ricardo de la Torre, a spokesperson for the president, called the media with financial problems "victims of bad management."[33]

Perez de Antón countered by revealing a leaked government memo that not only outlined the boycott but also instructed government officials to refuse to conduct interviews with reporters from *Crónica* and *elPeriodico*. These publications were cut from the list of those informed about media availabilities and other government functions. Arzú's spokesperson denied the authenticity of the memo and the existence of the blockade, which was now moving from advertising to information, thus blocking the media's essential function in a democracy: to gather information about the government.

Beyond its attempts to hide the boycott, the Arzú administration was fairly open in its criticisms of the media, which it claimed were overly negative, biased, and frequently inaccurate. The president complained bitterly that the media focused too much on the nation's escalating crime rate and that the constant attention to this type of news was damaging Guatemala's international reputation, not to mention the tourist industry. Before ascending to the presidency, Arzú had built a business empire based on enterprises connected to tourism. Some critics felt that the president turned his ire on the nation's media because they refused to muzzle their crime reporting.

"You would think the president has more important things to do than phone up his friends and ask them to stop advertising in *Crónica*," said Estuardo Zapeta, the influential columnist at *Siglo Veintiuno*.[34] Zapeta may have been much freer than others to criticize, however. Despite reports that the Arzú government occasionally pulled advertising to show its displeasure with the paper's editorial stance, *Siglo Veintiuno* weathered the boycott relatively untouched, no doubt because of the pro-PAN position of its ownership group.

Eventually *Crónica*'s owners capitulated in the face of the government's actions. Mario David Waelti and Jorge Rodas bought control of the distressed magazine after it had endured more than two years of the boycott. They appointed Mario David Garcia, a pro-Arzú journalist, as the editor. Most of the magazine's staff quit in protest.[35]

The boycott also forced the sale of a Guatemalan media institution, the independent syndicated radio news program "Guatemala Flash." The program, one of the first nationwide news programs, was begun by Ramiro McDonald Sr. in 1945. In the mid-1990s, with his son, Ramiro McDonald Jr., behind the microphone, the program was broadcast several times daily and translated into the Mayan dialect K'icheé. At its high point "Guatemala Flash" was distributed to a network of stations that gave it 1.5 million listeners daily and made it one of the most influential programs in the country. With its signature marimba theme music, the *radio periódico* was a staple in most Guatemalan households, but it too could not withstand the economic pressures of the boycott. Like *Crónica*, the program was sold to investors friendly with the Arzú faction of the PAN in late 1998.

As happened in El Salvador, the state amplified its advertising boycott by coaxing its political allies to join the economic blockade. Not only was Arzú able to force distressed sales of media outlets, but his hardball tactics ultimately pushed the properties into the hands of his political allies. One might argue Arzú was even more successful in this part of the antimedia campaign, because it forced some owners to sell their properties and others to close operations altogether.

Nonetheless, the Arzú administration was unable to hurt the largest publishing group in the nation and its flagship newspaper, *Prensa Libre*. With the highest circulation rate in the country, *Prensa Libre* seemed immune from the government's attempts to pull advertising. Even without government publicity, the paper was too important and too popular among Guatemala's readers for advertisers to desert it as they had other publications and programs on the blacklist.

The government thus used other tactics. One of President Arzú's key aides, Mariano Rayo, came up with a scheme for the government to create a radio program masquerading as an independent *radio periódico* and run by anonymous *noticieros*. The program, called "Hoy por Hoy," featured political analysis, commentary, and gossip, but above all it criticized prominent members of the media. Journalists at *Prensa Libre* became the program's favorite targets. One of the owners of the *Prensa Libre* group, Dina Garcia, was often portrayed as promiscuous. Garcia's daughter, Dina Fernández, a popular columnist for the newspaper, was ridiculed as a bad journalist, and she too was called a "loose woman."[36]

Investigative reporters at *elPeriodico* decided to dig into who was behind the controversial and mysterious program. The reporters revealed Rayo as the mastermind behind "Hoy por Hoy." He had created a shell company to produce the program and had secretly financed the productions, which were run by radio stations owned by the media mogul Angel González.

Both González and Rayo faced criticism for their roles in the scandal, but they escaped relatively unharmed. The IAPA condemned González for supporting the government's smear campaign.[37] Meanwhile the FRG, at that time the minority party, dragged Rayo in front of Guatemala's Congress for special hearings. Although Rayo offered Arzú his resignation, the president refused to accept it. Rayo ultimately benefited from the public exposure and his devious manipulation of the media: in 1999 he won a seat in Guatemala's legislative elections.

This was not the first collaboration between the Arzú administration and González. Early in his tenure President Arzú put González's monopoly ownership of the nation's commercial television system to the test. In 1996 reporters at González's stations began complaining that the government was screening and filtering newscasts, especially the popular "Notisiete." After their public outcry, however, the reporters on "Notisiete" who had complained were fired. They claimed that President Arzú had asked to have them removed.[38]

In addition, the government-produced daily information program "Avances" moved into the prime-time spot preceding "Notisiete," which let it take advantage of the latter program's large audience. "Avances" had run on Canal 5, the government's station operated by the military, but Arzú wanted it changed to a commercial operation with a wider reach. The government's program had begun as a nonpartisan informational newscast under the administration of President de León Carpio, but the Arzú administration changed its purpose and approach. Instead of having it air press conferences or interviews, the government began using "Avances" simply to make statements, without inviting journalists to attend. In addition, members of the PAN used it to attack other parties. Arzú and others in the administration also assailed the media during "Avances," which became infamous for disputing news accounts from the nation's radio programs and the print media. Eventually international media groups such as the CPJ condemned "Avances" as a publicly funded program used for partisan propaganda purposes.[39] By giving space to "Avances" on Canal 7, González gave the government program legitimacy, because it was formatted to appear as a news program. The undiscerning viewer might have been unaware of the program's origins, and because much of the information programming on Guatemalan television was purposely kept low key, nonconfrontational, and progovernment, "Avances" might not have seemed out of place.

Given González's history of supporting conservative causes and political groups, his collusion with Arzú and the probusiness, right-wing PAN was not unusual. To build his monopoly in Guatemala, González often appeased powerful politicians with little regard to their ideology as long as they did not represent socialist or left-wing views. González's stations had welcomed government censors during the unsuccessful Serrano *autogolpe*. One of González's earliest contributions to the Guatemalan political scene was to donate 4 million quetzales (about $650,000) of airtime to the successful 1986 presidential campaign of Vinicio Cerezo, a centrist Christian Democrat.[40] This was the first election in Guatemala after the military decided to return power to civilian government. Since that time González has often given free airtime to politicians running for election, with little regard to their political affiliations. This has endeared the Mexican media owner to various groups inside the Guatemalan political establishment and ensured that no one would try to challenge his broadcasting licenses, which although legal certainly ran counter to the spirit of the laws meant to restrict media ownership to Guatemalans.

So far González has been just as generous with the far-right FRG. During the 1999 presidential campaign, González donated $2.5 million of airtime for the political promotions of the successful FRG presidential candidate Alfonso Portillo.[41] As had Arzú, Portillo tested González's loyalty early and was not disappointed.

The test involved the only independent television *noticiero* in Guatemala, José Eduardo Zarco, the host of "Temas de Noche," a program that blended a talk-show format with magazine-style in-depth stories to yield something akin to the U.S. program "Nightline," although it was broadcast in prime time. "Temas de Noche" was the only Guatemalan television program willing to take on controversial topics.

Zarco is a member of one of Guatemala's leading journalism families and one of the nation's most prominent journalists. The Zarco family joined four others to form the investment group behind *Prensa Libre*, and José Eduardo served as that popular newspaper's editor for a time. During those days Zarco was named Guatemala's representative for the high-profile publishing association the IAPA, and he became a leader in the Guatemalan Cámara de Periodistas, one of many trade groups representing journalists. After leaving his post at the newspaper, Zarco drifted to television. While maintaining a popular column at the family's newspaper, he started a production company to produce "Temas de Noche." With the strong economic support of his family and years of experience, Zarco became one of the most daring journalists in the country. On his show he boldly confronted issues such as the military's record of human rights abuses during the war. During the 1999 election campaign he often focused on the FRG's Portillo.

Portillo was a colorful speaker, a former university professor who had adapted his rhetoric to meet the macho politics of the FRG. He became international news, however, because of revelations from his past. In the early 1980s Portillo had taught at a university in Mexico's state of Guerrero, a region known for harboring bandits and guerrilla groups. In 1982 he had attended a party where faculty and students alike mingled. According to Portillo, a trio of drunken law students began to debate him about his political views, which in the 1980s were somewhat to the left. In Portillo's account, the debate became overheated, and the students decided to attack him. With three students launching themselves at him, ready to use their fists, Portillo drew a gun and started shooting, leaving two of the students dead and the third wounded. To escape murder charges, Portillo fled back to Guatemala.

Portillo kept his secret despite an unsuccessful bid for the presidency in 1995. The Mexican statute of limitations on the killings elapsed in 1995, so Portillo's revelations seventeen years after the deadly shoot-out put him at peril only with Guatemalan voters. Portillo cleverly turned the confession to his advantage, however. His campaign team crafted a commercial stressing that Portillo knew how to protect himself in dangerous situations and was not afraid of using force when necessary. In a nation scarred by death squads and the military's human rights abuses during the guerrilla war, some commentators, including Zarco, thought that Portillo's campaign tactic played like a sick joke. The voters felt otherwise. Portillo's tough-guy pose was attractive to many Guatemalans who were tired and afraid of the nation's soaring crime rate, one of the worst in the hemisphere. The PAN had tried to ignore and cover up the nation's crime problems during the Arzú administration, but Portillo's confession placed the issue squarely at the center of the election campaign. "I have made mistakes like any human being, and I accept my responsibilities," Portillo told Guatemalan voters during the campaign.[42] Despite harsh criticisms of Portillo in the media, the voters believed him, electing him handily over his *PANista* opposition.

After his inauguration, however, Portillo exacted his revenge on the media, especially one of his harshest critics, Zarco. Two weeks after Portillo's inauguration, media owner González made a major programming change for Guatemalan television viewers. A message was sent to Zarco, informing him that he would no longer be able to rent time on González's stations for "Temas de Noche." Because González holds a monopoly concession on Guatemalan television, this effectively canceled Zarco's independent television programming efforts.

Zarco was told the decision stemmed from low ratings, but many Guatemalans doubted that explanation. The timing of the actions against Zarco, an outspoken critic of the new president, looked suspicious. Many began to compare the cancellation of Zarco's program to the closing of "Aqui el Mundo," a respected *telenoticiero* that the Cerezo administration had closed in the 1980s for what the government called seditious commentary. Most television viewers saw through the ratings explanation because they understood how the independent *noticiero* system worked. Zarco paid González for a block of time. Zarco would then sell part of that time to advertisers. Ideally the commercial sales would offset Zarco's production costs and González's fees, with any remainder as profit. Low ratings would thus affect only the price Zarco could charge advertisers, not González's bottom line.

Of course, ratings might have some effect on the fees González could charge Zarco. For example, a popular slot in prime-time hours would be worth more than a time slot outside prime time. Ratings provide one way of measuring the worth of time slots, so fees can be based on them. This business model does not seem to apply to the Guatemalan situation, however. Because González owns a monopoly on the television spectrum, he can charge whatever he wishes for time. As his activities during the political campaign season show, he can even give time away if he wishes. Ratings are still a useful tool for establishing rates, but they can change at the owner's whim. So González could have charged Zarco whatever he wished for time, no matter what the ratings showed. If ratings had truly been a concern, González could have asked Zarco to move his program to a different hour, perhaps outside prime time. Instead he simply refused to sell Zarco air time, and "Temas de Noche" was canceled.

Noticieros throughout Central America often lose their leasing agreements with station owners. That is an accepted part of the business. Several factors made González's actions controversial, however: "Temas de Noche" was recognized as the only television information program airing a variety of viewpoints, and criticism of the government; González's television monopoly meant Zarco could not shop his program to another television outlet; the cancellation was announced almost immediately after President Portillo came to office; and González was seen as strengthening his connections to the Portillo administration.

Indeed, these connections were quite strong. González, who lives in Miami and closely programs his stations throughout Latin America from his headquarters in Florida, was represented in Guatemala by Louis Rabbe.[43] Rabbe had just been appointed minister of information in the Portillo administration when Zarco's program was canceled; Rabbe also happened to be González's brother-in-law.[44] Given these connections, the media and some discriminating viewers cried foul over what they saw as a blatant conflict of interest: the new president's chief critic had lost his most visible media vehicle, and the decision to cut the program was made by the new minister of information in concert with one of the new president's chief political contributors.

As might be expected, *Prensa Libre* led the charge against the cancellation, but other Guatemalan media outlets also criticized this act of collusion between the country's principal broadcaster and the government. In an editorial condemning González's actions, *Prensa Libre* noted with some irony that Zarco's program had been canceled a day after President Portillo had promised the Association of Guatemalan Journalists (Spanish acronym, APG), one of the country's fourteen different journalism trade groups, that he would support free expression. The paper criticized both the government and González by writing: "This arbitrary closing of the program demonstrates a problem of tolerance, and this time bares the purpose of the national television facilities to see their way clear to manipulate in favor of whichever government is in power, a danger that is too large for whichever nation that pretends to be supporting democracy."[45]

To deflect criticism, President Portillo stated that his media spokesperson, Fernanda Castejon, a former CNN correspondent, had lobbied

González by phone to reconsider the decision to cancel "Temas de Noche," but the owner would not change his mind. Neither Portillo or Castejon explained why they did not discuss this with cabinet minister Rabbe. They also failed to question the current ownership structure of Guatemalan television, because González's absentee ownership certainly runs counter to the spirit of Guatemala's laws, which require local ownership of the nation's television networks. This politically convenient move painted González, the outsider, a Mexican living in Miami, as the sole decision maker responsible for ending Zarco's program. Although González would have his image tarnished in the scandal, his business interests and their interconnections with the government were actually strengthened by the incident. No wonder one of González's nicknames is *el fantasma*, the ghost.[46]

Later in 2000 the OAS ombudsman on free expression investigated Portillo's role in the incident, but that was the least of the new president's worries. By that summer, less than six months into his administration, threats from Guatemala's powerful crime syndicates and gangs forced Portillo to send his family to Canada. He also ordered 10,000 troops to patrol the nation's key cities as crime spiraled out of control.[47] As usual in Guatemala, concern over violence canceled out any solid debate about the need for more free expression.

Through all these media scandals—the cancellation of Zarco's program, the smear campaign of "Hoy por Hoy," the substitution of "Avances" for real news, the firings and censorship at Canal 7, and the advertising boycott—Guatemala's leaders demonstrated a disdain for the basic concept of free speech in a system attempting to appear democratic. Their actions to undercut the independent transfer of information and free communication reinforce the notion that only through brutal power can one make headway in Guatemala. If anything, such brash power plays by the nation's leadership embolden the nation's criminal elements. If there is no respect for the rule of law, division of powers, or strong independent institutions outside the semiauthoritarian office of president, why should anyone respect any attempts at building a civil, democratic society? The use of raw political power to eliminate critics from the system provides a poor example in a nation attempting to build a democratic foundation after decades of warfare.

Some scholars studying the connections between the state and the media have lower expectations, untarnished by idealism. As Keane has written: "The core of all democratic regimes today contain [sic] the seeds of despotism."[48] The media boycotts in Guatemala and El Salvador certainly demonstrate how some of those seeds can flower into action.

The media owner González's complicity helped the government consolidate power: González gave the government flexibility to attack its most vocal critics in the remaining sectors of the media and provided it safe harbor on the television airwaves. The way his monopoly barred Zarco from the television market also illustrates how further concentration of media ownership threatens free expression. "González's control of TV and radio means he gives support to political candidates or can cover up politicians' misdeeds to manipulate public opinion," warned Zamora, the editor of *elPeriodico*.[49]

Nicaragua

Advertising boycotts, which the governments of Guatemala and El Salvador had used successfully against their critics in the media, became a convenient mechanism of control when political retrenchment came to Nicaragua. President Alemán Lacayo used advertising boycotts and other economic means in attempts to turn back the clock.

During the Chamorro era, in the early 1990s, media freedom had become a major issue for the president. The story of Pres. Violeta Chamorro's newspaper, *La Prensa*, parallels that of Nicaragua's state-media conflict during most of the past century (see chapter 4). With her publisher-husband assassinated—some might say in the name of a free press—and her children leading the nation's major newspapers, President Chamorro initiated policies that would give her nation the most open media environment it had ever enjoyed.

Chamorro's government was responsible for ending a long tradition of censoring independent news outlets, a history that includes most of the twentieth century. President Chamorro did use censors to review, filter, and sometimes spike news material broadcast on Canal 6 and Radio Nicaragua, the state's television and radio operations, respectively. This certainly diverges from independent state media as exemplified by PBS in the United States or the BBC in the United Kingdom. In Latin America, however, states have traditionally used their broadcast properties as propaganda organs. As she did in most of her endeavors, President Chamorro found a middle ground. Although the Chamorro administration sought to manage news content by ordering specific staff changes at the two broadcast operations in the early 1990s, most of the Sandinistas on both staffs were retained, in keeping with the Chamorro-era theme of reconciliation.[50] President Chamorro also employed a number of prominent Sandinistas in the public relations arm of her government.

Under President Chamorro the government began equitably dividing its advertising and publicity contracts among media outlets, regardless of political affiliation. Because the government remains the largest single advertiser in Nicaragua, accounting for more than one-third of all advertising there, this system provided fertile ground for new media operations. The number of radio stations tripled during this period of open and relatively free media. A number of important weekly publications started printing, and *La Tribuna* entered the market. Numerous VHF and UHF television channels opened. Nicaragua had never before seen such a lively media scene. Admittedly, this increase stemmed partly from the relaxed state controls on licensing and oversight at the end of the Sandinista era, but the Chamorro administration's economic policies and impartial support for independent media, either directly or indirectly through state advertising, played a role as well.

This was not completely good news for the media still controlled by ardent Sandinistas. When the FSLN controlled the government, state subsidies went solely to its media operations, and most state advertising was placed at media operations friendly to its cause. By sharing the state's advertising across the board, President Chamorro reduced revenues for the Sandinista-inspired media outlets, which now had to split the pot with other outlets. These economic changes helped spark the first wave of editorial changes at *Barricada*.

The Chamorro administration's policy toward equitable sharing of its media budget also provided a key example of the reconciliation necessary for the country to end some of its political polarization. During the Sandinista era, not only had the FSLN closed and censored *La Prensa*, but the government had used economic tactics to squeeze the Chamorro family newspaper. Cristiana Chamorro still has the order from the Sandinista government preventing the placement of advertising in *La Prensa*.[51]

With the installation of the Alemán administration in 1997, however, the spirit of reconciliation was lost. President Alemán immediately made decisions about the country's media based on ideology. Alemán acted forcefully against his critics in the media, first the Sandinistas and then others. Alemán's tactics, although not as heavy-handed as those of the Somoza or Sandinista eras, came as a blow after the Chamorro period.

Alemán purged all Sandinistas whom the Chamorro administration had allowed to stay in the government. Rather than censor state television or fire just the Sandinistas there, Alemán ordered Canal 6 to be closed, putting all its 150 employees out of work. Sandinistas in the state's public relations apparatus were fired as well.

Alemán also decided to use his own advertising boycott to flush the Sandinistas from the Nicaraguan media system. The government promptly pulled all subsidies and canceled advertising from media outlets judged to be friendly to the Sandinistas. The primary targets included the most popular newspaper in the country, *El Nuevo Diario;* the most popular radio station, Radio Ya; the Sandinista's Canal 4; and the party's newspaper, *Barricada.* President Alemán also redirected the state's considerable resources to support media outlets that backed his Liberal Party. To amplify the government's advertising boycott, the owners of Radio Corporación, the pro-Liberal network with an ultraright-wing political line, called on the president's supporters in private industry to show their "patriotism" by not advertising in media outlets critical of the government, especially those associated with the FSLN.[52]

The boycott yielded results, as had similar ones in Guatemala and El Salvador. Beset by its own internal political struggles and editorial makeovers, *Barricada* folded, with the boycott providing the coup de grâce. The distressed sale of Canal 4 to Mexican media mogul González followed soon thereafter. The former director and founder of *Barricada,* Carlos Chamorro, later remarked that although "tense relations between a president and the press [are] a symptom of good health" in a political system, President Alemán's policies had stepped over the line and amounted to "fiscal terrorism."[53]

Alemán, who had survived an assassination attempt during his election campaign, seemed more than willing to tough out the criticism as he consolidated his power. Radio Corporación became the voice of his administration on the radio, with most government advertising running on that outlet. Under Alemán the government actually spent more on Radio Corporación than it budgeted for the state's Radio Nicaragua.[54] In a policy perhaps left over from Alemán's stint as mayor of Managua, the capital city, too, placed most of its official advertising with Radio Corporación. For television, the government chose the friendly venues of the Liberal Sacasa family's Canal 2 and Carlos Briceño's Canal 8. Briceño was also directing public relations for the president. Alemán's friends and political allies in the media were reaping the rewards of his presidency, uncomfortably reminding some critics of the Somoza era. As for media outlets neither favored nor blacklisted, the government pressured them to properly slant stories and firmly requested that certain government events and Liberal Party political functions receive full coverage. By using an economic fulcrum, Alemán was effectively leveraging much of the media.

For a time the struggling *La Tribuna* attempted to hitch its economic fortunes to the president's gravy train. Always a probusiness, conservative publication, *La Tribuna* was nevertheless the political base for Haroldo Montealegre, a political rival of the president in the Liberal Party. At the beginning of the Alemán era, as much as 70 percent of *La Tribuna*'s advertising space was devoted to government publicity. After the paper veered from complete support of the government on a number of occasions, it, too, was cut off from the government advertising concession.

Joel Gutiérrez, formerly with Miami's *El Nuevo Herald* and later *La Tribuna*'s senior editor, brushed off the government's actions as part of the Nicaraguan newspaper business's political nature. Although he viewed the Chamorro era as having been relatively open for media relations, Gutiérrez remembered how President Chamorro had sometimes ordered the government to reduce or block *La Tribuna*'s importation of newsprint or ink.[55] In that regard, the vagaries of the government advertising budget, which fluctuated with the political mood of the Chamorro administration as well, were just more challenges for the struggling newspaper. Nevertheless, the Alemán administration's decision to cut off *La Tribuna* would eventually doom that newspaper, too.

All these tactics, from using government advertising as both carrot and stick to cutting the importation of newsprint or ink, are hoary traditions employed elsewhere in Latin America whenever the state wants to hide its coercion of the media. In some ways, these tactics were honed to perfection in Mexico during the PRI's long reign there.

Soon President Alemán imported another sophisticated tactic to combat the nation's independent media outlets. Unhappy with the way the nation's newspapers were delivering the government's message, in late 1999 the Alemán administration rechanneled 25 percent of its advertising budget to support the publication of a new daily newspaper called *La Noticia*.[56]

The managing editor of *La Noticia*, Xavier Reyes, claimed the paper circulates about 6,000 copies daily,[57] but estimates based on the audit of *La Prensa*, its competitor, put circulation for *La Noticia* at 2,000.[58] Other media observers in Nicaragua have estimated its circulation to be lower than Reyes claimed, more likely 3,000 copies daily. *La Noticia* began as an afternoon paper with an initial press run of 8,000 copies.[59] Not only has circulation shrunk, but the paper switched to morning distribution.

Despite its circulation, *La Noticia* has attracted notable journalistic talent to its staff. The editorial and graphic changes at *La Prensa* inspired some of that paper's staff to migrate. Pablo Antonio Cuadra, a respected Nicaraguan poet who has often served as one of *La Prensa*'s editors, came aboard *La Noticia* as a columnist. Horacio Ruíz, another leader at *La Prensa*, defected to the new publication as well. *La Noticia* also attracted a number of journalists who had been on the staff of *La Tribuna*. Elizabeth Romero and Fidelina Suarez were among the key writers who found new posts at *La Noticia* after *La Tribuna* collapsed. Reyes himself had been part of *Barricada*'s staff and a radio host at Cadena de Oro.

Although the newspaper has been able to build a staff from a variety of political backgrounds, it is still considered the Liberal Party's mouthpiece. Some people have thus begun to compare *La Noticia* to its forerunner, the Somoza-era propaganda sheet *Novedades*.

The Alemán administration invested heavily in its new daily paper, but it remains a minor player in Nicaragua. Most of the dominant media outlets have some tilt toward the FSLN and away from the Liberals. Despite the advertising boycott and the government's attempts to aid conservative media outlets, Radio Ya and *El Nuevo Diario* continued to flourish. Given Radio Ya's national reach and large audience, many private advertisers decided joining the so-called patriotic boycott was bad business. In the case of *El Nuevo Diario*, it kept afloat by emphasizing profits from circulation rather than ads. Both these examples support our claim that a media organ can positively affect the overall media system only when it exists as an independent market force, with its profitability uncoupled from state support and subsidies. Admittedly, these two media outlets, with their Sandinista leanings, were not changing the system, but their opposition to Alemán's policies helped prevent further retrenchment. As was true in Guatemala, the largest and most popular media outlets were proving to be immune from the government's pressure tactics, although those tactics were still hurtful.

In November 2000, perhaps realizing that the media boycott was not yielding the best results, the Alemán administration relented and once again began advertising in *El Nuevo Diario*. At one point the government was sending about 25 percent of its newspaper advertising budget to the paper, although *La Noticia* was still receiving the lion's share.[60] With the important 2001 elections approaching, however, *El Nuevo Diario* again sparked Alemán's ire. Just eight months after the policy shift, the government's advertising boycott returned in full force.[61] For a time the paper was still receiving about 10 percent of the government's newspaper advertising budget, but only because of previously incurred contractual obligations. This time the president was so upset with the tabloid paper that he banned the government's television channel, Canal 6, from even mentioning it. But the boycott did not kill the paper. Once again, *El Nuevo Diario* survived because it relied on its circulation and readership.

The Alemán administration decided to employ yet other state powers to tame its critics. Alemán's ordered audits of the tax returns of unruly media outlets.[62] The IAPA criticized this practice, labeling it "a policy of confrontation with the national press." Journalists of various outlets criticized the practice as well; for example, Reyes, of *La Noticia*, said that the policy encourages self-censorship.[63] Even for journalists who want to support the government or a conservative line, one misstep could result in a time-consuming and costly tax audit. For independent *noticieros* such an audit could make the difference between broadcasting or going out of business.

Although *La Prensa* had supported Alemán during his election campaign, his antimedia policies made it only a matter of time before the nation's oldest publication fell back into its watchdog role. When Alemán delayed calling a state of emergency during Hurricane Mitch, criticism of his administration's incompetencies began rising in the media, including the columns of *La Prensa*. The paper sent its reporters searching for corruption in the Alemán administration, and they scored numerous scoops. The president then turned his antimedia rhetoric on *La Prensa* and ordered an intensive audit of the newspaper's books in 1999.[64] Eventually the Nicaraguan government slapped a large fine on the newspaper, which *La Prensa* has appealed. The IAPA once again found itself defending *La Prensa* internationally against the pressures of Nicaragua's central government, a recurrent message since the 1960s.

As this pattern of behavior plays out in Nicaragua, it becomes necessary to compare similar patterns in other countries on the isthmus. As Gorriti of Panama has noted, many of these Central American countries are marked by highly centralized government structures, where power resides in a strong president and countervailing institutions are weak. Some might describe such countries as having weak state structures where government is run mainly through force of personality and leadership style. These systems are set up to maintain strong executive power. In such weak states, supranational actors sometimes become necessary allies for the state. In addition, the cases of Nicaragua, El Salvador, and Guatemala clearly show that the centralized executive power dominating these weak states must have key allies in the country's oligarchy and media.

Some media scholars have noted this rise of the so-called media-political complex in a variety of other countries and regions: the various nations of Eastern Europe, Russia, Malaysia, South Korea, Japan, and Egypt, among others.[65] In these areas, as in some of the countries of Central America, an intricate web of relationships is spun among key sectors of the landed and business oligarchy, major media owners, and the state. In Honduras those structures are actually merging. The economic boycotts of critical media outlets in El Salvador, Nicaragua, and Guatemala show these relationships acting—sometimes successfully—to strangle debate. In effect, the state and some elements of a country's media become extensions of a conservative oligarchy regulating speech and discourse. Although the owners of Nicaragua's *La Prensa* are arguably part of an oligarchic structure, the structure of oligarchies throughout the region is far from monolithic. So, for instance, progressive elements of oligarchies in El Salvador (with Canal 12), Panama (with *El Panamá América*), and Nicaragua (through *La Prensa*) have consistently challenged the conservative viewpoints of strong executives and competing elements within the oligarchic structure. This is an important reason explaining why certain media outlets sometimes find themselves engaged in decades-long ideological battles with executive power. These conflicts reflect interelite conflicts raging inside oligarchies and, consequently, inside these media systems.

In some of Latin America's cornerstone states, such as Mexico and Brazil, the government's alliances with dominant media monopolies or near-monopolies have constituted a key element in maintaining the dominance of particular parties or conservative elites. The Sacasas of Nicaragua, Esersky in El Salvador, and Ferrari in Honduras serve similar functions as dominant broadcasters aligned with the state. In Central America, however, supranational broadcasting entities have also played crucial roles. Thus, his broadcast monopoly in Guatemala makes González important there, but his supranational force in the region magnifies that importance. His broadcast ownership in Nicaragua, which has worked as a buffer between the conservative state and Sandinista broadcasters, cannot be discounted as an important factor in that broadcasting system. Likewise, the Mexican network TV Azteca has played a similar buffering role in El Salvador. Although the controversial González has comfortable monopoly control in Guatemala, he perhaps might have been bolder if he were not already flouting the spirit of Guatemala's national broadcast ownership laws. As we have seen in Guatemala and Honduras, though, the state's relationship with the media is designed in part to remove unfriendly voices from the media system when the occasion arises.

Costa Rica

Considering the glowing reports of media freedom in Costa Rica (see chapter 6) and the discussion of the sophisticated advances of that country's media system, it may seem unusual to see Costa Rica listed among nations where the state has impinged on the rights of journalists and threatened free expression. Nevertheless, journalists inside and outside Costa Rica recognize the system's limitations and the threats that some of the country's laws pose to pure media freedom. The issues in Costa

Rica, however, unlike those elsewhere in Central America, involve the rule of law and acceptable ways in which democratically constituted laws may constrain expression. The Costa Rican system has occasionally been subject to the type of personalized political feuding between government leaders and the media not uncommon among its neighbors—although the state most affecting the Costa Rican media has sometimes been the one centered in Washington, D.C. Some of these cases will be examined here.

Violence from the early days of the Contra War in Nicaragua spilled across the border, giving Costa Rican president Oscar Arias Sánchez one of several reasons to launch his Central American peace initiatives, which eventually led to peace throughout the isthmus. President Arias won the Nobel Peace Prize for his efforts.

The Arias peace initiatives were also meant to quell the activities of armed Costa Rican right-wing and anticommunist groups that threatened to destabilize the country, a democracy without a regular military. In 1980 one of those groups, the Free Costa Rica Movement (Spanish acronym, MCRL), participated with the Nicaraguan Contras in an armed attack on a Costa Rican radio station known as News of the Continent. The station had broadcast news items that the MCRL regarded as procommunist.[66]

Besides attacking radio stations, the Contras set up their own network of anti-Sandinista radio outlets inside Costa Rica to beam propaganda messages into Nicaragua. One of the stations was operated by Voice of America.[67] This coincided with the buildup of Contra bases in Costa Rica during the early 1980s, all part of U.S. strategy to contain the Sandinistas. San José and other parts of Costa Rica became centers for the Nicaraguan exile community, and refugees from the war streamed into the country. The refugees strained Costa Rica's social welfare system, a problem that continues today.

With CIA funding, *La Nación*, Costa Rica's most popular newspaper, began printing a publication aimed directly at the Nicaraguan exiles, *Nicaragua Hoy*. The publication was inserted in *La Nación* on a weekly basis and was edited by Pedro Chamorro Barrios, an exile who had played a prominent role at Nicaragua's *La Prensa*.[68] This arrangement was in keeping with the conservative, anticommunist stance of *La Nación*'s majority owners, the Jimenez family. The paper thus became a base for criticism of the Arias peace initiatives.[69] The newspaper was not alone, however; *La Republica* and *La Prensa Libre* also tilted noticeably toward the Contras.

Nonetheless, *La Nación* stood at the forefront of the anti-Sandinista cause. During the 1980s the publication's assistant director was José Sánchez Alonso, the vice-president of the MCRL. One notorious incident illustrating the paper's bias followed an MCRL attack on the Nicaraguan embassy in San José in 1985. *La Nación* blacked out portions of a photograph of MCRL militants so they could not be identified as members of the armed right-wing group. The incident showed the newspaper's vaunted independence from politics had been breached.

Other ethical lapses fueled by the heated political situation soon surfaced. To build further support for the Contra cause, the CIA and the Contras began a covert propaganda campaign by paying various Costa Rican journalists to slant their stories. Journalists who refused to take these bribes reported that they were pressured to resign from their positions, and others simply quit in frustration at the turn toward propaganda in the nation's media. Some of the country's high-profile journalists hired security guards during this period to ward off assaults or kidnappings by right-wing groups that might not like their reporting.

The divisiveness and unease that these activities spread through the country spurred President Arias to action. The propaganda campaign not only threatened free expression but also directly challenged Costa Rica's independence and neutrality. Besides leading the peace initiatives, President Arias criticized the nation's media for being in Washington's pocket. "The democratic system demands that its citizens and journalists comment, debate, and criticize the actions of public figures. However, the democratic system suffers when its citizens and journalists guard silence, slant facts or words, thereby confusing public opinion," Arias noted.[70]

With the success of President Arias's peace initiatives and the eventual end of the wars in Nicaragua and El Salvador, this sad chapter of U.S. attempts to subvert opposing opinions in Costa Rica came to an end. The United States had forcefully inserted its agenda into the region during this period, interfering in Costa Rica as intrusively as it ever had over the past century. It showed that policy initiatives made in Washington could supersede the power of the Costa Rican government and directly affect the nation's media.

This is not to say that the Costa Rican government never pressures the media. Close examination shows that some of the sophisticated policies for media manipulation used elsewhere in Central America have been used in Costa Rica as well. They are generally used less often and more subtly, although the government's finesse sometimes gives way to more direct forms of confrontation.

For instance, government pressure to fire journalists is still possible in Costa Rica, although such cases are rare. Such pressure has generally faded from the scene over the last twenty years. As the prominent Costa

Rican *noticiero* Rolando Angulo Zeledón remarked: "Before, if a government minister didn't like a journalist, he asked for a replacement and the journalist was changed. Now, it would be very difficult for a minister to request such a thing."[71]

Such cases do still surface, however, one of which began with reports concerning foreign contributions to Miguel Angel Rodríguez's ultimately successful presidential campaign. In 1997 then candidate Rodríguez and other PUSC leaders, including former Costa Rican president Rafael Angel Calderón, met with a group of Mexican entrepreneurs in Mexico. Long afterward journalists reported that Rodríguez had obtained a $1 million campaign donation from Carlos Hank González, a Mexican entrepreneur. Hank was a former Mexican agriculture minister, the governor of the state of Mexico, and a leader of the PRI.

Investigative reports published in Costa Rica and Mexico raised questions about the Hank family's ties to corruption in the PRI and the possibility of corrupt influences on the PUSC. Officials from the PUSC denied that Hank had given any money to Rodríguez's campaign. The reports prompted Costa Rica's legislature to promise its own investigation into the various business and political connections of the Hanks and other Mexican entrepreneurs investing in Costa Rica. All this strained relations between the countries and proved to be an embarrassing start to Rodríguez's term in office.[72] The administration failed to contain the spread of the story, which no doubt left the president somewhat unhappy with the media, including Julio Suñol, the editor of *La Republica*. Suñol said that Rodríguez was upset by his newspaper's investigations into the Hank affair and that the president pressured the Canadian chain that owns *La Republica* to dismiss him.[73]

The Costa Rican government further manipulates the media by providing all-expenses-paid international trips for journalists covering the president or other top officials. Because Costa Rican news organization do not always have the resources of *La Nación*, such coverage might otherwise be limited. Some Costa Rican journalists thus accept the practice, arguing that it allows greater coverage of the government by a wider variety of news organizations. Media codes of ethics in other countries, such as the United States, often require that news organizations reimburse the government for such travel expenses to preclude any conflict of interest. The Costa Rican media make no such demands, an attitude common in other Latin American countries, especially Mexico, where such trips have often been used to gain favorable news coverage for the government. In 1994, when José María Figueres Olsen was elected to the presidency (he is the son of President Figueres Ferrer, the controversial hero of Costa Rica's 1948 civil war), the Costa Rican government promised to review this travel policy, but no changes were made.

"One could say that it is a way to pressure the media. How impartial are those journalists? Are they as independent as those who pay for their own way?" asked Elbert Durán Hidalgo, the news director of "Radio Periodicos Reloj." "One does see colleagues who are not hindered by these circumstances and have no qualms asking the president what they need to know and expressing what they have to say. They are perhaps in an ethically compromising position, but if you limit yourself to analyzing their final product, you may find that they have done their job well."[74]

In 1993 Costa Rican journalists led the way in drawing up a code of ethics for Central American journalists as part of training programs to improve journalism throughout the region sponsored by Florida International University. At a meeting in New Orleans, representatives from throughout the isthmus agreed to try to institute ethical standards. One section of their ethical code directs journalists to avoid accepting benefits or payments that would compromise their standing as independent witnesses and analysts of events. The customary practice of accepting the government's travel perks seems to conflict with this standard, regardless of the appearance of objective reporting by some of the Costa Rican media.

Of course, the CIA-sponsored bribery of the 1980s already suggests the Costa Rican media are not as neutral, nonaligned, or ethical as they often portray themselves. Compromised and unethical journalists in Costa Rica are referred to by a slang term that mixes English and Spanish: *howmucheros*. Reporters accepting the government's friendly travel stipends are not considered *howmucheros*, which shows that Costa Rican standards for ethical behavior can be much closer to their neighbors' than the Costa Ricans would like to admit. The government's tactics for compromising these ethical standards are more subtle than are the illicit direct payments to journalists found in other countries (see chapter 8), but the policy exists because the government sees some benefit from its largesse.

As do others in the region, Costa Rica's government places a significant amount of advertising in the national media. Although nothing on the scale of the advertising boycotts in El Salvador, Guatemala, or Nicaragua has occurred in modern Costa Rica, some concerns have been raised about the government's persuasive tactics in placing advertising. In their 1995 analysis of Costa Rica, Vanden Heuvel and Dennis note: "The government can either reward or punish media organizations by giving to or withholding from them ad money from state-owned businesses."[75]

Armando González, the director of *Al Día*, the sister publication of

La Nación, said there have been occasions when the government used advertising to influence coverage and to "reward or punish the media: media that pester the government can lose state advertising."[76] Large publishing companies such as *La Nación* can often ignore such government tactics, however. As was true of *Prensa Libre* in Guatemala or *El Nuevo Diario* in Nicaragua, publications with large circulations or other revenue sources are insulated from these advertising pressure campaigns. In Costa Rica, without state media boycotts amplified by pressure from private sources, large media outlets can rely either on various other advertising sources, thus picking up the slack caused by absent government revenue, or on their elite owners' economic resources, patiently waiting out the pressure tactics.

An intricate series of Costa Rican laws, however, provides the government with leverage against the country's media organizations. Until 1995 all journalists were legally required to be members of the Colegio de Periodistas de Costa Rica, a trade guild that licensed and sanctioned journalists. This type of journalistic licensing runs counter to many models of media freedom espoused in the United States and European nations and is often an important concern when considering the legal limits of media freedom in Costa Rica. Until 1999 Panama had a similar system. Honduras still has a *colegio* system restricting who can work as a journalist. In the 1980s a reporter from the United States working at the English-language *Tico Times* challenged the constitutionality of this system. Although the Costa Rican Supreme Court ruled against him, the OAS's Inter-American Commission on Human Rights asked the court to review the case again because it saw the *colegio* system of licensing as limiting free expression. The licensing requirement was overturned, but the *colegio* remained influential as a trade association.

By comparison, the strength of the *colegio* system in Honduras has grown under President Flores, despite the opinion of the OAS and Costa Rica's example. In 1998 Elan Reyes became the head of Honduras's *colegio* system. This move strengthened Flores's clout in journalism circles because Reyes had strong ties to the Flores family. He had served as official spokesperson for the president's wife, Mary Flake de Flores, before heading the *colegio.* Given the president's already smothering behind-the-scenes influence with media owners, some journalists felt that letting Reyes head the *colegio* gave the president too much power. They protested, but Reyes did not back down.

Elsewhere in Latin America, the *colegio* system has served as a backdoor system where the state controlled the trade guild, which regulated the standards, practices, wages, and often licensing of journalists. By controlling the *colegio*, politicians could use it to sanction their enemies in the media or even have their licenses revoked. In some countries certain taxes are redirected to the guild to finance its activities (this was true of Costa Rica before the previously cited court decision).

Before the Costa Rican *colegio* lost some of its clout, it challenged the journalistic practices of the nation's favorite anchorwoman, Pilar Cisneros Gallo. In 1994 the elections that brought President Figueres Olsen of the PLN to power were clouded by controversy. Figueres Olsen was dogged by rumors linking him to the murder of a suspected drug dealer in 1973, when he was eighteen years old. Memories of Figueres Olsen's father, who ran for president thrice and served as president twice—the nearest the modern democratic Costa Rican system had to the traditional Latin American *caudillo*—also hovered around the campaign. Cisneros, Canal 7's anchor and news director, questioned Figueres aggressively during the nation's presidential debates. Canal 7, owned by the conservative Picado Cozza family, and the *La Nación* publications of the Jimenez family were accused of running exceptionally negative coverage of Figueres Olsen. The Picado and Jimenez families have traditionally opposed the PLN in Costa Rican politics.

The Costa Rican *colegio* investigated the election coverage and decided to reprimand Canal 7, *La Nación*, and *Al Día* for colluding to negatively slant their coverage of Figueres Olsen. The investigation revealed that Cisneros of Canal 7 had met with representatives of *La Nación* and *Al Día* to share information about Figueres Olsen.[77] The decision against the media outlets was controversial, however, because some journalists felt that the *colegio* should not be legislating standards that might curb investigative reporting, especially when the information might decide a race for the presidency.

In the wake of the ruling, Cisneros and other reporters linked to the affair were fired. Cisneros proved too popular, however, and Canal 7 eventually rehired her. Lafitte Fernandez, one of the journalists reprimanded by the *colegio*, went on to a successful career as the architect behind the redesign and reorientation of *El Diario de Hoy* in El Salvador.

Despite the negative coverage, Figueres Olsen was elected to office, but the campaign coverage controversy tainted his relations with the media for most of his presidency. The president often gave special access to certain news organizations and shared information or made pronouncements to journalists considered friendly to his administration, avoiding Canal 7 or the Jimenez family outlets. Although journalists everywhere decry such behavior, they experience it often enough, even from the president of the

United States. Many journalists have grown accustomed to such peevish behavior by presidents and have stopped commenting about it.

In a separate case from the *colegio* review, Humberto Arce, an editor at *La Republica*, claimed he was forced to pay the price for his aggressive coverage of the Figueres Olsen campaign. Arce had run a number of investigative pieces about Figueres Olsen's business practices and linked the new president to fraudulent mining deals. Arce claimed that the newspaper's owners forced him out of his position after pressure from Figueres Olsen's representatives.[78]

Cisneros seems rather matter-of-fact about the criticisms leveled at her by politicians. "We listen to their complaints, know that they are unhappy about some situations, but continue our work," she said.[79]

While in office President Figueres Olsen acquired a reputation for hiding important developments from the media. That reputation for secrecy intensified in 1996 when he issued a presidential decree labeling certain security issues, such as police operations against drug trafficking and money laundering, as official state secrets to prevent the media from discussing them. "The Figueres government, which was confrontational, mistrusted the media and lacked transparency," said Eduardo Ulibarri, the director of *La Nación*.[80]

During President Figueres Olsen's term in office the distrust between government and the media grew to extremely high levels. The Costa Rican judicial system set aside the *colegio* system of licensing and review during this administration, so politicians and members of the government sought other legal mechanisms to use against journalists. One such mechanism was the right of reply. The right of reply requires that newspapers provide space for people named in news stories to present their own views as to the stories the paper has printed about them. This legal concept is similar to the "personal attack" regulation once enforced by the Federal Communications Commission (FCC) in the United States. The right of reply in Costa Rica stems from an interpretation of the country's 1902 press law, which holds that a person whose honor is offended may demand a retraction, regardless of a story's truth.

In 1996 Costa Rica's Constitutional Court strengthened its support of this law when ruling on a petition brought by a PUSC leader who disliked *La Republica*'s coverage of his disputes with his legal clients. The newspaper had run the politician's reply on its editorial page, but the court ruled that the response must occupy the same place as the original stories in the news section of the paper and include the politician's photo.[81]

In 1997 *Diario Extra* was almost forced to close after a Costa Rican court garnisheed $130,000 from the publication to cover the legal costs of a case concerning the right of reply. The newspaper's story concerned police suspects detained in a stolen car. Although the newspaper had printed the suspects' reply, as required by law, it had waited longer than the legally stipulated three days. The court eventually reversed itself concerning the garnisheed legal fees, and the newspaper went on publishing.

Costa Rica's laws also restrict what the media may report concerning police investigations and limit criticism of legal rulings. Furthermore, journalists sued for libel must prove that what they printed is true. (In contrast, if a journalist in the United States prints or broadcasts a potentially defamatory falsehood, the plaintiff must prove the journalist acted with malice.) Some journalists in Costa Rica believe that nation's laws restrict the media and have the classic "chilling effect" of self-censorship that prevents journalists from probing too deeply. "I don't think that there are any democratic countries in Latin America with legislation and an enforcement of the laws pertaining to crimes by the media as restrictive as in Costa Rica," Ulibarri said, despite his feelings that the media in his country remained relatively free.

Andrés Borrasé, the publisher of *La Prensa Libre* and the dean of Costa Rican journalism, has a different opinion. "The press law is old and somewhat out-of-date," he said. "It looks restrictive on paper, but in practice it is not."[82] Nevertheless, Ulibarri sees difficulties in the status quo: "Our freedom of expression is limited by laws. The great difference between Costa Rica and other countries is that all of this happens in the legislative and judicial arenas. It happens within the established channels but that doesn't mean that it is not restrictive. I think that we have a serious problem there."

Ulibarri knows firsthand about the country's libel laws. In 1999 Costa Rica's Supreme Court ruled against Ulibarri and two of his reporters at *La Nación*. The case involved a scandal and allegations between the National Association of Public Employees and a former justice minister. The minister was accused of taking state-owned weapons and an official car for his personal use. The court ruled *La Nación* must pay $34,000 in libel damages and print seven pages of the court ruling in the newspaper.

In a separate case three weeks later, *La Nación* was ordered to pay $203,000 in damages to the Costa Rican diplomat Felix Przedborski for defamation. The paper had questioned the diplomat's activities based on reports in various European publications.[83]

Ulibarri and *La Nación* are also facing prosecution under Costa Rica's Public Spectacles Law, which was intended to deal with morality in the media. The paper ran various stills from the Stanley Kubrick film *Eyes*

Wide Shut, which prompted the legal case. Ulibarri said he now regrets publishing the photo sequence, which stretched what might be normally acceptable in a conservative family publication. He nevertheless noted that this was another restriction on expression, which shows that although the Costa Rican system is freer than most in the hemisphere, it still has limits. "If you interpreted all this legislative avalanche in its most restrictive sense, you could paralyze Costa Rica's media," Ulibarri said. "The fact is that there is a growing tendency to interpret the legislation in very restrictive ways. This conditions, limits, and scares some of the media outlets. They might publish less controversial stories to prevent complications. This affects the efficacy of democracy."

Because *La Nación* has the most resources of any of Costa Rica's newspapers, it is often at the forefront of the fight with the nation's courts over the boundaries of expression. For that, Ulibarri and his colleagues have earned the respect of their colleagues. As Marcela Angulo Grillo, the director of *El Financiero,* said of Ulibarri and his staff: "*La Nación* is an admirable example. Even when they have faced so many trials and know that they are always vulnerable to such claims from groups interested in hiding the truth, the paper continues to practice strong and consistent investigative and revealing journalism."[84]

La Nación has clashed not only with the president and the courts but also with Costa Rica's Legislative Assembly. The newspaper's investigative reports about drug dealing attracted the attention of legislators, who subpoenaed journalists at the paper to testify before a formal legislative panel. The stories that had sparked the assembly's interest linked drug cartels in Colombia to leading Costa Rican businessmen and politicians.[85]

The Costa Rican system of media laws are troubling because they effectively create a two-tiered system of rights. Media outlets such as the *La Nación* group of publications or others with deep resources can sometimes write off legal fees as the cost of doing business. At the very least, the laws seem to establish a system in which only media enterprises with sufficient resources may practice investigative reporting or other types of expression that challenge conservative boundaries. Smaller media organizations may tempt fate if they try to challenge the status quo. The legal case of *Diario Extra,* which almost closed the publication, shows that even everyday stories may put a media organization at risk in such a system. For small, alternative media outlets, whose political affiliations may differ markedly from those of conservative media outlets such as *La Nación* or Canal 7, the Costa Rican system seems to preclude their full participation in the freedom granted to larger enterprises. Such a system marks them as vulnerable, peripheral, and ultimately inferior.

As Ulibarri noted, however, Costa Rica—unlike its neighbors in Central America—uses a system of laws to channel these disputes between the media and the state. Although the force of personality sometimes comes into play, as with the suspension of Suñol at *La Republica,* which is similar to the Zarco and Sarmiento cases, concerns in Costa Rica have usually related to friction between media stretching to challenge a traditional order and a system of laws and codes meant to create that order. Some of this friction reflects the plurality of voices in an evolving democratic system, but some of it relates to the origins of the Costa Rican political order, which still remains largely in the hands of powerful elite forces. Like all systems we have examined here, the Costa Rican system is evolving, with a constant push and pull of different forces. For every legal decision that grants more freedom, such as the end to the *colegio* system, other decisions counter these new openings.

8 The Threats to Central American Journalism

During the 1990s Latin America became the most dangerous place in the world for journalists: about 150 journalists were killed, and many more were kidnapped, threatened, or attacked.[1] International journalism groups have monitored Latin America carefully, and despite important declines in the region's lethal numbers during recent years, violence and death continued to challenge freedom of expression. Although Colombia and Mexico present the greatest danger for journalists, Central America has been the locus of much of this violence. In 1997 the IAPA held a special conference in Guatemala City to discuss violence aimed at journalists in the region. The group highlighted two murders of prominent Guatemalan journalists, including publisher Jorge Carpio Nicolle, along with the assassinations of other journalists from Latin America.[2]

But Guatemala was not the only Central American nation feeling external pressure about its treatment of the media. In 1999 the OAS condemned Panama for the overt and direct threats facing the media there. Given the shared borders, it seems only natural that the antimedia violence common in Mexico and Colombia might cross into Guatemala and Panama, respectively. Nevertheless, although Guatemala and Panama have received the most attention for this violence, other Central American nations have experienced problems as well. As Central American elites move beyond hiring goons to eliminate their media problems and turn to more sophisticated means, even normally quiet Costa Rica has found itself embroiled in debates concerning how to protect free expression.

In the early 1990s members of the media in El Salvador and Guatemala faced direct threats of violence due to civil wars. Panama faced General Noriega's crackdowns, which included the firebombing of radio stations and direct physical assaults on reporters the dictator viewed as threats to his regime. The end of armed conflict across the isthmus ushered in a new period, however, and threats became less overt. Journalists cannot always tell whether violence aimed at their colleagues carries a message, but it has nevertheless created an atmosphere of self-censorship in most countries in the region.

Crimes against journalists designed to silence them rarely receive satisfactory investigation, either because officials cover them up or because they are committed by the police, the military, or forces working for them. This lack of information often makes it impossible to substantiate the exact motives behind such violence. But the violence itself has a ripple effect throughout the journalistic community in a country. We focus on that violence and other direct threats to the safety of journalists in this section.

Because each country is unique, we examine the trends in each one separately from the others. These case studies, although perhaps limited, prove illuminating. More important, we refuse to overreach by making broad claims about the conditions of violence and personal threats across the region. Trends and commonalities certainly exist, but it would be a mistake to lump together all these nations without first examining the specifics of each. In this sense our analysis here takes less a macroview, and more a case-by-case approach. Without a complete examination of these specific cases, we believe, the plight of journalists in the region gets lost in discussions of democratization and the evolution of communication systems.

El Salvador

According to the CPJ, Laura Saravia may have been the first journalist whose work led to her murder in post–civil war El Salvador. Saravia was a newscaster on Radio RCS, a national radio network based in the capital and featuring political talk shows hosted by both former military officers and former guerrillas, a politically volatile blend. In the summer of 1997 Saravia was abducted from her car and then killed by a single gunshot to the head. Police later found her abandoned car fifty kilometers outside the capital. At the time of her murder, the CPJ issued a media alert nevertheless acknowledging that she might have fallen victim to the postwar crime wave plaguing San Salvador, which made the city one of the most dangerous places in the hemisphere.

The investigation into Saravia's murder became more complex, however. In 1998 thirteen men, including several former police officers, were charged with her murder. At the time charges were filed, police said that one of Saravia's former lovers had hired the men. In such cases authorities in Latin America often claim a journalist's murder was a crime of passion rather than an assassination linked to the reporter's work. By the end of 1998, however, the reason behind Saravia's murder was again clouded in obscurity. The judge assigned to the case released five of the accused killers for lack of evidence. When the case came to trial, he freed the remaining men. He ruled that instead of murdering Saravia, the men had been framed by their former colleagues on the police force as part of an elaborate feud.[3]

The motive for Saravia's murder is still undetermined, and no one has been convicted of the crime. This is not unusual in Latin America, where authorities seldom pursue or prosecute those who kill journalists.[4] Often, as in the Saravia case, a cover-up seems to be the safest and most expedient course of action.

Adding to the mystery in the Saravia case was the judge's decision to bar reporters from the legal proceedings. In this case, the judge invoked Article 272, a controversial new addition to the Salvadoran penal code that allows judges to bar reporters from covering trials where, as the CPJ notes, "the moral order, the public interest, or national security could be affected."[5] The judge's action in this case prompted members of the journalism community to question the type of cover-up protecting Saravia's killers.

El Salvador's Article 272 may prevent journalists from doing their jobs, but other legal measures directly threaten journalists and their livelihood in many Central American countries. Most advocates for free expression note that most of these countries have devised criminal contempt laws (*leyes de desacato*) and criminal libel statutes that both the government and private parties can use to control journalists.

In Mexico, for example, drug cartels and politicians linked to narcotics traffickers have used such laws to silence critical reporters.[6] These laws threaten the safety and livelihood of journalists throughout Latin America. Jail time, large fines, and legal fees can be daunting to poorly paid reporters. The powerful have used these laws to stifle reporters in Central America, too.

As we have noted, Costa Rica has sometimes used laws to control the media and limit expression. Although the application of these laws has had a mixed result, and journalists there often describe the country's system as one of the most free in Latin America, the concept of *desacato* and other mechanisms are used to threaten journalists. In the Costa Rican system, however, *desacato* has been applied to very few cases.

Although Costa Rica's *desacato* law had been on the books for decades, the first conviction came in 1994. Columnist Bosco Valverde, of *La Nación,* was convicted after he characterized several justices on the country's Supreme Court as "pigheaded." Under the law Valverde could have served jail time for the comment, but he was instead given a suspended three-year sentence and fined $10,000.[7] The Valverde case is still regarded as one reason Costa Rican journalists tread lightly in their reporting on the nation's court system. Such laws point not just to the limits in the Costa Rican system, but also to the dangers facing journalists who decide to cross these legal lines in the sand. The Valverde case also provides a good comparative reference point for media freedom outside Latin America, where such aggressive criticism would be not only legal but regarded as fair commentary or protected speech.

Some Costa Rican journalists support the system, however. Marcela Angulo Grillo, the director of *El Financiero,* noted: "Here the government doesn't rule the media or determine who can work in it, not like in Panama. But the government does protest media actions directly and I think that is legitimate."[8]

Criminal libel statutes have been used to quell similar criticism in Nicaragua, even when the criticism did not originate there. In 1998 the Nicaraguan subsidiary of Zeta Gas, a Mexico-based multinational firm, sued TeleNica 8, one of the nation's minor television stations, because the station rebroadcast a report from CBS's "Sixty Minutes" about reputed ties between Zeta Gas and drug traffickers. Zeta Gas sought $1.25 million in damages from the station and pursued criminal libel charges against the station's general manager, Carlos Briceño, and the independent producer of the program where the CBS story was rebroadcast, *noticiero* Miguel Mora of "100% Noticias." Unlike those of other nations, the criminal libel statutes in Nicaragua carry only monetary penalties, but the suit nevertheless created problems for the station, because the trial judge froze the station's assets until a ruling could be made.[9] Briceño said Zeta Gas had threatened to seize the station and its assets if it won the libel suit. From his viewpoint, nothing positive emerged from the legal flap except that ratings went up because viewers became interested in the controversy and the station's fight against a foreign firm.[10]

Again, this was the legal response to a simple rebroadcast of a U.S. story on links between business in the region and the drug trade; original reporting on anything connected to drugs has become even more worrisome for reporters there. Both the physical and economic risks of covering stories concerned with the drug trade have kept reporters from aggressively writing about what is emerging as an important economic and legal battleground in the postwar era. "There is only one type of story we stay away from and that is anything to do with drugs and drug trafficking," warned Ramiro McDonald Jr., the former director of the independent radio newsmagazine "Guatemala Flash" and one of Central America's most respected radio journalists. Other journalists in El Salvador and Honduras have backed McDonald's assertion that reporting on drugs currently seems too dangerous for most reporters in the region. "We've just come out of a time when our lives were in danger. Why should we put our families through that again? In a sense, the profession is tired right now of this type of dangerous reporting," he added.[11]

The potential for violence that haunts anyone reporting on the narcotics trade and the threat of legal action through *desacato*, which can put journalists in prison, provide yet another chilling combination adding to the fear confronting those who work in the media in Central America. These are palpable reasons for the widespread practice of self-censorship.

Panama

One journalist who has bucked the trend of self-censorship is Gustavo Gorriti, the associate editor of Panama's *La Prensa*. Gorriti has run afoul of Panamanian authorities because of his investigative work. Having worn out his welcome in his native Peru, he nearly did the same in Panama. After his writing infuriated Peru's president Alberto Fujimori, Gorriti was forced into virtual exile.

Gorriti's reputation as one of the best investigative reporters in Latin America began to take shape during his coverage of Peru's guerrilla war. In 1990, during President Fujimori's first presidential campaign, Gorriti's investigative stories connected Fujimori to Vladimiro Montesinos, a CIA informant and former officer in the Peruvian Army. Gorriti's reporting about Fujimori's questionable connections and the men behind his rise to power looked prescient later on, when Montesinos was appointed to head Peru's National Intelligence Services (Spanish acronym, SIN). Two years after Fujimori was elected, when he moved to grab extraconstitutional powers, an elite team of Peruvian commandos acting under orders from the SIN, kidnapped Gorriti. After his release, Gorriti left Peru, taking a position at Washington's Carnegie Endowment for International Peace before moving to Panama.

The SIN would go on to pressure and harass other journalists in Peru. In 1999 the OAS's special ombudsman on freedom of expression condemned the SIN for attempting to restrain expression through a concerted campaign of harassment and for keeping an enemies list of journalists critical of the Fujimori regime. The report noted "that certain sectors of the Peruvian government have the intention of silencing journalists who have expressed opinions critical of authorities."[12] Almost all the journalists on the SIN's enemies list have received death threats. Like Gorriti, some have gone into self-imposed exile for their own safety and that of their families.

Several challenges lured Gorriti to Panama, however, despite its dangers. The leaders at *La Prensa* wanted to give the newsroom a jolt, and they saw Gorriti as a catalyst who would spark more investigative reporting.[13] Because Colombia, the world's largest cocaine producer, is right next door, much of the hemisphere's drug money is laundered in Panama. From Gorriti's standpoint, such a location could be "an investigative reporter's paradise."[14] When Gorriti arrived in Panama in 1996, he wondered about the collapse of the Panamanian Agro-Industrial and Commercial Bank (Banaico). How could a bank fail in such a rich environment? Gorriti found the answers in the bank's links to the Cali drug cartel. But Gorriti's investigation went beyond the bank to show the complicity of Panamanian government officials. While Colombian drug lords were using the bank to launder money, government officials were helping them cover their tracks.[15]

Gorriti managed to find their trail. His search of records eventually turned up a link between the Cali cartel and Panama's former president Perez Balladares—specifically, a $51,000 campaign contribution from a cartel leader to Perez Balladares's election campaign fund.[16] To Gorriti, the links between the corruption at Banaico and the president were evident: the bank's vice-president, Alfredo Alemán Chiari, was Perez Balladares's top fundraiser.[17] At first President Perez Balladares accused Gorriti of printing falsehoods and inaccuracies, but eventually he was the one forced to retract his statements, admitting that Gorriti's allegations were correct. In discussing his motivations for his investigations, Gorriti mentioned the media's responsibilities. "In Latin America, because of the fragility of democracy, there's a burden for the independent press to have a substantial role in the balance of power equation," he said.[18]

As we have documented, however, attempting to balance authoritarian or semiauthoritarian centralized power often comes with dangers. Gorriti had the courage of his convictions and followed his philosophy in his investigative work, which provided a counterweight to the PRD's attempts to return to long-term power in Panama. Gorriti gleaned some protection from *La Prensa,* an influential paper with strong ties to the nation's progressive political power structure and its allies in some sectors of the business class, but the investigative editor was still vulnerable. If he was sent back to Peru, he might be jailed or threatened or face a worse fate at the hands of Fujimori's security apparatus. But he was willing to risk that in his search for the truth.

Although *La Prensa* has a long history of opposing the Panamanian government, the media in general fell into a culture of self-censorship in the years of dictatorship. Gorriti's brand of hard-knuckled reporting not only reinvigorated his paper but showed others that perhaps they should not retreat into old patterns, even though the party of dictatorship, the PRD, once again controlled the country.

In the 1990s many journalists in Latin America have found a new mission for themselves in the type of watchdog journalism Gorriti practices. They could turn to the work of *Veja, Jornal do Brasil,* and *Fólha de Sao Paulo,* publications that cracked stories of corruption in the administration of Fernando Collor de Mello and brought down the Brazilian president. These stories were not just inspiring; they showed that the media could be an important factor in leveraging power in emerging democratic systems.

Nevertheless, the composition of the media is also an important consideration. As we have seen, media oligopolies are often merely supports for national oligarchies. Those oligarchies in turn support authoritarian or semiauthoritarian power.

The history of Panama's electronic media demonstrates this tendency. The increasing consolidation of Panama's television and radio properties became another target of Gorriti's investigative work. Gorriti started feuding with the president's cousin, Nicholas González Revilla, one of Panama's major media owners (see chapter 4). González Revilla caught Goritti's attention just as he was consolidating his Panamanian holdings. González Revilla's company, MEDCOM, controls Panama's two most powerful television networks and the country's most popular radio news outlet. Gorriti wrote critically about González Revilla's attempts to gain a monopoly in the electronic media market, where his television stations already attracted three-fourths of the nation's viewers.

Asked about his concerns regarding the consolidation of Panama's electronic media, Gorriti replied: "Vertical integration of the media is much more dangerous here than in the States. The effect of the acquisition of independent media by one source runs at counterpurposes with the quality of journalism. How can a journalist report when they are controlled by those who represent the most powerful political sectors?"

The Panamanian government under Perez Balladares tried to make the Peruvian editor pay for his ideals. In the summer of 1997, when Gorriti's work permit was up for renewal, the government moved against him. The government issued an order to expel him from the country and deny his work permit. In addition, the government said Gorriti and *La Prensa* were violating laws, enacted under dictator General Torrijos, that banned foreigners from holding management positions in the Panamanian media.

The international journalism community rallied around the besieged editor. Groups such as the CPJ and the International Press Institute (IPI) publicized the Panamanian government's attack on the editor for his investigative work. Gorriti also asked the Inter-American Human Rights Commission of the OAS to intervene and used his contacts in the U.S. media to gather more support. Indeed, how could journalists in the United States resist a story with such interesting characters? It was the classic tale, a contest between Gorriti's pen and the state's swordlike power. The editor's vulnerability to deportation to Peru, where he risked worse repression, further put him in the classic position of someone facing the violation of his human rights. The media latched on to the editor's cause, and he was profiled by some of the United States' largest newspapers. After months of international pressure, the Panamanian government retreated. Looking somewhat foolish after the international flap, the Perez Balladares government reissued a visa and work permit for the embattled editor.

The Panamanian government appeared to be trying this tactic again in 1998, when Gorriti's application to renew his documents was held up in processing. Instead, the government took the opposite tack. It decided to restrict Gorriti's travels. The travel restrictions grew out of Gorriti's battles with Panama's attorney general, José Antonio Sossa. In 1998 Sossa filed criminal libel charges against Gorriti and one of his reporters at *La Prensa*, Rolando Rodríguez. In 1996 Gorriti and Rodríguez had written an investigative story about Sossa's legislative reelection campaign. They revealed that Sossa's campaign had accepted a $5,000 donation from a Panamanian firm linked to drug dealers. As part of the legal proceedings, Gorriti and Rodríguez were barred from leaving the country, forcing Gorriti to cancel various appearances in the United States. Once again, however, the government eventually relented, and he was able to pick up his International Press Freedom Award from the CPJ in

New York City. "Bureaucrats, kleptocrats, narcocrats, they don't want a strong media and free expression," Gorriti said of his problems with the Panamanian system during this trip. "For them, image laundering is more important than money laundering."[19]

Gorriti's staff also faced the government's wrath. In 1998 President Perez Balladares sent police to raid *La Prensa*'s offices and arrest the reporter Herasto Reyes. Reyes had written an article tying the president to corruption in the 1980s, when he was the minister of finance under the Torrijos and Noriega regimes. Reyes's story linked the president to corruption in a federal housing program. Panama's gag laws allow as much as a one-year jail sentence and fines for anyone found guilty of offending or insulting the president. Reyes was saved from arrest when his colleagues at the newspaper surrounded him, creating a human wall to separate him from the police, who eventually retreated. The president also backed down in an attempt to have Reyes arrested later, but he pursued other legal action related to the investigative article.

With *La Prensa* continuing the feisty role it had played under the Noriega dictatorship, Gorriti's problems in his Panamanian exile were not over. During the summer of 1999 Gorriti wrote another story criticizing Sossa. The story took issue with the attorney general, who would soon be leaving office at the end of the Perez Balladares administration. Gorriti wrote that Sossa had not pursued an investigation into two suspected drug traffickers from the United States, as requested by the FBI.

This time Sossa fought back, not just with a flurry of new lawsuits, but with the aid of allies in the PRD. After the PRD lost the presidential election in 1999, and after Gorriti's latest string of revealing stories on Sossa, a group called the Committee for Freedom of Expression in Panama began a smear campaign against Gorriti. Many believed the secretive committee had links to the PRD. They were less interested in free expression than in ruining Gorriti's reputation in an attempt to undercut the credibility of his reporting and the impact of *La Prensa*'s stories. The group papered the capital with posters accusing the Peruvian editor of stifling free expression. The posters included pictures of Gorriti and accused him of being a spy. Similar charges were leveled at the editor by the head of one of the country's associations for lawyers, a group that called for the government to expel the controversial editor. Although the mysterious anti-Gorriti committee never revealed its members to the public, the embattled editor accused Sossa and the media mogul González Revilla of backing the smear campaign.[20]

So even with the end of the Perez Balladares government, Gorriti's problems were not over. The former president, his attorney general, and others friendly to the PRD carried their fight with *La Prensa* and its investigative editor to the courts. By using the country's *desacato* laws, they could attempt to neutralize the newspaper's aggressive reporting in the future. The laws carry a penalty of up to two years in prison and allow judges to levy fines.

Mounting legal problems and the shifting political winds in Peru and Panama eventually pushed Gorriti back home. During 2000 Gorriti took a leave from his duties at *La Prensa* to become a long-distance adviser to the political campaign of Alejandro Toledo in Peru. Although Toledo did not win, his accusations of government fraud helped unravel Fujimori's regime.[21] (Ironically, when Fujimori's spymaster, Montesinos, fled briefly to Panama seeking exile, Gorriti was one of the media leaders calling for him to be expelled. Gorriti was also instrumental in arranging media coverage of Montesinos when he flew back to Peru and attempted to hide there.) The bold investigative editor did leave Panama in 2001 to help with Toledo's successful campaign to become Peru's president. Although Gorriti was asked to become part of Toledo's government, he chose to go back to journalism and start a television program featuring his strong blend of investigative and political coverage. A change in the leadership of the board of directors of *La Prensa* in Panama (see chapter 10) was also instrumental in showing Gorriti that the Panamanian chapter of his career was over.

During the 1990s Panama's legal system increasingly became the weapon of choice to choke off investigative reporting. "They use restrictive press laws to threaten us, to keep the press from digging up all the embarrassing facts," complained Elizabeth Brannan, *La Prensa*'s Washington correspondent.[22] The OAS's ombudsman on free expression had identified these laws as one of the main obstacles to free expression in the hemisphere, and Panama ranked among the top trouble spots on the OAS list because of the way it used its laws. Panamanian reporters did not like being on a list that compared conditions in their country to media restrictions in Peru and Cuba. They were forced to choose between fighting the laws or restricting their reporting. Not only do these laws give the state increased leverage over reporters who wish to analyze government activities, but entrepreneurs, lawyers, and others in the private sector have used them to hem in freedom of expression. Brannan reported that the country's press laws have created an atmosphere in which reporters are afraid to dig too deeply, for otherwise they may be dragged into a seemingly unending judicial process.

One Panamanian journalist, Tomás Cabal, had to fight the same court case thirty-four times. Cabal, a freelance correspondent for several publications, was still fighting libel accusations more than seven years after he wrote a story in 1991 for *U.S. News and World Report*. In that story, Cabal linked the Panamanian attorney Hernán Delgado to drug cartels operating in the region. Delgado filed libel charges against Cabal thirty-four times: under Panama's press laws, a plaintiff is allowed to file charges several times as long as they are filed with different judges. Although Cabal won thirty-one times, three other judges saw it differently. One fined him $1,000; another gave him a twelve-month suspended sentence. Cabal is appealing a third ruling that sentenced him to fifteen months in jail.

Before leaving office the Perez Balladares administration also turned its attention to *El Siglo*'s reporters, who were known for aggressive investigative work. In just one of several cases aimed at the newspaper, a group of journalists connected to *El Siglo* were hit with defamation suits related to their reporting on a corruption scandal known in Panama as the *piñata*. Not to be confused with the *piñata* scandal in Nicaragua at the end of the Sandinista era, the Panamanian *piñata* involved official corruption related to the handover of properties when the Canal Zone reverted to Panamanian control. An official bidding process had been established to open the sale of homes and other properties to all Panamanians who might be able to afford them. Gorriti's investigative team at *La Prensa* had broken the story, showing how some powerful members of government had secured the rights to properties before the bidding process had started or had intervened for friends or political allies. *El Siglo* followed up aggressively, however, further detailing the *piñata* story. The *El Siglo* investigation revealed how a prominent federal prosecutor had obtained an expensive home in the zone as part of the *piñata*. The targets of these investigations responded by taking the journalists to court.

The new administration of President Moscoso, however, decided to reverse this trend toward using the nation's laws to keep reporters in check. In one of the first major acts of her administration, Moscoso signed a bill that reduced the scope of the nation's so-called gag laws, as well as ending the *colegio* practice of licensing journalists in Panama.[23] The bill also eliminated potential six-month jail sentences for journalists convicted of publishing reports that "discredited government institutions" and revoked the government's power to close news outlets, which had been used effectively to stifle dissent during the years of dictatorship (see chapter 3). Moscoso promised to work with Panama's legislature to abolish more of the sweeping media laws on the books, including those instituting presidential powers of censorship. Although these laws have not been used since the Noriega era, they remain a concern for journalists. In addition, Moscoso promised to work on repealing the punitive *desacato* laws, which make libel a criminal offense and threaten journalists with prison time, even for stories that are true.

At the bill-signing ceremony, President Moscoso characterized the gag laws as "a Damocles Sword hanging over the media in Panama." She added: "There should be no law or action that restricts press freedom. Whenever freedom of expression and the press is restricted, for whatever reason, other liberties also disappear."[24]

Although President Moscoso's intervention may come too late to lessen the burden on journalists such as Cabal, Rodríguez, Reyes, and Gorriti, her actions are an important shift from the repressive policies of the past. Not only did these policies give the state a major tool to mute critical journalists; in addition, the laws gave members of the private sector—sometimes corrupt members of the entrepreneurial class—a way to keep journalists from poking too deeply into the shady dealings that have undermined Panama's image.

As we have noted, outside forces that threaten the primacy of the state's relations with the media will invoke a backlash that may result in violence or in the state's using mechanisms to control media output. Although Panama did not spiral down into the violence the system has experienced in the past, neither has it entirely escaped that past. The strong state reaction against Gorriti, who energized Panama's investigative reporting scene, and his colleagues provides an abject example showing how such outside influences can spark negative reaction from state power. The open-minded policies of President Moscoso, however, whose closest advisers include former journalists, seem to signal that Panama is now headed away from those vengeful policies.

Guatemala

Since peace accords were signed at the end of 1996, security issues for the Guatemalan media have improved. Like those in El Salvador, many journalists in Guatemala perceived that they were safer once the war was officially over. Reports of killings and attacks against journalists dropped. Previously reporters who wrote controversial stories had faced violence and even assassination. With peace came the feeling that the old rules no longer applied.

This assessment is partially based on anecdotal information from journalists. The feelings, however, are to some extent based on wishful thinking. Like others in Guatemala, journalists there want to enjoy some of the glow from the peace, and they do not want to focus on the potential for a return to violence. Nevertheless, much of that feeling of safety may be based solely on the impressions of conditions in the capital.

Provincial journalists have a different view. "Those reporters in the capital don't even come out to cover the news, so how do they know?" asked Timoteo Tobar Salazar, the president of a cooperative group of small provincial newspapers.[25] According to studies cited by the news agency Cerigua, only 5 percent of stories in the nation's newspapers originate outside the capital.[26] Tobar said journalists working outside the capital reported that the atmosphere there had changed very little since the accords.

Top journalists in the capital brush off such concerns. They say complaints from provincial reporters do not reflect the mood in the country. In a general way, however, this attitude may express the usual arrogance and self-importance of journalists who report from a nation's capital. One-third of Guatemala's population lives in the capital, so the shift in attitudes about safety is important, but the blanket generalization that the country is safe for journalists to report freely may nevertheless reflect conditions only for elite journalists or for journalists at elite media outlets. For example, in 1998 Tobar noted that members of his news cooperative, COOPEDEGUA, reported that members of the military had confronted a reporter and threatened him with a grenade because of his reporting. According to Tobar, another reporter in Coban had his home firebombed.

Neither of these incidents was investigated or independently confirmed by international journalism groups, but international groups such as the CPJ did report that at least four journalists have been killed in Guatemala since the peace accords, which equals the deaths the group reported during the ten years preceding the accords.[27] Unfortunately, different groups cite different numbers of deaths and use different documentation to link them to the journalists' work. For example, at the Forum for the Democratization of Communications held in Guatemala City in 2000, forty-nine journalists were listed as killed for trying to do their jobs from 1960 to 1996, making Guatemala one of the most dangerous countries in the hemisphere during that era.[28] Editors of small provincial papers reported that even after the peace accords local government officials had delivered threats with a view to curbing critical reporting. One high-level media manager in Guatemala City also reported receiving serious phone threats from the military or paramilitary groups in 1998.

The murder of one editor in the COOPEDEGUA consortium in 1997 led provincial editors to take such threats seriously. International journalism groups believe Jorge Luis Marroquín Sagastume, the editor of the monthly *Sol Chortí*, was murdered for reporting on corruption in Jocotán. Two men gunned down Marroquín in Jocotán. The men charged with the murder were ultimately convicted and sentenced to thirty years in prison. During one trial they implicated the town's mayor, José Manuel Ohajaca, saying that he had hired them to kill the editor. Guatemalan law protects mayors from prosecution in many crimes, however, including this one. The Human Rights Office of the archbishop of Guatemala City then petitioned to have the mayor's immunity lifted. A court of appeals rejected the request, but the case is pending before the country's Supreme Court. The same court that sentenced the gunmen said it, too, is reviewing Ohajaca's immunity, since he is no longer the mayor of Jocotán.[29] The review may be a moot point, however; at last report Ohajaca had fled the country, and some people believed he was in hiding in the United States, possibly in Los Angeles.

In addition, the CPJ lists three provincial journalists among the murder victims in Guatemala since 1996. Unfortunately, it could not determine whether their deaths resulted from their journalistic endeavors or from Guatemala's current crime wave, due in part to the postwar availability of guns and a high poverty rate.[30]

Although journalists in the capital have generally claimed to feel safer since the war ended, *Prensa Libre*, the country's most popular paper, has seen significant violence aimed at their journalists. Journalists at *Prensa Libre* trace its problems with repressive violence to 1970 and the assassination of Isidoro Zarco, an editor at the paper and one of its owners during the war.

In 1997 Luis Ronaldo De León Godoy, the editor of *Prensa Libre's* weekend supplement, was stabbed outside his home. Because witnesses said De León's attacker had waited for him for several hours, and because nothing was stolen, the CPJ noted that De León had probably not simply fallen victim to Guatemala City's crime wave.[31]

In 2000 Roberto Martinez, a photographer for *Prensa Libre*, was killed while covering a protest over public transportation in the capital. A private security guard fired his gun into a crowd of protesters, killing the photographer.

Despite a perception that violence has decreased in Guatemala, for journalists it remained the most dangerous country in Central America. Why is this so? Guatemala, El Salvador, Nicaragua, and Panama all experienced violent upheavals—wars or invasions—during the past generation, yet violence seems to have been used against journalists differently in each country. After the years of dictatorship, Panama's Dignity Battalions ceased using violence against journalists and politicians. Revenge shifted squarely into the judicial arena, and punitive laws that threatened journalists with prison or expulsion became the stick used to beat them into submission. Following the revolution in Nicaragua, the assassination of journalists lost its popularity as a means to control information. In El Salvador, too, with the notable exception of the deadly attack on Saravia, murder seems to have lost its appeal as an option of control. In Guatemala, however, despite perceptions to the contrary, the practice of killing the offending messenger endures.

Recall our earlier claim concerning Central America: forces that threaten the primacy of the state's relations with media owners will meet with backlash, which may result in violence or in the state's use of mechanisms to control media output. But what happens when the state changes the equation?

In Guatemala, as we have explored in previous chapters, the Arzú administration sought to gain more authority over the media by pressuring media owners to sell properties to the president's *PANista* supporters. Owners who failed to sell were forced either to close their enterprises or to conform to editorial boundaries prescribed by the president's office. To pressure owners into line, the Arzú administration eliminated government subsidies, stopped regular government advertising, and cut its payroll to individual journalists. Ironically, this policy not only created economic pressure but allowed forces striving for independence and ethical standards to fight corruption inside the ranks of journalists (see chapter 9 for more details on these issues in Guatemala and elsewhere). When President Arzú deployed these economic means to manipulate the media, he also discontinued the government's illicit payments to journalists. Because the government was one of the chief sources of journalistic corruption, this policy resonated throughout the journalistic community. It became easier for publications to enforce ethics codes that prohibited illicit payments for biased coverage. When the main source of such payments—the central government—eliminated this source of corruption, it became easier for journalists to accept a higher standard of behavior, although acceptance was not universal. What made Guatemala's government different from most others in the region was the state's public exposure of corrupt journalists and Arzú's promise that state-sanctioned corruption of the journalism community had ended.

By removing payoffs and bribes from the system, however, the central government also removed one of the more effective means for controlling the media. Smaller governments outside the capital found they had fewer weapons to suppress information. In the postwar era, when the media began to search for ways to test their free expression rights, provincial media discovered that they were held on a shorter leash than were their colleagues in the capital. The military, local governments, and other forces in the Guatemalan system found that without economic measures, violence was still a handy tool for sending messages to the media. Another factor: Guatemala was the last Central American nation to emerge from its violent civil war era, making the violence of the past less far removed from the present than it was elsewhere in the region.

In addition, as we have documented, the economic pressure of the Arzú administration, although hurtful, failed to control *Prensa Libre*. Other measures were aimed at the owners of the paper and its publishing group—for example, a smear campaign was mounted against the Garcias. The publishing group's immunity to the state's economic pressures perhaps opened *Prensa Libre* to more repressive tactics. Smear campaigns and even murder thus became increasingly useful devices to instill more self-censorship in the system.

Journalists must also take some responsibility for the violence in the Central American system. By accepting the conflicts of interest that payoffs entail, journalists in Central America and indeed in much of Latin America also open themselves to violent reactions from narcotics cartels, paramilitaries, criminals, or corrupt members of government and the military who feel that they have not received their money's worth.

We thus add the following corollary to our earlier claim about external pressures: when bribery and corruption are accepted inside the culture of journalism in a nation, removing or reducing those methods of controlling the media may stimulate other controlling measures, such as violence, unless the system's elites agree that freedom of expression should increase. In the case of Guatemala, the Arzú administration sought not more free expression but a different manner of controlling the media. Likewise, in maneuvering to have José Zarco removed from network television, the Portillo administration signaled that free expression could easily be sacrificed for the needs of the state. Outside media circles, no one in the postwar Guatemalan system promoted freedom of expression as a liberty that should be honored. Instead, the use of terror and fear to inhibit free speech remained a solution for those who sought to retain the conservative status quo in the country.

Honduras

Political or policy changes within Central American states provide important indicators of violence levels. For instance, violence in Honduras has often been linked to political change in the 1990s. Many of the problems facing the media in Honduras can be traced to friction between the nation's military and civilian authorities. This classic competition between elite forces sometimes produced collateral damage where journalists were the victims.

During the 1980s the military's grip on the nation seemed absolute, and the media were held on a tight leash. During this era, when Honduras served as a base for monitoring El Salvador and supporting the Contra War, dissent was stamped out (see chapter 7). The government allowed a military terror campaign against civilians, including journalists. The popular anchorman Rodrigo Wong Arévalo, who is known for his strong opinions, especially about U.S. intervention in Honduran affairs, discovered a bomb in his home. Most reporters took the bombing attempt to signal that controversial views would not be tolerated. Nevertheless, Manuel Gamero, of *El Tiempo*, is an exception in that he managed to campaign against U.S. foreign policy and its effects on Honduran society and politics without facing such security problems.

In 1993, after most wars in the region had subsided, the relation between civilians and the military began to shift. Honduras saw its military role as a forward base for the United States reduced. At the same time, civilian forces began to test the boundaries of their growing power in the Honduran system. Some of these changes could be seen in the media.

As the power of civilian government grew, the media felt freer to criticize the military regime, which largely controlled the country behind a shroud of democracy. During this period the media published their first reports of extrajudicial killings by the military, which eventually led to full reporting about the military's campaign to kill left-wing sympathizers in the country during the 1980s. The media were not behind this investigative work, however; they were merely amplifying releases from the nation's human rights ombudsman, Leo Valladares.

During this period one of the nation's television stations ran a story linking members of the military to the murder of a prominent businessman in San Pedro Sula. This was followed by articles in *El Tiempo* about the threats the television journalists had received because of this story. The Honduran system convulsed violently in reaction to these expressions of media freedom.[32] Eduardo Coto Garcia, the television reporter who broke the San Pedro Sula murder story, was forced to flee to Spain after receiving death threats.[33] Yani Rosenthal, one of the owners of *El Tiempo*, had his house firebombed immediately after the newspaper reported the threats to journalists covering the murder story. The newspaper had information that linked elements of the military and its death squad Battalion 316 to the firebombing, the murder, and drug trafficking, but military intervention slowed the release of this information, which leaked out only gradually.

A week after the firebombing, Colonel Hung Pacheco, the head of the military's police forces, ominously revealed that the military was keeping files on all journalists. He also said the nation's security forces routinely monitored their activities. Hung Pacheco's military police patrolled the capital and San Pedro Sula as law enforcement agents, but his comments about tracking reporters were a revelation to the country's journalists. Hung Pacheco was later promoted to general and eventually to leader of Honduras's armed forces, a move that did not need presidential review and that the Honduran legislature rubber stamped. Hung Pacheco's announcement and his later ascension to ultimate power in Honduras prompted the domestic media to cease probing into military wrongdoing. Even more ominously, within a month of Hung Pacheco's announcement the Honduran military moved armored vehicles and extra units into Tegucigalpa in a show of force. The message that the military was in charge was clear to civilian authorities and the media alike. The Honduran media would not return to the subject of the military and human rights in any significant way until 1996 and Serapio Umanzor's groundbreaking series in *La Prensa,* which followed reporting on the topic from the United States. In effect, Hung Pacheco had established the boundaries of expression through his direct announcement and its subsequent chilling effect on the system. At the same time, his words were backed with the violence and threats others had already visited on the journalists who dared to test the boundary. Because the military enjoyed overriding power in Honduras, making it perhaps more powerful than Guatemala's military (the Honduran military was not forced to fight a civil war and went virtually unchallenged), its powers to shut down free expression were more nearly absolute. With respect to democratization, Honduras lags far behind others; indeed, the chilling effect of violent threats has gained wide international notice.[34]

Although the military's practices of human rights abuses, torture, and execution have been exposed, they have not eased quietly into the background of the Honduran political system. In 1999, when President Flores shook up the nation's military establishment, the most aggressive reporter working on the story faced frightening consequences for his work. As noted in chapter 1, Renato Alvarez, a television reporter, had tied Flores's actions to a possible coup. Days after his revelations, Alvarez found himself escaping from a possible kidnapping.[35] Like the events of the early 1990s, this incident sent a stern message to those willing to delve into the politics of the nation's military: this territory would remain dangerous, and those wishing to tread on this ground would do so at their own risk.

Likewise, when Sandra Maribel Sanchez reported on corruption in the Honduran military and legislature in 1996, she too found the system reacted strongly against her.[36] She received a number of telephone death threats warning her to stop focusing on stories of corruption. Unlike Umanzor's important series of the same era, Sanchez's stories concerned actors in the current political system with considerable power. Perhaps it was all right to expose the sins of the early 1980s, but the corruption of the present was still too dangerous to touch.

In 1999 Rossana Guevara, a television journalist and longtime critic of the Honduran political system, received her own alarming message. After Guevara wrote a series of investigative stories on government corruption, her dog was killed. Police said the dog had been deliberately poisoned. "The right to free expression doesn't exist in Honduras, and without a free press, there cannot be a democracy," Guevara said. "The situation has gotten worse."[37]

These two cases from the latter portion of the 1990s illustrate the clear limits for journalists in Honduras. Although the system has not often turned to deadly measures, as it has in Guatemala, journalists still remain in the crosshairs of those with an inclination toward violence. The journalists act accordingly, restraining their reporting to fit within the boundaries of expression when one of their colleagues receives a warning. The Guevara and Sanchez cases further show that reporters brave enough to challenge those in power will often be sent violent messages to restrain themselves, lest they provoke worse violence. Few are willing to accept the challenge.

Less clear is the case of Yadira Ramos, who was murdered in 1998. A television journalist, Ramos had reported on drug trafficking in San Pedro Sula and detailed the operation of some of the city's drug gangs. This too provoked a reaction. Gang members went hunting for Ramos. They ambushed the television reporter and shot her several times. Ramos was left comatose and died several months later.

Clouding the cause for the murder was Ramos's long personal relationship with the controversial television owner Rafael Nodarse. Ramos had sued Nodarse for mistreatment and abuse in their relationship, which made headlines nationwide and resulted in yet another scandal pinned to the Cuban American media owner. Nodarse had long-standing connections to the nation's military and was linked to a variety of questionable practices, including piracy of satellite signals. After months of legal maneuvering, Ramos eventually settled with Nodarse out of court.[38]

The timing of Ramos's murder, not long after the legal settlement, raised questions. Nodarse offered a 25,000 lempira award (about $1,900) for information leading to the arrest of Ramos's killers. Police captured one of the gang members who participated in Ramos's killing, but another, Fernando Rizzo Abudeye, ended up dead. Police found Rizzo's body in a canal outside San Pedro Sula about four months after Ramos was shot. Rizzo had been killed execution style, with a single bullet to the head. His family said a group of men had stormed into his aunt's house, where Rizzo was hiding, and kidnapped the fugitive. Rizzo's family was quick to blame Nodarse for the gang member's murder. The media owner turned up in Acapulco, Mexico, not long after Rizzo's body was found. It remained unclear whether Rizzo's murder was just the fallout of gang warfare among narcotics traffickers or some other type of revenge. No one was charged with the murder.

If anything, the killing of Ramos, a television anchorwoman and reporter, points to the obvious dangers facing reporters who are willing to take on journalism connected to drug trafficking. As Ramiro McDonald Jr., of "Guatemala Flash," sagely advised, such reporting was to be avoided for all but the most experienced, because the drug war is fought with little concern for anyone's perceived rights. To anger someone in this hazy, dark underworld was to trip a violent response, every bit as brutal and lethal as those of the death squads during the civil wars of the 1980s.

Although these messages of violence from drug gangs and the military in Honduras are certainly more chilling and ominous than the legal actions against reporters in Panama or television stations in Nicaragua, they all have the same effect. In the case of Nicaragua's TeleNica 8, the station was not reporting on corruption or Nicaraguan elites, but a company accused of having links to drug lords reacted much as the government might react, taking strong legal action to muzzle the station and thus signaling the Nicaraguan media that linking companies to drug cartels would exact a high price. Zeta Gas, the company that filed suit, was attempting to keep the media inside prescribed lines of control common in Central America, where most journalists have decided that investigative reports about drugs and the drug economy are too dangerous to run.

Likewise, when Gorriti established himself in Panama and began exposing corruption, the state used various mechanisms in response. Direct attacks on Gorriti, although legal and nonviolent, were nevertheless attempts to limit his free-speech rights and send a message to his colleagues in the Panamanian system. They also implied the threat of expulsion to

Peru, where he might have faced violent threats. Other investigative reporters who were brave enough to follow Gorriti's lead found that the targets of their investigative reports would seek revenge in a similar fashion.

The difference in many of these nations may relate to the role of the military. Neither Panama nor Costa Rica maintains a standing military force. As our examples show, the battle over free expression has therefore shifted to a new arena: the courts. Although the judiciary in Panama has supported a more punitive system in the past, the reforms proposed by the Moscoso administration suggest that freedom of expression and therefore democracy are advancing there.

In Guatemala and Honduras, however, the opposite is true. Both nations have strong militaries that continue to support violence. Look no further than the Guatemalan military's complicity in the 1998 murder of Archbishop Juan Gerardi following the Catholic church's report on human rights during the war years. This act showed the dangers facing anyone who wanted to probe Guatemala's genocidal past. Taking a cue from this culture of violence, those with disputes against reporters, as in the case of Marroquín at *Sol Chortí* or the unsolved murder of *Prensa Libre*'s De León, see that the lives of those searching for the truth are not valued highly by the harsh powers that lurk beneath the surface in Guatemala's political system.

Honduras is searching for a new political equilibrium where the military will take a less prominent role, but the road to that future resembles a rollercoaster, with extreme dips and turns. The military retains ownership of key economic holdings, such as banks, insurance companies, and construction firms that it operates independent of the civilian government. Although President Flores has won the most important arm-wrestling matches with the Honduran military, the future is far from certain, especially when the military continues to threaten those who criticize its operations. Given the country's modest movement toward democratic forms, the media may continue to test the limits. If they once again meet with the violent convulsions and threats common in the past, the media will retreat prudently again. Although media owners have seen their power grow exponentially in the past decade, the battles to put the Honduran military squarely under the control of civilian leaders are far from over.

None of this intolerance may be very surprising to those who have studied the history of human rights abuses and military strength in Central America. Nonetheless, the basic human rights of free thought, free expression, and free speech cannot exist in a culture of terror and fear. Writing of Latin America, Silvio Waisbord notes: "The authoritarian regimes that ruled these countries for most of their modern history were antithetical to the development of an 'independent' and professional press. Such journalistic practice was a chimera and a matter of life or death when military governments closed down media firms, tightly censored newsrooms, and persecuted and killed dissident journalists. The few journalists and editors who remained committed to investigative reporting often paid with prison, torture, exile and death."[39]

Although Waisbord was writing about the development of media systems throughout the hemisphere in the past century, our documentation clearly shows that conditions continue to raise similar concerns in Central America. In the worst cases, the threats remain the same: prison, exile, terror, torture, or death. In Central America, and likely in other regions where this type of relationship between the state and the media exists, actors and forces that attempt to reduce the state's leverage on media affairs often provoke a strong, sometimes violent response.

9 Corruption and Corporate Censorship

Until now we have focused on the state's overwhelming power to influence or control the information the media transmit. As we have noted, however, each country in Central America has developed its own unique media culture, and that culture exists in a dynamic system affected by many factors, not just central governments or militaries. As the whirlwind of change tears through the region, the concerns of the state often blend with those of the private sector, or even of criminal elements, all of them conspiring to control the media. We will explore those influences here.

To understand the complex competing pressures that affect the media, one must consider the economic climate and culture of corruption in the region. Although some may complain that such an examination strengthens negative stereotypes, to ignore the rampant corruption seeping into many facets of Central American society would be to ignore a factor that affects the media's ability to contribute to or detract from movements to build democracy in the region.

The problems of corruption in Central America are fairly well documented, but a few recent examples may support our analysis and indicate the atmosphere in which reporters must work. For instance, in 1999 Transparency International, an independent international NGO that monitors corruption, ranked Honduras as the second-worst country in Latin America.[1] For example, one Honduran car-smuggling ring encompassed prosecutors, lawyers, judges, and high-profile businessmen, along with the regional chief of Interpol. The ring would take stolen vehicles seized by Interpol and then issue false documentation for them so they could be smuggled into Guatemala, El Salvador, and other countries, where they were sold. Honduras suffers from private-sector corruption and smuggling, too. To avoid tariffs and customs charges, producers smuggled out about one-sixth of the country's coffee crop in 1998.[2]

Honduras has been a center of corruption for a generation. In the 1980s various parties diverted economic aid sent from the United States, especially the U.S. Agency for International Development (USAID).[3] Police and customs corruption was rampant. When Colombia's drug cartels expanded into Honduras in the mid-1980s, senior officers, members of the legislature, and the country's top politicians were added to the list of people receiving funds tainted by the drug trade.

But Honduras was not alone. As Gustavo Gorriti, the editor at Panama City's *La Prensa,* has pointed out, his adopted country has become a nefarious center for money laundering and the corruption needed to hush up those activities. Gorriti was not the only one pointing a finger, however. The Financial Action Task Force put Panama on its so-called blacklist for complicity in money laundering. The task force, which is part of the Organization for Economic Cooperation and Development, reports its findings to the International Monetary Fund (IMF) and other international lenders. It cited Panama partly because the country had never convicted anyone for money laundering, although some leaders of corrupt financial institutions had been extradited or charged.[4]

Gorriti and his investigative team at *La Prensa* documented links between money laundering and funds that narcotics cartels and drug lords donated to various political candidates in Panama. Others have also written about similar political donations elsewhere in the region. In a 1998 report the Center for Strategic and International Studies, based in Washington, warned that such drug payments likely constituted part of the $15 million that Honduran candidates spent on media campaigns in the 1997 elections.[5] Aside from criticizing politicians for accepting money from drug gangs, the report condemned such overspending in a country with a variety of other, more fundamental needs—indeed, the poverty rate there was one of the worst in the hemisphere, ranking, along with Nicaragua and Guatemala, near the bottom of the scale.

In Guatemala the PAN corruption scandals that were revealed after President Arzú left office almost led to the complete collapse of the party. One major concern involved the state telephone system; many Guatemalans believed the state had tremendously undervalued it before selling it to private investors friendly to Arzú and the PAN. Such a cut-rate sale of state enterprises in the move toward privatization exemplifies the more subtle corruption plaguing Guatemala's political system. Some members of Arzú's government publicly expressed concern that they would lose the next elections based on the public's perception that the sale of the state's phone system had been a gift to friendly elements in the country's oligarchy.[6] Subsequent events proved them right.

Too often analyses of the media in Latin America tend to portray journalists as the lone enemies of corruption. In this one-dimensional portrayal, they are the white-hatted good guys riding into town to clean up the mess that society has made of itself. They fight pitched battles with corrupt governments, banks, and multinational companies, along with a few real criminals, and eventually they save the day or go down fighting.

Of course, as we have documented, a few journalists in Central America try to live up to this idealized image. Their reality is much more complex, however, and they are not alone in their fight, although sometimes they feel that way. More important, this one-dimensional story leaves out the other, corrupt members of the media in Central America. It leaves out human nature and the temptations that corrupt forces with many resources may offer. They are not always monetary. In poor countries such as these, however, where many journalists can barely scratch their way into the middle class, the opportunity to grab some financial security exerts a strong allure.

In some cases journalists in the region face problems when they report on government corruption or drug gangs because the targets of their investigations move in a culture that calls for a less public approach, the culture of extortion. The targets expect journalists to approach them before publication, not for an interview—as might be expected—but for a payoff. Journalists who perpetrate such shakedowns, extorting money for their silence, thus participate in the region's all-too-common corruption. Journalists who are unwilling to accept these cultural norms, or who perhaps have a change of heart, may face the sometimes violent wrath of angry patrons who feel they should be able to pay for a journalist's complicity.

An analysis of media systems in Central America must consider the role of corruption, for the media cannot counterbalance power if they join in such criminal games. If the media are to rise above the political fray, they must not be encumbered by conflicts of interest, monetary and otherwise. Of course, as our discussions of state advertising budgets have shown, such independence is a rare commodity in Central America. Nonetheless, if the media hope to contribute to a democratic transition and strengthen the rule of law while turning government institutions

toward working for the populace, then they must above all deal honest-
ly with corruption in their own ranks.

Although each nation in Central America developed its own responses to bribery and journalistic corruption—so much so that each of
the six nations we discuss has a different word that refers to journalistic
corruption—we have found some general factors that affect the level of
corruption in a media system. Cultural acceptance of corruption is of
course important, and some systems, such as that of Costa Rica, seem
to have backed away from such acceptance more than others. The general level of crime and the government's ability to fight it is another
important consideration. Governments riddled with corruption will use
their influence to cover up their activities and pressure the media to help
in the cover-up. Our examination of state power over the media seems
to indicate that this is an inevitable outcome. In addition, we have identified several other important factors as well: general economic conditions
for journalists, recent wars, generational shifts in ideology and ethics,
government policies to eliminate corrupt practices, and the influence of
the United States.

Corruption can flourish in a media system only when it constitutes
an accepted practice. Of the South American journalists polled in a 1995
study, slightly more than 58 percent knew of a journalist who had accepted illicit payoffs.[7] A few years later, in 2000, the Center for U.S.-Mexico
Studies at the University of California at San Diego reported that 52 percent of the journalists it had polled in Mexico knew of journalists who
accepted bribes.[8] Such polls and studies are often met with cynicism in
Latin America. Most journalists in the region say these polls strongly
undercount the problem throughout Latin America, where journalists
may be too embarrassed to admit the extent of the problem to outsiders.

These studies have connected the widespread practice of bribery with
the economic needs of journalists. According to the 1995 study, salaries
for Latin American journalists averaged about $400 a month. In Central
America the salaries are about the same, if not lower. In 1998 some radio journalists in El Salvador earned as little as $100 per month. In neigh-
boring Nicaragua beginning journalists earned as little as $300 per month,
although more experienced journalists made $700 monthly. Likewise,
Panamanian salaries in 1998 were as low as $300 per month. Despite the
differences between the Panamanian and Nicaraguan economies, all these
salaries for journalists seem relatively low.

Again, Central American media owners often support conservative
political systems and established oligarchies; sometimes they push to
create media oligopolies as well. As we have shown, such allegiances can

lead to bias and even censorship. At the same time, these owners seem unwilling or unable to share their wealth by paying their employees decent wages. They thus help create the economic conditions in which corruption can take root. Although such selfishness, which underlies the upper class's general unwillingness to help others of lower strata, is only one reason journalists' wages are depressed across much of the region—job competition plays an important role as well—by helping to keep wage rates low, it tends to allow corruption to flourish.

Sandra Maribel Sanchez, an outspoken reporter at Honduras's Radio America in Tegucigalpa, charged owners with complicity, laying the roots of corruption at their feet. Such owners, she said, merely wave off the problems this causes for journalistic credibility. "A media owner who knows that his journalist is making $300 or $400 a month and who sees him drive into the media parking lot in a BMW—he either gave it to him or is participating in the corruption," she said.[9] Sanchez has worked to expose corruption of all types in Honduras. As noted earlier, she received death threats following her work to uncover corruption in the country's military and legislature.

Sanchez's colleague, Rossana Guevara, a television reporter in San Pedro Sula, has also worked for years to expose corruption in Honduras. Guevara has complained that investigative reporting in her country is undercut by a system where the government bars reporters from access to documents and tries to pay off reporters who become persistent pests. Most reporters take the bribes, she said, because salaries are "miserable."[10]

These two reporters share more than a mission to expose corruption in Honduras: both show what can happen to journalists who buck the system. As noted earlier, Guevara was sent a clear message when her dog was poisoned by forces who did not like her reporting on government corruption.

The cases of Guevara and Sanchez provide the most obvious examples of journalists in Honduras who have been threatened because of their efforts to tear down the accepted culture of corruption. They also support our claim that forces threatening the primacy of the state's relations with the media will invoke a backlash in the system, wherein the state uses violence or other mechanisms to control media output. In the case of Honduras, this violent pattern can be charted through the 1990s.

As we have noted previously, 1993 was a watershed year in Honduras. The country's human rights ombudsman was exposing the military's poor human rights record from the 1980s, and even Carlos Reina, who would soon be the nation's president, was campaigning on a platform that included human rights and anticorruption themes. The country was swinging away from the ultraconservative period of the 1980s, and old habits were changing. Journalistic attitudes were also evolving.

Managers at San Pedro Sula's *El Tiempo* decided to confront the open and endemic corruption in their newsroom during this period. Vilma Gloria Rosales, the paper's editor, said part of the reason she decided to attack this corrupt culture was her exposure to journalistic ethics courses at Florida International University (FIU). During this period, FIU also organized a conference in New Orleans where Central American journalists drew up their own code of ethics. Without this intervention and advice from the United States, the first Honduran challenges to corruption might never have moved forward.

Rosales had a more direct reason for intervening, however. The flagrantly open bribery in her newsroom left complicity or action as the only possible choices. One of the reporters at *El Tiempo* had organized a pool of reporters who were accepting regular payments from Honduras's National Election Tribunal. These were important payoffs in an election year. The organizer of the corrupt pool mistakenly left his list of participants and the amounts they were due on a photocopier, where they were discovered by management. In the spirit of the newly adopted ethical code, Rosales decided not only to confront the reporters in her newsroom but also to publish the list. She further decided to share the list with her competition. Even though the reporter who had forgotten the list threatened her at gunpoint, Rosales followed through on her decision to clean up the problem.

At Rosales's crosstown rival, *La Prensa,* managing editor Nelson Fernandez also decided to print the list. Fernandez was closely tied to the FIU training program, and he was a driving force to improve journalistic ethics in the region. Fernandez and Rosales both decided to fire members of their staffs who had accepted payments from the government. Because *La Prensa* and *El Tiempo* are among the most respected and popular publications in Honduras, this very public action was influential in driving overt corruption out of most newsrooms in Honduras.[11] Both papers further used their influence to encourage the country's media organizations to draft firm policies designed to prevent corrupt practices. For his part, Fernandez was able to show concrete advances and improvements in Honduran journalism because of his connections with FIU and its work in the region—and, of course, the bravery of his competitor, Rosales. Fernandez would also prove influential in supporting Serapio Umanzor's important series on the human rights violations of the Honduran military several years later, before passing on his day-to-day duties at *La Prensa* to others.

Nevertheless, the dramatic actions and revelations of Rosales and

Fernandez were not enough to cleanse the system of corruption. Less than six years later, the managing editor of *La Prensa*, Maria Antonia Martinez, admitted that corruption still existed in her newsroom. Instead of enjoying a semi-open system, however, reporters who participated in these shady dealings had become extremely secretive. They knew that if management were to get a whiff of their activities, they would be fired. In general, she said, most Honduran newsrooms were still infected by corrupt practices, although the number of journalists accepting bribes had decreased. She had tried to fight for higher salaries at her newspaper to combat the underground influence of bribery, but the paper's owners were generally unwilling to raise pay significantly.

Martinez described a system where individual journalists who wanted extra income would strike deals to drop embarrassing stories or write favorable ones. Sometimes powerful people would pay journalists to dig up stories on their rivals or enemies. Journalists throughout Central America describe similar corrupt practices.

In 1998 Martinez discovered that certain individuals had bribed a member of her staff to write negative stories about their rivals. Although she did not dismiss this reporter, she did change his assignments and demote him. Indeed, editors and reporters have sometimes collaborated in steering coverage to satisfy hidden patrons, selling stories, airtime, and column inches much as advertising is sold. In Honduras this system of bribery and corruption is called *machaca*. Martinez said she believes this practice had been eliminated at most Honduran newspapers.

The leaders of NGOs in Honduras reported a somewhat different story. Although they believed that corruption had decreased in Honduras, they said the practice of *machaca* remained very much alive throughout the media. For instance, newspaper coverage of an event always had a price tag attached, an expensive figure for the front page and a smaller rate for a location inside the newspaper.

Very few journalists in Honduras are brave enough to admit that corruption still influences reporting. Nevertheless, Radio America's Sanchez stepped out at an international forum on Central American journalism held in Panama in 1999 to dispute the view that *machaca* had been reduced in the Honduran media scene. Sanchez revealed that a group of journalists who covered President Flores received illicit monthly payments from the government. She said these journalists and other corrupt members of the media in Honduras were regarded as "insatiable gangsters."[12] This was an important revelation because President Flores has often protested international reports about corruption in Honduras as "irresponsible and biased."[13]

What has caused this retrenchment from higher standards? Why would a system moving toward these new standards revert to older habits, where a media owner and president would not only accept corruption but allow his administration to participate in it and attempt to cover it up?

Part of the answer may rest with the ominous presence of the military in Honduran society. In 1993, when the journalism corruption scandal broke, Honduran journalists decided to challenge the military's ability to stifle their critical reporting (see chapter 8). The result was the firebombing incident at the home of *El Tiempo*'s publisher, Yani Rosenthal.

During the critical juncture of 1993, Honduran media owners were moving to reduce corruption in their newsrooms. This movement was started not by the state but by media owners who sought to loosen the state's controlling mechanisms. This attempt coincided with the media's move toward more open criticism of the military. The result was a reduction in corruption in newsrooms, although the media owners' attempts to eradicate *machaca* were only partially successful. Likewise, after a brief convulsion of violence, threats subsided, as the media lowered their level of criticism of the military. This provides a good example supporting our fundamental tenet: that forces threatening state control of the media will provoke a reaction against the media, a reaction that may include violent episodes.

At this juncture it may be important to consider other theories about the development of professionalism in media systems. The media scholar John Nerone has noted that journalism in the United States underwent increased professionalization only after the Civil War, when the social divisions afflicting society began to heal. Until then, Nerone asserts, it was acceptable to use violence against journalists and publishers; this violence was often spurred by off-duty members of the military or paramilitary groups. Until the number of elites who believed firmly in civil liberties reached a crucial point, violence remained a means to control journalistic product. In turn, Nerone continues, diminishing partisanship and increasing objectivity helped reduce these violent reactions against the press.[14] At this point, in the latter part of the nineteenth century, the market, not violence, played the major role in determining the life of a publication, and elite forces worked to professionalize journalism. The process of professionalizing journalism continued for more than a century, until professional ethical standards reached a level where bribery and many other types of conflicts of interest were regarded as inappropriate in journalism circles.

Although Central American systems have a very different cultural history, the same forces may be at work. As we have documented, partisanship remains a driving force in most of the region's media outlets. Elites there seek to use the media more as incubators for their ideas and political careers than as some objective common ground where democratic debate can flourish. Elites outside the media systems give only tepid support for civil liberties and human rights. The oligarchies of these nations remain dominant forces, as do strong centralized governments. Paramilitaries and military forces seem willing to use violence if the media tread into sensitive areas. Even in Costa Rica, which has been the most successful at moving toward an objective media, old political enmities among the dominant families still lurk just below the surface. The controversial way the major media outlets reacted to the Figueres Olsen administration suffices to show that the country's culture of objectivity is still but a shallow pool.

Using elite acceptance of opposing partisan views as one of our standards, we can examine the Honduran media system in relation to its neighbors in an attempt to explain why corruption continues to grow there. As we have noted, this is just one factor in a multidimensional media environment, but an important one: has the nation attempted to resolve its social cleavages, and if so, did that happen in a sudden outburst, such as a civil war?

Honduras, unlike other countries in the region, has not experienced a modern civil war, and its military continues to shape ideas about civil liberties and human rights. Compare this history to that of Costa Rica, which experienced a short civil war in 1948 and then solidified its nascent democracy by, among other things, abolishing its military. Costa Rica is generally regarded as the most peaceful country on the isthmus, and its media system is respected as the most developed and professional. Conversely, Honduras has one of the most corrupt systems. By examining the nations of the isthmus one can clearly see how the various conflicts of the past generation have affected the media systems and their relations with power in each country. Therefore, Nerone's suggestion that civil war can provide a yardstick for gauging the advance of professionalism in a media system may apply to the Central American context.

Other factors also apply to the case of Honduras, however. Although media owners were urged to increase salaries to combat corruption, they ignored this advice. The central government retained its policies of under-the-table payments, not wishing to relinquish the control they offered. Major ideological or policy shifts inside journalism circles either failed to materialize or were stunted by the military in the 1990s, whose repressive messages were reinforced by the high-profile cases of Guevara and

Sanchez. Finally, after FIU's journalism training programs were disman-
tled in the mid-1990s, the influence of journalists from outside the Honduran system diminished significantly. Given all these factors, it is not
surprising that those who worked to stop corruption failed to attain all
their goals.

Corruption helps explain the strong reactions that investigative reporting faced in Panama during the 1990s. Investigative reporters there
sought to expose corruption in all facets of society, yet journalists continued to accept payoffs. Gorriti and his colleagues encountered problems
and resistance because their ethical model conflicted with the conditions
prevailing in the country. Indeed, Panamanian journalists were infamous
for practicing a special type of extortion. They would work on a story for
weeks not to publish or broadcast it but to extort hush money from the
targets of the investigation. During the Perez Balladares administration,
journalists reported they could easily obtain payoffs from legislators, the
national prosecutor's office, and the office of the president.

Dishonest practices remain common in Panamanian journalism. In
fact, corruption is sufficiently common to have attracted several slang
terms, including *coima* and *choyoté*. A person who accepts a bribe is
known as *la botella*, "the bottle." In 1995 Panamanian journalists tried
to cleanse their system of corruption, with mixed results.

Like their counterparts in Honduras, several prominent media outlets set out to stop the practice by publicizing the issue. *La Prensa, El
Panamá América, Crítica Libre,* and *El Siglo,* along with Canal 2's news
department, all crafted stories about graft flowing from the Legislative
Assembly. The main source for the stories was Edwin Wald, a journalist
who worked in the assembly's public relations office. Wald told the media that the president of the assembly, Balbina Herrera, had approved illicit payments to reporters ranging from $400 to $2,600 per month. In
some cases, this quadrupled a reporter's monthly salary. The stories centered on a group of influential journalists who covered the assembly and
accepted bribes to slant their reports. The media outlets aggressively
exposed the members of their staffs who were involved. Journalists from
La Prensa and *El Panamá América* were accused, along with reporters
from MEDCOM's Canal 4 and one of the nation's top news radio stations,
Radio KW Continente.[15]

The reaction to these revelations was swift. Herrera denied that the
assembly was paying anyone for positive coverage except for its official
public relations staff. The leaders of the national association of journalists (El Colegio Nacional de Periodistas) and the journalists' union also
closed ranks to defend the system. The *colegio* and its president at the

time, Barbara Bloise, staunchly defended the accused journalists. Bloise said that because salaries are low, journalists were free to moonlight as long as they did not endorse particular positions solely for money. Bloise dressed up the bribes as payments for public relations work, despite the fact this work was obviously intermingled with work done for their main employers.

Bloise's defense of this practice was undercut, however, when *La Prensa* revealed that she held positions beyond her job as a reporter at MEDCOM's Canal 13. Not only was Bloise moonlighting for a Panamanian business concern; she was also holding down a public relations job at the University of Panama, a position that linked her directly to the government and that might have compromised her views on this subject. The university received its funding through the Legislative Assembly, so that Bloise had at least some allegiance to politicians tainted by the scandal. Such conflicts of interest undermined Bloise's independence, a fundamental ethical tenet at *La Prensa*.

La Prensa led the push for ethical journalism in Panama, partly because of the paper's connections to the FIU journalism training program. As it had in Honduras, support for exposing graft in the journalistic system had come from FIU. Eventually *La Prensa* led the way toward creating a training center based in Panama City. The center was designed to take on the mission of improving journalistic standards in Latin America once FIU's program terminated in the mid-1990s. Cleaning its own house in the Legislative Assembly scandal was an important first step in pushing for higher ethical standards.

Most Panamanian media organizations follow different rules regarding *coima*, however. An organization that wants its activities covered or a press release run must usually offer cash or some other benefit. This remains true for all the media. Such a system can be especially burdensome for nonprofit organizations. Some media outlets, such as *La Prensa*, would ask such organizations to buy an advertisement if the story they wanted run had little news value. Most media outlets, however, would merely fashion a story masquerading as a news item, much like the *campos pagados* of El Salvador or the *gacetillas* in Mexico. A system where only those who pay for it can get coverage casts doubt on the inclusiveness and objectivity of what is published, for the system is open only to people or organizations with sufficient power or cash.

The Panamanian media's attempts to cleanse and professionalize the system met with mixed results for reasons we have already identified. Salaries at some media outlets, such as *La Prensa*, were improving and thus undercutting the temptations of *coima*, but this was not universal.

In addition, a younger generation of reporters was being trained, first by FIU and then by Panama's own training center, to bring higher standards to the profession. Meanwhile government practices, at least during the Perez Balladares administration, had often been antimedia, and a system of journalistic graft was maintained. In its early years the Moscoso administration instituted policies that broke with this tainted past. Finally, like Honduras, Panama never underwent a modern civil war that set aside disputes among its elite factions. Although Operation Just Cause, the 1989 U.S. invasion, altered the political, media, and social climate, along with eliminating the military, the polarized nature of Panamanian politics speaks to the divisions that remain. In all these cases, despite the progress in this dynamic system, factors that encourage corruption persist.

As noted earlier, in Guatemala the reduction in media corruption seen elsewhere in the region unintentionally resulted from new government policy. Attempting to cow the media through economic pressure, the Arzú administration curtailed regular cash payments to journalists. When the president cut official government contracts with members of the media, he also revealed a list of corrupt journalists accepting bribes. He discontinued these ties.

This government cutoff of bribery was intended to intensify the government's advertising boycott, but it produced ripples elsewhere. Not only were media outlets forced to confront some journalists about their corrupt practices, but other businesses and institutions that had used bribery both to place stories and to prevent their publication also discontinued the use of graft, which Guatemalan journalists call *fa-fa.*

Guatemalan media managers estimated the amount of corruption was cut in half during the Arzú era. They credit the stronger ethical base among younger journalists as another reason for the reduction. Higher salaries for journalists have also reduced the need to solicit bribes. These factors have driven *fa-fa* under the table.

Much like their peers in Honduras, however, managers at the biggest media outlets still must be vigilant about corruption. Businesses and publicity firms still offer bribes despite the government's turn away from that practice. "*Fa-fa* allows reporters to round out their salaries and invites businessmen to incur major costs by paying long lists of reporters," noted Gustavo Berganza, the managing editor of *Siglo Veintiuno.* "This obviously has consequences for the quality of information that is transmitted, in the style and language that is used, and constitutes a painful limitation on our rights."[16]

Editors at Guatemala's largest dailies have taken Berganza's words to heart and enforced stricter ethical codes. Some said they had disciplined several of their reporters in 1998 for accepting bribes. Some newspapers implemented written personnel policies explicitly prohibiting the acceptance of bribes. Explaining the need for these higher standards, Berganza commented, "One reporter can make us all lose our credibility."[17]

As noted earlier, although the Arzú administration had also stopped its practice of giving government subsidies and advertising to publications as a way of exerting editorial control, *Siglo Veintiuno* was one of the few publications that retained some government accounts, mainly because it was perceived as being tacitly aligned with Arzú's branch of the PAN.

Unfortunately, despite the reduction of overt corruption and the attempts to follow higher ethical standards, some Guatemalan media outlets still charge to place stories. A few outlets charged as much as $5,000 to have a story covered in 1998. Guatemala's widespread poverty continues to leave journalists and others vulnerable to the temptation of using graft to supplement their income. Although Guatemala has the largest economy in Central America, it ranked second-lowest on the United Nations' development index, surpassed in misery only by Haiti.[18] Income is concentrated in the hands of a tiny elite faction, exposing the remainder of Guatemalans to economic coercion. One might expect the reduction of government subsidies, advertising, and under-the-table payments in Guatemala to pressure other sectors of the economy to take up some of the economic slack, but NGOs there have few complaints about the problem of payment for placement.

In this context, however, television may be lagging behind the other media. Television journalists generally receive the lowest salaries of all the country's media workers. Some Guatemalan journalists blame monopoly ownership of Guatemalan television for this low pay.

Before his turbulent run-in with the Portillo administration, José Eduardo Zarco, the former host of "Temas de Noche" and the former leader of *Prensa Libre*, openly criticized the poor ethical standards of his country's television journalists. Through his work with FIU and the IAPA, Zarco has campaigned for higher journalistic standards for many years. Although he said direct cash payments had lost favor in Guatemala in the late 1990s, a marked improvement from the past, reporters were still offered expensive "gifts," such as watches or jewelry. In his opinion, the low pay for television reporters left them vulnerable to these temptations.[19]

In any event, Guatemala appears to be making more progress toward reducing corruption than are other countries in the region. Although the results were mixed, Guatemala did significantly better than Honduras. The factors we have identified explain why. First, although Guatemala was the last country on the isthmus to end a civil war, it was working to heal the fractious divisions that started that conflict. Second, the government halted all types of media subsidies and illicit payments to journalists. The government's advertising boycott, coupled with this new policy to curb journalistic graft, forced many media outlets into a nonpartisan posture, if not an antigovernment position. Younger journalists were also rejecting *fa-fa,* partly because of rising salaries. Improved salaries were not a universal solution, however, especially in the area of television, which seemed to lag behind the rest of the media culture. The country's continued problems with poverty indicate that it may slide backward in this area. Training programs from the United States have also scaled back in Guatemala since the mid-1990s, although some journalists, including Zarco, have carried on very public campaigns for improvements. Guatemala thus showed significant improvement in most of our key factors. The result was still a mixed system of various standards, but considerably more positive answers yielded stronger results. Perhaps the one major area of concern was the debate in Guatemala over human rights and civil liberties. Until the country's elites promote a system to grant universal human rights to the country's population, the foundation for stronger ethical supports will continue to have crucial weak spots.

In El Salvador the transition to a more professional media system began during the civil war. Correspondents from all over the world descended on San Salvador to cover the war, and they hired many local journalists as guides and assistants. The Salvadoran journalists needed the extra work to supplement their meager paychecks. Many observers of Central American media view the presence of journalists from the United States and Europe as having been a key positive influence on Salvadoran media standards in the postwar years. Until the Gulf War, all the major U.S. media outlets, along with worldwide news services, maintained permanent bureaus in San Salvador.[20] This differed markedly from the situation elsewhere on the isthmus. Often reporters from the permanent San Salvador bureau would "parachute" into one of the neighboring countries. When bureaus were established in countries such as Guatemala or Nicaragua during their war years, they were often temporary: the reporters might work out of a hotel room for an extended period.

This outside presence proved to be most influential with younger journalists, who, as we noted earlier, rejected the culture of the older *empiricos.* The *empiricos* had less contact with the international media. Unlike the younger reporters, who took university classes, the *empiricos* had learned journalism on the rough-and-tumble streets. They were not above taking a bribe or extorting payoffs, a corrupt system Salvadoran journalists call *la menta.* The younger journalists who admired the international media soon moved into newsrooms en masse. The generational shift at *El Diario de Hoy* was the most concentrated example of this rejection of an older journalistic culture.

Through the war years, low pay led many journalists to take second or third jobs with political parties or government agencies. They would write a press release for one employer and then guarantee it would be published or broadcast through their main employer. Many journalists who accepted the culture of *la menta* failed to see this conflict of interest as problematic. This attitude changed, however, as these journalists retired.

While younger journalists were moving to replace the *empiricos,* some of the media owners were also standing up to corruption. The fight against corruption crystallized during the Calderón Sol administration when the president accused the media of infiltration by communists. The president charged these infiltrators with having shifted the way the Salvadoran media presented themselves; he furthermore attributed his plummeting popularity to these newly critical media. One of President Calderón Sol's targets was Lafitte Fernandez Rojas, the Costa Rican journalist who had come to San Salvador to redesign *El Diario de Hoy.* Instead of buckling to the government's criticism, Enrique Altamirano defended the editorial changes that made his newspaper independent of the president's party, ARENA. He turned the criticism around on the president and accused him of being surrounded by corruption.[21]

"That day I became convinced we had won," Fernandez Rojas said. He viewed the owners' support in fighting corruption and moving toward a more independent newspaper as a firm break with the culture of the past. This also sent an important signal to other media owners, who have often turned a blind eye to corruption because bribery reduced the pressure for higher salaries.

The Altamirano family showed it was willing to fight corruption beyond its own newsroom when it supported an investigation into the corruption of ARENA leaders. One high-profile investigation showed how the party's chair had imported a car under the forged name of a priest to avoid taxes. The stories from *El Diario de Hoy* played a critical role in forcing the ouster of that ARENA leader.[22]

Although the Altamiranos were torn between their longtime loyalties to ARENA and their ethical standards, as their newspaper staff continued to sift through the dirt of the party's operations, the Altamiranos became convinced the party did not deserve their full support until it cleansed itself. This stand against corruption was part of the reason *El Diario de Hoy* decided to back the Christian Democrats in the 1999 elections, a significant break with the newspaper's past. Taken together, the paper's changes showed the Altamirano family's conviction to combat corruption in all forms.

These strong positions toward fighting *la menta* on all levels jolted the journalistic community and sparked change at other media outlets. The fight for higher ethical standards and more journalistic independence became a rallying cry at *El Diario de Hoy*'s main competitor, *La Prensa Grafica*. Although *La Prensa Grafica* instituted a stronger ethical code and purged its newsroom of journalists who accepted *la menta*, the paper's management was unable to wrest complete independence from ARENA or the nation's oligarchy. Managing editor Ricardo Chacón led a high-profile walkout of key managers when journalists there discovered that they could not replicate the editorial freedom of their chief competitor.[23] Chacón and others who left *La Prensa Grafica* faced hard times for following their convictions. Some claimed that they had been blacklisted after they discovered that few if any media outlets would hire them following the walkout.

In any case, the cultural changes toward more transparency in Salvadoran newspapers benefited the nation's readers. These changes directly affected the treatment of *campos pagados*. Newspapers began clearly labeling these pieces of copy as "advertisement" or "paid space."[24] When running *campos pagados*, the Costa Rican press also follows this practice, as do ethical publications in the United States when they sell space to advertisers or others who pay to post their ideas.

But this progress toward professionalization was not universal. Radio continues to lack transparency in the Salvadoran system. As noted earlier, radio stations actively hid their *campos pagados* during the 1999 elections, so that listeners could not distinguish programs supported by ARENA from those produced independently by news departments. Radio stations remain strapped for cash, so their economic needs eventually override any pressure for higher ethical standards and accountability. The large number of commercial stations and consequent hypercompetition in the medium contribute to this economic pressure. The improvements in the Salvadoran media economy have not yet caught up to radio, which also encourages this "business-first" philosophy.

When analyzing the entire media scene in El Salvador, though, it becomes evident that great strides have been made in the past decade. Many of the factors we have identified for measuring advancements in professionalized journalistic systems show El Salvador's progress. The country has had a decade to heal from its civil war. Many media outlets have moved toward more objectivity in the postwar years, although partisanship remains apparent at many media outlets. The attitudes of a new generation of journalists have pushed out many of the nation's *empiri-cos,* however, and with them the influence of *la menta.* Individuals in the international media who worked in El Salvador throughout the war deserve much of the credit for this shift in journalistic standards. Although the government continued to use economic incentives, both above and below the table, to influence journalists, some media owners have been pressuring the government to change its policies.

Despite the mixed results, El Salvador is making progress against corruption, as is apparent to those beyond its borders. In 1999 El Salvador ranked forty-ninth on Transparency International's overall corruption index, almost at the median point and at the second-best spot in Central America. Costa Rica ranked thirty-second; Guatemala, sixty-eighth; Nicaragua, seventieth; and Honduras, ninety-fourth. Panama was not ranked. (During the same year, the United States ranked eighteenth on the same scale.)[25]

If any Central American media system is moving backward in the area of corruption, it may be in Nicaragua. Although bribery and corruption were deemphasized as mechanisms for controlling journalists during the Sandinista era, in the 1990s it became easier to find a corrupt journalist, whom Nicaraguans call *el venado.* This may stem from Nicaragua's economic conditions, which are some of the worst in Latin America. The country suffers from rampant unemployment, resulting from the U.S. economic boycott, the war, and mismanagement. In fact, only 2 percent of Nicaraguans can afford a phone.[26]

Given these economic conditions, journalists must supplement their low pay. Most turn to soliciting payoffs, doing so more openly than their counterparts elsewhere in the region. In Managua the mayor's office publishes and circulates a list of journalists and how much they receive for slanting or suppressing stories. The media consultant Harold Moore wrote of his time in Nicaragua: "With the possible exception of the leading television news reporters, none of the journalists I met were at all disconcerted by any attempt to influence their reporting, ranging from free food to outright cash bribes."[27]

In Nicaragua, as in Honduras and Panama, organizations and public relations firms pay journalists to place their press releases in the various media outlets. This is an accepted business practice.

Some of the resurgence of journalistic corruption in Nicaragua is blamed on *empiricos,* who have not received university training or been exposed to international journalism training programs. These *empiricos* stayed in the media system throughout the Sandinista era and fell back on old habits when capitalist systems were more welcome. Because Nicaragua never converted to a completely centralized communist system and maintained a mixed economy, some of these *empiricos* kept up a low level of corruption even through the Sandinista years. These *empiricos*, who learned their trade during the Somoza years of blatant corruption, are often referred to in Nicaraguan slang as *papas fritas*, literally, "fried potatoes," or "french fries." The term derives from a practice common among older journalists: attending events where free food is served and taking large amounts of it home. Of course, given the poverty and high unemployment in Nicaragua, such habits may look like survival mechanisms rather than an ethical faux pas. *Papas fritas* are not necessarily corrupt, but they tend to tolerate a journalistic style that allows partisanship and slanting of news for vendettas and other personal agendas. They often eschew professional standards of any type, however, losing themselves completely in the search for profit. Some see these *papas fritas* as having had their ethical standards changed by their rough environment: they have been fried in the greasy environment where they work.

In addition, the country's poor economy and the Alemán government's polarizing advertising policies have prompted some of the nation's publications to increase their use of unlabeled *campos pagados* in search of additional revenue.[28]

Much like Nicaraugua's politics, the media seem to be returning to older traditions of corruption. Once again, the previously identified factors speak to the current climate. Although a younger generation of journalists has moved on to the scene, it has not pushed out all the *empiricos* and *papas fritas*. Many of these younger journalists were trained under a system influenced by Sandinista ideology, according to which the media should transmit the state's message, not seek a balance of different opinions. Although international training programs for journalists, such as FIU's, did move into the country in the Chamorro era, their influence now has waned. As such, the advance of professionalism among journalists has slowed and faltered. Younger journalists who had touted improved professional standards have succumbed to the temptations in the system, as the case of Canal 23's Danilo Lacayo shows. Lacayo's involvement in the bribery scandal at the comptroller general's office (see chapter 4) revealed that high-minded talk among the new generation did not always translate into heartfelt action. Salaries remain low, and there has been no dramatic attempt among owners or journalists—as there has in Honduras, Panama, El Salvador—to expose journalists who perpetuate the system of corruption.

Although the nation's revolution in 1979 could be considered the starting point for the implementation of journalistic professionalism, the Chamorro era marks the true end of Nicaragua's civil war period. In the decade following the Chamorro administration, many of the key indicators for professional advancement have been stagnant or slid backward. Salaries, ideological shifts, and government policies relating to journalistic corruption all exhibit this trend. Although a few government agencies have openly listed journalists who are accepting payments, as did the Guatemalan government, the journalistic system has not moved to penalize *los venados*. Nevertheless, unlike Guatemala, which never developed a sense of human rights, Nicaragua has remained a relatively safe country to practice journalism, despite its fall backward into the complicated shadows of corruption.

Such corruption has gone far underground in neighboring Costa Rica, where the exploits of the *howmucheros* of the 1980s and their Contra and CIA patrons are now just a dark splotch on the country's journalistic memory. All the indicators suggest professionalism and little journalistic corruption in Costa Rica: more than half a century since its civil war, a time free from the pressures of a standing military; one of the most transparent political systems in Latin America; a tradition of international journalism training programs, allowing it to, among other things, export influential journalism educators to its neighbors throughout the isthmus; and the strongest economy in the region, with salaries for journalists generally putting them in the middle class of the country, and usually not so low as to invite corruption. Although the media have not shed all their partisan ways, they strive for objectivity and fairness and strongly oppose corruption in journalism and elsewhere in society. Perhaps this explains why many of the region's journalists envy the Costa Ricans and sometimes criticize them for what they see as the arrogance and aloofness of those who consider themselves ethically superior.

Economic Restraints

As we have documented, economic means to manipulate the media have been popular in Central America. Although we have focused on the state and the military, some believe that the private sector presents a more insidious threat to information media, every bit as influential as the state in maintaining the atmosphere of self-censorship that fogs the minds of journalists throughout the region. Mauricio Funes, the popular news anchor at Canal 12 in San Salvador, is often considered one of the most independent voices in Central American journalism. Nevertheless, he likes to invoke a popular saying: "He who pays for the *mariachi* chooses the song that is played."[29]

By running advertising, the media can become a voice for powerful forces. Advertising is universally accepted in the media, as is the subsequent tug of war between advertisers and journalists. Journalists do not like advertisers to dictate their ideas, spin messages, or block stories, but they understand that they exist in a capitalist industry and navigate accordingly. Advertisers play a legitimate role in attempting to get their products noticed and accepted in a competitive market. They may view journalistic coverage of their product as a preview of the reaction they can expect from consumers or as a nuisance that upsets their marketing plan. Each side often sees the other as a necessary evil.

As we have shown, however, the rules of engagement are sometimes a bit rougher in Central America than in, say, the United States. Furthermore, the cultures and business practices of all these nations differ from border to border. Some of the crude battles occurring in the Guatemalan marketplace might well be judged unethical and illegal in Costa Rica. For example, in 1997 competition among Guatemalan cable operators was often so intense that companies sometimes sabotaged their competitors' equipment. One cable operator in Guatemala City attacked another that had obtained exclusive rights to broadcast an important national soccer match. The attacker toppled the victim's transmission pole by attaching a chain to a car that was then driven away at high speed. The victim's once exclusive rights to the game were severed, thus leveling the playing field.[30] The legal remedies for such actions in the Guatemalan system of justice apparently did little to deter such activity. Transplant the same activity to Costa Rica, however, and the offending cable operator would likely be in jail while facing a stiff civil suit that they would probably lose. This type of business climate has made it acceptable for some broadcasters to steal satellite signals in Honduras, Nicaragua, and other parts of the region.

In such an atmosphere, advertisers and other business concerns are quite willing to use their clout to get the media to carry the perspectives they believe are important while filtering out messages viewed as overtly negative. Waisbord writes: "Economic independence is the only ticket for arriving at press freedom and making concrete the ideal of a watchdog press. The market rather than the state is mainly responsible for keeping the press subordinate."[31]

This seems to support our notion that only when a media outlet becomes financially independent from special interests, drawing mass support, will it be able to change the overall media system and act independently. Our analysis tends to place the state as the primary force in Central America, because the state is usually the dominant advertiser in these small, niche markets. We do not dispute that market forces significantly influence media systems; in Central America, however, those mechanisms are used directly and most efficiently by the state. Private-sector forces may use the same tactics, but their power is equal only to the capital they bring to the table. In other systems the state may benefit indirectly because elites with the power to advertise are steering media systems. In the case of Central America, both the state and the elites are exerting strong guiding forces on the media. Furthermore, as we have discussed, the state has often sought to coerce or silence media outlets by initiating advertising boycotts that the private sector later joined. Finally, as we have shown, both the state and the private sector are often willing to move beyond the accepted legal bounds of advertising and use corruption to control the media even further.

Even for media outlets unwilling to be sucked into the dark maw of corruption, however, advertising remains an important mechanism of manipulation. Indeed, as Herman and Chomsky have noted, concentrated media ownership combines with the media's profit orientation to create a system ripe for manipulation, where the propaganda of the marketplace will dominate. Advertising provides most media outlets their lifeblood, and thus outlets and programs that have perspectives in line with advertisers will benefit, while others may wither.[32] These forces are present in Central America, as they are elsewhere. Huge multinational conglomerates in particular, which can marshal tremendous economic power, may threaten a media organization through the courts or by the withdrawal of advertising accounts. Few media owners are willing to risk losing these profitable accounts, nor are they willing to stare down these corporations in a legal duel.

The liberty and judgment of writers should be the paramount concern in a system espousing free expression, but as Cristiana Chamorro, the former director of Nicaragua's *La Prensa*, told us: "Freedom of the press belongs to media owners only. Reporters, the workers, are afraid."[33] One of those Nicaraguan reporters, Eduardo Marencko of *La Tribuna*, agreed. "The rules aren't written but they are quite clear," he said. "If you step over the line, you will be pushed back. You write a story covering a certain subject and the editor calls you to tell you: 'You know what? This won't work. This guy's the brother-in-law of the newspaper's owner.' The article doesn't run, even if you have all the supporting documents. We can cover some subjects but not others. There's a lot of communication between the different political and economic sectors and the media owners in a small country like Nicaragua."[34]

Nicaragua's *La Prensa* is not above catering to advertisers with flattering stories, and some media observers criticize the paper for containing too much advertising, as much as 80 percent on some occasions.[35] Likewise, in El Salvador *La Prensa Grafica* and *El Diario de Hoy* have sometimes been called catalogs rather than newspapers, for they are filled with advertisements for various types of merchandise.[36] In Costa Rica *noticiero* Rolando Angulo has also criticized the media for overemphasizing advertising and losing a balanced mix of content in the process.[37]

When he was at *Crónica,* Berganza criticized Guatemalan newspapers and other media outlets that carried 70 percent or more advertising.[38] But critics have a way of changing their minds. Eventually Berganza became the editor of *Siglo Veintiuno,* one of the more profitable media outlets in his country, which carries a large volume of advertising. The group of business owners who started *Siglo Veintiuno* were originally looking for a platform to promote their businesses and their political ideals, so the newspaper always has plenty of advertising space devoted to their concerns: groceries, restaurants, and liquor stores. The owners of *Siglo Veintiuno* include the Castillo family, which manufactures glass and distributes beer; the Botrán family, which distributes liquor; the Gutiérrez family, which owns a chain of restaurants; and the Paiz family, which owns a chain of supermarkets. This newspaper is not alone, however. Other media outlets in Guatemala exist as a base for their owners to use to promote their various enterprises. A similar pattern of vertical integration appears in Honduras. "Many times journalists are obligated to transform truth in favor of economic power," noted Guevara, the Honduran television journalist who has often tested the system. "Some communication media have direct or indirect links with economic power."[39]

Critics have attacked *La Estrella de Panama* not just because it has made ideological compromises but also because some of its staff members hold second jobs at large businesses that could become the targets of the newspaper's stories. Such conflicts can dictate which business and consumer stories may be covered. The newspaper's managing editor, James Aparicio, holds such a second position at one of Panama's largest banking firms, writing press releases and performing other public relations chores. Despite the obvious conflict of interest, Aparicio said he felt he could retain objectivity even if a story about the bank demanded coverage.[40] As noted earlier, the culture at many Panamanian media outlets accepts this type of complex web of secondary positions, although many of Panama's media outlets now have stricter ethics codes preventing such arrangements.

Some advertisers have instilled a sense of fear and self-censorship among journalists, media executives, and public relations firms in the region. Journalists in El Salvador still discuss a case from the 1980s when Volkswagen pulled advertising from a newspaper because it ran a photo showing one of the company's cars involved in an accident. After that some publications in the region practiced a type of self-censorship on photographs: they would airbrush over names of prominent advertisers who otherwise might feel they had been tied to the focus of the picture. For years photographers and photo editors tried to crop or otherwise modify photos to remove the region's ubiquitous Pepsi signs, fearing that their publications could lose the company's account if they failed to do so. This self-censorship came at no prompting from the company.

At El Salvador's Radio YSKL, news director Nery Mabel Reyes admitted making generic references in stories instead of naming specific companies. For example, if an environmental story concerned the local Pepsi bottling company, she would sometimes refer merely to "a soft drink company" instead of naming the brand. At other times she would name the brand once and use only generic references thereafter to downplay the company's involvement. Reyes said she was not sure where the pressure to weaken these stories originated, but she hears from her station's management about their fears of losing advertising when such a story runs.[41]

Likewise, she said, she would cover an accident involving TACA, one of Central America's international airlines and perhaps the region's biggest sacred cow, but she would do so carefully. When such accidents have happened, the station's owners have called to tell her a TACA representative should be consulted to guide coverage in the proper direction. "Economic interests compete to show which businessmen are in control of the media, and they establish links with owners of the same political persuasion, consequently affecting the orientation and message of the news that is transmitted," Reyes noted. "The journalist in this case is converted into a manual laborer."[42]

Funes, at El Salvador's Canal 12, has also criticized the media's weakness. He cited the case of an auditing report that criticized the construction of a venue for the 1994 Central American games. The executive director of a large Salvadoran banking concern was the games' local chairman. As a result, said Funes, only three media outlets carried the story: Canal 12, *La Prensa Grafica*, and *El Diario de Hoy*. Funes characterized the other media outlets in San Salvador as having practiced self-censorship. Although they received no pressure from the banker, they decided not to cover the story for fear there might be repercussions. "That is not freedom of the press," Funes said.[43]

In fact, some of the bolder Salvadoran media outlets have learned that advertisers will cancel their contracts if they do not like a media organization's coverage. For example, in 1998 *El Diario de Hoy* lost six months of advertising, worth $800,000, when the paper refused to give a supermarket chain editorial control over stories that mentioned the supermarket.[44] The Altamirano family's willingness to take these losses to build the credibility of their newspapers, however, demonstrated their commitment to higher standards. David Rivas, of APES, the association of El Salvador's journalists, hailed this type of behavior in the face of economic pressure, but he pointed to the predominance of other attitudes. "Media are not a public service," he said. "There is no public right to know. Advertising is the most important client."[45]

Similar stories have transpired in Guatemala. After running a series about the quality of Guatemala's phone company and several editorial cartoons mocking the poor service, *Prensa Libre*'s group of publications lost the company's lucrative advertising account. Gonzalo Marroquín, *Prensa Libre*'s chief editor, labeled this reaction "economic persecution" of the media.[46] In fact, however, the reaction may have been part of the jousting between the *Prensa Libre* group and the Arzú administration. At that time the phone company was a state-run service in the process of privatizing. President Arzú's advertising boycott may also have been the underlying reason the ads were yanked, so this example is not completely a private-sector matter.

These battles for editorial control resemble fights that journalists have with advertising concerns in Europe and the United States. The main difference is the size of these markets. In these smaller, less-developed economies, losing the main airline account, a soft drink company's ad campaign, a fast-food chain's advertising, or the telephone company's marketing can spell disaster for all but the largest media organizations. In El Salvador *El Diario de Hoy* was able to withstand such pressure, just as the *Prensa Libre* group could cope with advertising losses, because these were large, well-established media companies with high circulation rates and a wide variety of advertisers. With sufficient alternative means of revenue—such as that enjoyed by Nicaragua's *El Nuevo Diario*, which depends on street sales—media outlets can withstand even well-organized advertising boycotts. The media outlet must have wide mass appeal, however, and find ways to turn that appeal into a revenue stream. *El Nuevo Diario* survives because it is one of the most popular newspapers in Nicaragua. The fact that the paper carries the least amount of advertising does not seem to deter its readers.

When media outlets become dependent on a few large advertisers, they lose their independence, becoming slaves to the whims of those advertisers. By taking an independent tack and retaining editorial control, media organizations retain the ability to walk away from large accounts. If the advertiser wants to reach the outlet's audience, it will have to return or find another outlet that reaches the same demographic group. Of course, such courageous independence usually fails in media markets as oversaturated as the market for Central American radio. A media organization must be able to appeal to a critical mass of the population and have a varied advertising base to be able to stand up to a single large advertiser, or even a group of advertisers who may put together a boycott. Admittedly, radio stations and local television owners in the United States can face similar problems when they anger car dealers with consumer reporting. Because car dealers are often the largest advertiser for small and medium-sized media outlets in the United States, they retain significant clout and can often muzzle reporting about consumer issues. By hitching themselves to the advertising system, the media in effect abdicate most of their responsibility to provide objective and unbiased information to the public, becoming instead an avenue for the ideas of the commercial and political interests that have purchased the power to control the messages these media outlets broadcast.

The autonomy of media organizations is therefore usually determined by the marketplace of advertisers rather than the marketplace of ideas, where the public weighs in by making a particular media outlet popular. Only those media organizations that combine mass popularity with a commitment to take an independent stand will be able to resist these market pressures. Journalists working for such organizations therefore depend on the owner to establish the boundaries of expression and fight for those standards in the marketplace. For those working for owners without such convictions, freedom remains an elusive goal. Unfortunately, in the battle for market position, media owners often lose sight of the strange dichotomy of media products. When owners see media products as a business like any other and bow to the whims of advertisers, the increasingly sophisticated audience they seek to attract is often repelled by the crass commercialism or slanted information dressed up as fair and balanced reporting. Media outlets that seem to be more independent of commercial and political ties often establish a strong bond of credibility with an audience. This credibility eventually builds extremely strong customer loyalty, which trumps the efforts of the compromised competition. Certainly, there are those who profit in the Information Age without taking these concerns into account. Nevertheless, a few media owners realize they have responsibilities that come with the right to make a profit.

El Diario de Hoy of El Salvador and its subsidiary *Mas, Prensa Libre* and its subsidiary publications in Guatemala, and *El Nuevo Diario* in Nicaragua demonstrate that owners in Central America can understand those responsibilities, too.

10   *The Postwar Evolution*

A facile reading of our analysis of the Central American media may leave a reader with pessimistic questions. What hopes do these varied media outlets in differing political systems have to work as a true Fourth Estate? What power do the media possess? Are these media organizations not merely tools of the elite?

Each of these questions expresses an often complex truth, neither completely positive nor completely negative. We prefer to see the media as an important web connecting elite factions and other powerful forces at work in each of the Central American countries. The media reflect inter-elite battles, but they also allow the government to speak to the populace and vice versa. In many of the countries we have profiled, the media are evolving in attempts to find their roles. In Guatemala, El Salvador, and Nicaragua, the media are fighting governments that try to impose their wills on the communications systems using sophisticated methods and thus make them into one-way devices: transmitting the message of the oligarchy and the powerful downward to the masses. In Honduras the media have become the ruling oligarchy and have forgotten, for the most part, their responsibilities to open channels to all sectors of society. In Panama, however, perhaps for the first time in the country's history, the media may find a central government more supportive of the open exchange of ideas. In Costa Rica a media system that has helped deepen democratic traditions nevertheless ponders its role of representing traditional conservative forces as the system witnesses the first major infusion of capital from media chains based outside the region. How these different battles for control are resolved will affect the future growth of civil society in each of these nations. The media may be the weaker force when opposing strong central governments, but they have the ability to inspire the populace or link diverse groups in calls to action. Governments that try to buy or suppress the media see this inherent characteristic and understand its explosive power. This power constitutes an important social and political factor, because a tool that can help a society's myriad groups build a unified community of interests can contribute to the development of democracy throughout the region.

This is not to say we agree with the one-dimensional thinking of those who see independent media as a panacea for the region's ills. It is not a singular solution, a magic bullet that will cure these nascent democracies of the problems that retard their growth. We believe a free media system is important in bolstering support for human rights and free expression. As many details in our analysis have shown, however, the media serve the conservative oligarchic forces ruling much of this region even when they are unfettered by overt censorship. Dependent on advertising, the media lapse into self-censorship and keep content politically conservative to appease the forces that support their existence. As McChesney has noted, the more a media system depends on advertising, the more it becomes antidemocratic.[1] Thus the media's turn toward sensationalism—entertainment and blood-spattered tabloidism—serves to distract the mass audience from important policies and issues. As the media specialist and author Leo Bogart has noted, these compromises show that the media are not inevitably agents of democratization.[2] Worldwide, the media are buffeted by political systems, ideological debates, strong central governments, various economic forces (major conglomerates and other advertisers among them), competitive jealousies, and greed. All these forces are at work in Central America.

As we noted in chapter 1, Shattuck and Atwood claim that successful pluralistic systems include a free media system along with political systems that allow debate among the ruling and the ruled through various opposition groups, and these systems inevitably produce strong economic foundations because the free flow of information allows for better economic decision making. Furthermore, Shattuck and Atwood write: "Democratic competition can also increase the incentive for officials to resist corruption. Facing regular elections, an organized opposition, and a free media, political leaders in democratizing societies have less room for wheeling and dealing."[3]

Central America provides a unique laboratory for testing these claims. The least corrupt nation on the isthmus, Costa Rica, also has the strongest economy and deepest roots in democracy. It supports the most sophisticated and richest media market, with a variety of organizations that are independent of the government. Meanwhile, Guatemala, Nicaragua, and Honduras all show aspects from the other end of the spectrum. Each of these nations has a media system that is compromised in its own unique way, often by corruption.

As we noted in the previous chapter, however, some media systems are making significant progress toward changing the cultures of collusion with conservative forces. Media systems such as Guatemala's have cleansed themselves significantly and fought for more independence during the latter part of the 1990s. Newspapers such as Panama's *La Prensa* led attempts to reform media systems. Throughout Central America the media must decide which role they will play: a force to protect conservative, elite systems or a mechanism to support a wider civil society with hopes for democratization. These remain the decisions of elite owners, but the decisions will mean the difference between countries that use democratic forms to mask their oligarchic faces and countries that use the media to reinforce the building blocks of a real democracy. Many of the media systems in Central America exist in the uneasy midground between these philosophies.

Again, the developing countries of Central America bear similarities to Eastern European countries in transition. Elites now dominate the media systems of the latter, although these elites may be different from those in control before the 1990s or the 1940s. As Colin Sparks has noted in his analysis of these Eastern European systems, if democratization is to advance, then elite control of the media systems must be loosened or broken.[4] In Central America, however, the elite systems have not gone through anywhere near the turbulence of Eastern Europe. We view these ossified elite systems as a barrier to further progress on the isthmus.

These oligarchies and their supporting media superstructures have long prevailed in part because they fit U.S. goals for the region. Nevertheless, our views are not set purely in this frame of dependency theory. Although we question why discussion of this influence has often been sublimated or ignored, our views have evolved along with the changes in the region. Those views may incorporate a "neodependency" cast, but our main goal is to encourage examination of the intricate ways that the media and power intersect and connect in this relatively unexplored region. In fact, the lack of analysis of these connections is partly responsible for the anemic status of these protodemocracies.

It is important to remember that, as the Salvadoran media scholar David Escobar Galindo has told us, the region's media have little experience with democracy, so that they and society in general must practice the habit of democratic forms before they can attain a real sense of democracy.[5] According to Escobar, overcoming state-sponsored violence was one form of practicing a basic type of democracy. In countries such as Escobar's El Salvador, democratic reforms have proceeded more quickly than the development of a democratic consciousness. Journalists thus often alternate between the bold advances of investigative journalism and the timid safety of the nonconfrontational past.

These media systems face an important era as most of the nations of the isthmus move beyond years of war and violence. Again, the relationship between a professionalized media system and corruption depends greatly on the extent to which the media outlets work to heal polarization and class differences. We maintain that as the media evolve into a more open system where various factions of society can communicate, they serve to amplify the forces of democracy. If more conservative forces retain power, however, they often rely on the media to smother dissent. Many of the region's countries are now witnessing a fight to determine which way their media systems will swing. We believe that the media systems will reflect the dynamic nature of each country's political and social system as they evolve in this postwar period.

We have identified the following factors as affecting the development of these nations' media: (1) media owners' attitudes about free expression; (2) the ideological foundations of media organizations and their abilities to set aside partisanship in the move toward professionalism; (3) concentration of ownership in conservative, elite hands versus movement toward diversification; (4) media outlets' abilities to find market support and avoid control via advertising; (5) the shift toward a codified and widely accepted ethical standard; (6) younger journalists' capacities to mold these systems quickly; (7) the influence of foreign investors (be they from Mexico, Canada, or the United States); (8) the abilities of journalists to insulate themselves from violence and to demand justice for the wrongs visited on them by repressive forces; (9) the reduction of conflicts of interest between journalists who provide information for media organizations and the sources of their coverage in the private or public sectors; and (10) the acknowledgment by central governments and military forces of the basic rights of expression that should be part of each citizen's role in a democratic system and these citizens' abilities to join in the debate essential to pluralistic systems.

Change is not unidirectional, however. Alemán's policies in Nicaragua show that progress is not linear, that systems sometimes take a few steps back before moving forward. These systems change in complex ways. Each of the previously identified ten factors can move in a direction opposite to the others, so that key improvements in one area have a way of neutralizing retrenchment elsewhere and vice versa. This contributes to the obvious friction in these media systems, which seem to be pushing in one direction while being pulled in another. Such is the maelstrom now underway in these dynamic systems.

The media's lack of progress toward some idealized pluralistic system is also related to the political limbo of many of these countries, stuck as they are in the gray zone between democracy and authoritarianism. The political scientist Thomas Carothers has identified much of Central America (but not Costa Rica), along with other developing democracies, as being caught in developmental stagnation; the media systems will play an important role in determining whether these countries move on to the next stage.[6] Likewise, the sociologist William Robinson has characterized certain Central and South American nations as standing between authoritarianism and democracy, a position that developed nations promote as a way to guarantee both stability and open markets. Robinson singles out Nicaragua, Panama, and Mexico to support his theoretical approach to democracy in the region.[7]

The stagnant systems Carothers and Robinson describe are typified by strong centralized governments that developed antipluralistic tendencies during years of authoritarianism. These governments are marked by the trappings of democracy: elections, political latitude for opposition groups, and independent voices on radio or in newspapers. The opposition has little real power relative to the entrenched oligarchy, however. Conservative incumbents are supported by overwhelming media campaigns, television tilts strongly in favor of these established conservative incumbents, and there are few checks on executive power in the political system. An examination of the country profiles we have provided shows that many of the characteristics of these gray-zone systems exist in Central America. For example, all the region's television systems tend to favor conservative elites, even in Costa Rica. More important, Guatemala, Nicaragua, Honduras, and El Salvador all exhibit the general political and media tendencies outlined by Carothers and by Robinson. In Panama, although progressive elements are in power now, the country's political system remains divided, and the television system remains dominated by elements of the nation's conservative oligarchy.

In her work on the development of broadcasting in Latin America, Fox to some extent predicted the monopolistic or near-monopolistic character of much of Central America's television systems.[8] Although Fox was comparing the authoritarian systems of Mexico and Brazil, her model showing how strong authoritarian systems eventually breed strong, monopolistic television industries applies to most nations on the isthmus, with the exception of Costa Rica. Of course, the consolidation of media properties and the intervention of outside investors in Costa Rica's system have raised new questions and concerns there.

As foreign interests have invested in Central American media systems, their roles there have depended on their adaptation to the unique political status of each country where they have invested. When Angel González moved into Guatemala, Nicaragua, and (briefly) El Salvador, his television networks supported conservative elite oligarchies and posed no threat to the state. Because foreign owners have not entered the Panamanian system in a significant way, that system's reactions to the inevitable investment invasion will be an important development over the next few decades.

As usual in Central America, the exceptions exist on opposite ends of the developmental spectrum: Costa Rica and Honduras. Nodarse, the controversial Cuban American media owner of Honduras, seems to be an exception to our analysis, but this claim is obscured by Nodarse's incursion into Honduras before the transition to civilian rule. The negative reactions to him, including attempts to eject him from the system, are twofold: they stem both from his long-established ties to the military elites who are giving up power in the Honduran system and from his status as an outsider who is not part of the cozy, Liberal Party, *turco* elite club that has come to dominate the system.

In Costa Rica González's major investment in the country's television system was greeted by controversy for many of the same reasons. González is not a native and thus threatens the dominance of native elites. Also, his ultraconservative reputation seems to run counter to the spirit of democracy at the foundation of Costa Rica's system, even though the major establishment media elites come from the conservative parts of that nation's oligarchy.

As we have noted, media ownership is the paramount factor in these small market systems, because the owners establish the boundaries of political discourse. As Waisbord and others have mentioned, a favorite expression in Latin America is "*libertad de prensa* (press freedom) means *libertad de empresa* (market freedom)."[9]

The Central American media have evolved and changed, sometimes in very important ways, since the prewar era and the lost wartime decade of the 1980s. The advances cannot be ignored, although they fall short of the hopes and dreams of those who expected the media would deliver the region to democracy. There is more *libertad de empresa* now than a generation ago, and therefore more overall freedom. To cynics who would point to the overall conservative nature of the media, we admit that this conservative political orientation has slowed progress. The progress we note here may be only enough to nudge the media and political systems a few degrees forward. Nevertheless, the advances are there for everyone to see.

The most obvious changes have perhaps been merely cosmetic, but in many cases these changes have attracted larger audiences. Most Central American newspapers have undergone major face-lifts in the past generation. Many have spawned new products looking for a younger audience. The most popular newspaper in each of these countries has led efforts to introduce color and contemporary design and photographic techniques to the region's print media. *La Prensa*'s recent return to market leadership in Managua perhaps speaks to the inevitability of that modernization trend. *La Prensa*'s circulation triumphs may also show the passing of the torch from one era to another.

At the same time, these cosmetic changes often signaled improvements in content. Panama's *La Prensa* and Guatemala's *Siglo Veintiuno* have consistently been mentioned among a handful of newspapers admired throughout Latin America.[10] Conservative retrenchment may be underway at both newspapers, but there has been progress.

El Diario de Hoy changed its entire composition in an effort to become one of the best papers in the region. In the process, the publication went through not just radical cosmetic surgery but also a sort of spiritual rebirth so that it would no longer merely be a mouthpiece for ARENA. Although recent events have shown that the newspaper's architects were more successful with the surface changes, attempts were made to separate the paper from its conservative past. The ideological battles for that publication's soul are not over.

In Guatemala *Prensa Libre* built a stable of publications with modern designs, and these publications increasingly became independent voices for the liberal business community and intelligentsia. Nicaragua's *La Prensa*, the Chamorro family newspaper, not only modernized but also moved toward a more objective and professional stance. In the process, as the new century began, it once again took the lead as Nicaragua's most popular paper.

Although television has remained tied to conservative political elites, the quality of programming has improved. Costa Rican, Panamanian, Salvadoran, and Nicaraguan broadcasters were all able to match the quality of information programs coming into the region from other prominent Latin American broadcasters, including those in Mexico and Venezuela. At Canal 12 in San Salvador, Jorge Zedan showed that maverick broadcasters could survive, even if they had to negotiate with foreign ownership groups such as TV Azteca. In addition, broadcasters with firm ties to conservative political elites toned down the political rhetoric on their networks, and bias became harder to detect as programming grew more sophisticated, as the examples of Panama's MEDCOM, Nicaragua's Sacasas, and El Salvador's Esersky all show.

The most prominent of these media organizations, regardless of political affiliation or ideology, have several aspects in common. They are not satisfied with stagnant market leadership; they have seen that to lead is to evolve. They have thus made changes to give their programming and publications a modern flair. Such renovations reflect both a millennial shift and generational change. All the previously cited leading broadcasting and print media organizations (except El Salvador's Canal 12, which may reorganize if TV Azteca sells the network) enjoy financial stability, which has allowed for modernization. The drive for improved appearance, and sometimes improved content (broadcasting lags behind print media with respect to the latter), often involves competition as well. Although many of these forward-looking media organizations are already the leaders in their countries, domestic and international competition spurs them to do even more.

The United States of course remains a powerful influence on the region, but the evolution of the region's media over the past generation clearly shows that regional, national, and Latin American cultural influences have contributed to the current media scene. As Straubhaar has noted in his studies of Brazil, Latin American media systems may be open to influences from beyond the region, but strong regional and national influences eventually predominate in their flavor and tone.[11]

The noted Brazilian editor and journalist Rosental Calmon Alves has proposed that some of the more impressive media outlets in Central America and Latin America in general have followed a European model, where outlets openly discuss their political orientations while exploring events. Alves has compared leading publications such as Guatemala's *Siglo Veintiuno* to Spain's *El Pais*, a publication that is widely read and admired throughout many parts of Latin America.[12]

Waisbord sees journalism in Latin America, and by extension Central America, as an amalgam, a hybrid of influences from the United States and Europe mixed with the sensibilities of media entrepreneurs who migrated to Latin America.[13] The influence of the United States came to the fore following World War II as that country became the world's predominant power. Cultural and media influence accompanied that political power. As we have seen, however, the professionalization and maturation of the region's media systems have tempered that influence.

Competition from various regional and transnational broadcasters from Latin America has diminished the United States' influence as well. Mexico's Televisa, Brazil's Globo, and even Mexico's TV Azteca network have influenced programming in the region and are major program suppliers to Central America. Angel González, the Mexican who has concentrated his holdings in Mexico and Central America but supplies programming and holds media investments throughout Latin America, has helped shape media environments and politics alike. The ascendancy of these regional Latin American entities in shaping Central American media systems tends to confirm the observations of Waisbord and Straubhaar, both of whom have noted the rise of influential Latin American programming and journalistic trends that have buffered the region from external cultural and political forces.

On a macro scale, all this evolution toward media systems with unique national characteristics has occurred in the crucial postwar era, which has seen an incomparable climate of liberty spread across the isthmus. Although the advancement of freedom has suffered setbacks, notably the advertising boycotts spurred by Cristiani, Arzú, and Alemán, overt government censorship is now part of the past. The heavy hand of the military has largely disappeared as well, although threats of violence from military forces or paramilitaries with little patience for free expression still surface from time to time in Guatemala and Honduras. The media have mostly sought to end their collusion with the military, although *La Estrella de Panama* remains tainted by its ties to military dictatorships. Again, the attacks on Nodarse may be due to this trend to cut ties with military control.

We have seen journalists courageously take stands, sometimes at gunpoint, to increase free expression. In Honduras *El Tiempo*'s Vilma Gloria Rosales worked to expose journalistic corruption and improve her media system. Rossana Guevara and Sandra Maribel Sanchez continue that tradition, fighting the plague of corruption in the Honduran system. Panamanian journalists and the Altamiranos of El Salvador likewise took stands against corruption, partially as a way toward more editorial independence. As younger journalists with higher ethical standards come to work at publications such as *El Diario de Hoy*, Guatemala's *elPeriodico*, and Nicaragua's *La Prensa*, the era of the *empiricos* and the *papas fritas* is waning.

Even small niche publications provide examples of media outlets fighting to provide independent voices and alternative political views.

Guatemala's *La Hora*, despite its shrinking circulation, continues to provide enlightened political analysis, which has inspired *elPeriodico* of the
Prensa Libre group. Panama's *El Universal*, despite the political views
of its originators, has tried to cut an independent, objective, and professional course. Such publications seem less interested in partisanship and
more interested in advancing the political debate in these evolving political systems. El Salvador's *Mas*, the spin-off from *El Diario de Hoy*, is
proving influential with young journalists and young readers alike, and
despite its light approach, it nevertheless goes after political stories. The
high ethical standards that *Mas* promotes to younger journalists have
made it a symbol to El Salvador's younger generation, who are struggling
to survive in a country with one of the highest crime rates in the hemisphere. Guatemala's Radio Nuevo Mundo, with its orientation toward the
nation's indigenous groups; Honduras's Radio America; El Salvador's RPC
Radio; and Panama's Radio KW Continente all show that their countries'
influential radio systems have made room for alternative voices.

Many of these media outlets seek above all else to provide a needed
counterbalance in their political and economic systems. As Carlos
Chamorro, the former director of *Barricada*, noted: "Journalism's role
should be to counterbalance power—not just in facing government, but
also in facing the economic and military powers that be."[14]

The future of the stronger Central American media outlets is perhaps
already on display in Costa Rica, the region's most developed nation with
the strongest democratic traditions and most sophisticated media market. Costa Rica enjoys the region's most diversified economy, so that the
importance of government advertising has been reduced (although not
eliminated), and a wider swath of advertisers frees the media from dependency on a few large patrons. Finding themselves just one of many advertisers, sponsors lose their leverage to control the content of programming. As advertisers become less politicized and polarized, the media will
find they will have fewer boundaries on expression.

Media outlets also need to develop strong circulation bases, as *El
Nuevo Diario* has done in Nicaragua, to buffer themselves against the
vagaries of the marketplace. Developing alternative strategies and alternative revenue streams not only reduces the media's vulnerability but
also fosters the democratic ideals for the media espoused by Fox and
McChesney. Some publications, such as *La Prensa* in Nicaragua, have
branched into private publishing and marketing music compact discs to
diversify their revenue sources and buffer themselves from governments
that have used coercive economic means against them.

Fox lays out the challenge for these evolving media systems, pointing out that private commercial media need not be democratic media.[15] As these countries move, however slowly, toward true democracy, they must understand from the beginning that media paradigms should change in ways that let the media better represent public interests and address the needs of the populace, not just those of an established elite. The abilities of the judicial and legislative institutions of these nascent democracies to legislate and enforce media codes will largely determine the future for the media in Central America. These new codes will need to guarantee public access, representation of a wide variety of voices, and competition that breaks apart concentrated media structures. Without such legal codes, the media, especially the electronic media, are bound to represent the same oligarchic interests that dominated the region's past. With more and more of the area turning to broadcast television as the main source of information, and those systems firmly in the hands of conservative elites, the moment for action may already be passing. Strong central governments are bound to kill such legislative agendas or fight them fiercely because they threaten the state's power to use advertising or other mechanisms against media organizations that do not fall into lockstep behind broadcasters who represent central authority.

Absent these remedies, however, some media organizations have found that popular support can let them resist organized advertising boycotts that attempt to control content. *El Nuevo Diario*'s ability to survive mainly on street sales is the leading example of a media outlet that bypassed the control of advertisers and the state by connecting directly with the populace. Nicaragua's Radio Sandino and Radio Ya and Guatemala's *Prensa Libre* have shown that popular support can make the boycotts backfire: advertisers were forced to ignore the blockades if they wanted to reach the lucrative audiences these important media outlets offered. In addition, Radio Sandino and Radio Ya both showed how formerly state-sponsored (and even communist) media outlets could adapt to a commercial marketplace without completely surrendering their political hearts. Radio Sandino and Radio Ya retain their ideology, but now they offer a necessary counterbalance to the far-right Alemán government.

Even in polarized nations such as Panama and Nicaragua, ideology is becoming less important for some journalists. In Panama *El Universal* has tried to open its pages to a variety of viewpoints, even though it was started by a family within the conservative faction of the elite, which was aligned with the nation's dictators. At the end of Nicaragua's Sandinista era, journalists were clearly labeled as belonging to the left or the right, and Sandinistas were often barred from working at publications that did not share their ideology. Less than a decade after the Sandinistas left power, however, when the Sandinista newspaper *Barricada* folded, Freddie Potoy, who wrote for the party organ and numbered among Nicaragua's best investigative journalists, was able to find a new home at *La Prensa*. *La Prensa* also welcomed one of *Barricada*'s top editors, Roberto Fonseca.

These media systems are in flux. Ideology and polarization have not been conquered, as is shown by the ownership change at Panama's *La Prensa* that ended the Gorriti era. This episode demonstrated that even a modern, multiple-owner system may remain vulnerable to the concentrated efforts of political rivals bent on revenge. In February 2001 Ricardo Alberto Arias, one of the founding board members of *La Prensa*, engineered a takeover of the board by soliciting proxies for votes. Members of Arias's family and political allies had been slowly buying shares in the paper and accumulating corporate power. In the twenty-one years since the newspaper's founding, Ricardo Arias's politics had drifted toward the PRD, the right-wing party bearing a longtime enmity with *La Prensa*. Arias had served as President Perez Balladares's foreign minister, and some saw his takeover as the former president's revenge on the newspaper for years of embarrassing investigative reports about him and his administration.

Arias's corporate maneuvering led to his being named president of the La Prensa Corporation, the publication's holding company.[16] Arias also used a board meeting to rescind support for Gorriti, the newspaper's famous investigative editor from Peru. The board voted not to renew Gorriti's work permit. Under Panamanian law, firms employing foreign workers must support their application for and renewal of work permits. With the board's vote, Gorriti was forced out.

After his return to Peru, Gorriti wrote: "*La Prensa* serves as proof that even under especially designed papers to withstand pressure, any serious attempt to conduct investigative journalism in thoroughly corrupt societies will be a very difficult and precarious endeavor. The sorry outcome of that specific experience does not mean, however, that serious journalism would be a foredoomed affair in those countries."[17]

Arias's corporate takeover of *La Prensa* is an example of retrenchment, but as Gorriti notes, it does not mean that alternative forms of ownership structures cannot yield more democratic media. Although media outlets continue to serve as bases for ideological battles, the media are evolving slowly. One paper in Costa Rica, for example, shows media owners moving away from the traditional *caudillo* role: *La Nación* is not a fiefdom for old-school, domineering owners. Panama's *La Prensa* may show the vulnerability of a shareholder-owned media organization when confronting the corporate onslaught of its political adversaries, but *La Nación* demonstrates how that system can succeed. Although *La Nación* is sometimes steered by the political viewpoints of key board members, the paper has a modern ownership structure that diffuses the personality feuds and political vendettas all too common in the columns of other newspapers. *La Nación* is not disengaged from politics, but it has been able to assume the role of investigative watchdog, which sometimes pushes the boundaries of freedom of expression and makes communication freer for all the media in Costa Rica.

As these markets become more sophisticated and media outlets diversify to serve niche audiences—processes already underway in Costa Rica—the media may come to play a more dominant role in establishing a sense of pluralism. Already in Guatemala, despite threats and violence, the indigenous programs emerging on Radio Nuevo Mundo have shown they can build popularity and credibility along with salability. Advertising agencies saw Radio Nuevo Mundo's indigenous audience as the fastest-growing sector of Guatemala's radio audience and new territory for programming.

The internet revolution has yet to hit Central America in a significant way outside elite circles. In most countries internet availability remains in single-digit percentages and is not expected to top 15 percent until after 2005. Costa Rica is already showing the way toward the future by experimenting with wireless cable television delivery systems. With plummeting costs for cell phone service and more wireless delivery systems moving into Central America, the internet revolution in Central America could become a "third generation" movement. Central America may emulate the Northern European or Filipino models and move directly to lower-cost wireless internet delivery using hand-held devices, leapfrogging hard-wired delivery. Issues of access for the poor, indigenous, or peripheral groups will remain important for this internet revolution to make a difference, however, much as they have for other media in the region.

More important, the internet revolution is making it much more difficult to control a country's media system. Although bribery and advertising will still offer tools for limiting the rights of free expression even on the internet, a Web presence carries relatively low overhead, and Central American journalists and information specialists working in the medium will likely feel less economic pressure than do their colleagues in other media. Already most major newspapers and other media outlets in the region have an internet presence. These sites will only grow in importance once the region manages to make phone service, whether wired or mobile, affordable to a majority of the population.

The internet revolution has great potential for steering more media outlets toward supporting pluralism and democracy. At this moment, at the beginning of a new millennium, the region's media bear great potential to grow, mature, and evolve into servicing all niche groups. Media leaders will shape Central America's future by choosing how they use this potential and harness the available resources. The media may gain more power to influence pluralism and governance, or they may slip back into the negative patterns of the past.

For now, although progress has been made, the future of the region remains precarious. Conservative oligarchies still control most of these countries. Although progressive politicians were elected recently in Panama, following the example Costa Rica carved out a half-century ago, the ultraconservative right holds most of the power everywhere else. The media barons who control most of the region's broadcast media have flexed their muscles to support this right-wing establishment while fighting to throttle any organizations brave enough to transmit the views of the left. Polarization of society is still a concern in Nicaragua and to a lesser degree in El Salvador. Panama, too, displays scars of a divisive past. Guatemalan politics form a constantly shifting maelstrom, as groups of all persuasions fight as easily with erstwhile allies as with those on the other side of the political divide. In Honduras civil society is still too small and fearful to confront the violent years of military oppression. Throughout Central America, with a few notable exceptions, media owners still fight to protect corrupt governments and entrepreneurs unwilling to address the poverty and low wages their business practices perpetuate. Instead of using the power of the media to aid voices for change, these media owners often turn away from their public responsibilities.

These conditions are not just the aftermath of the cold war era, which played out violently on the isthmus. Some of these divisions reflect centuries of clashes between liberal and conservative ideologies. Indeed, colonial-era politics continue to pulse underneath all these other divisions. *Criollo* elites and *ladinos* continue to constitute the ruling oligarchies and to produce the region's media barons, both groups colluding to keep Central America's resources for themselves. Despite notable exceptions, these political and media elites usually remain deaf to inclusive policies that would benefit indigenous groups or the poor masses who make up most of the media audiences.

All these divisions create the atmosphere of a fragile peace. With many of the past generation's economic and political issues unresolved, the media find themselves uniquely placed to negotiate between classes and political factions that still vehemently oppose one another. At least

one major media outlet in each of these countries has taken up that challenge by opening space to a variety of opinions and political views. On
balance, however, most of the media remain fronts for government propaganda or shills for oligarchies. The media must resolve these opposing
philosophies; in doing so they will tip the balance in many of these gray-
zone nations stuck in a limbo between pluralistic democracy and semiauthoritarianism. Those who guide the media in the region must decide
between playing to old, elite constituencies or branching out to make
their organizations more than profit centers. Will they be able to transform their holdings into information-service bases for a populace that has
been denied access to knowledge in the Information Age? The answer
awaits us in a brave new century.

NOTES

Introduction

1. J. S. Mill, "On Liberty," qtd. in *The Journalist's Moral Compass: Basic Principles*, ed. Steven R. Knowlton and Patrick Parsons (Westport, Conn.: Praeger, 1995), 72.

2. Silvio Waisbord, "Investigative Journalism and Political Accountability in South American Democracies," *Critical Studies in Mass Communication* 13 (1996): 351.

3. Upton Sinclair, *The Brass Check*, qtd. in *Journalist's Moral Compass*, ed. Knowlton and Parsons, 186.

4. Waisbord, "Investigative Journalism," 347.

5. Elizabeth Fox, *Latin American Broadcasting: From Tango to Telenovela* (Luton, U.K.: John Libbey Media, University of Luton, 1997), 131.

6. Thomas Carothers, "Democracy without Illusions," *Foreign Affairs* 76, no. 1 (Jan.–Feb. 1997): 85.

7. Jerome Aumente, "Struggles for Independent Journalism," *Media Studies Journal* 13, no. 3 (Fall 1999): 169–70.

8. Silvio Waisbord, "The Ties That Still Bind: Media and National Culture in Latin America," *Canadian Journal of Communication* 23, no. 3 (Summer 1998): 381.

9. Daniel C. Hallin, "Media, Political Power, and Democratization in Mexico," in *De-Westernizing Media Studies*, ed. James Curran and Myung-Jin Park (London: Routledge, 2000), 97.

10. Joseph Straubhaar, "Brazil: The Role of the State in World Television," in *Media and Globalization: Why the State Matters*, ed. Nancy Morris and Silvio Waisbord (Lanham, Md.: Rowman and Littlefield, 2001), 134–38.

11. Fox, *Latin American Broadcasting*, 129–32.

12. Waisbord, "Investigative Journalism," 356.

13. Robert W. McChesney, *Corporate Media and the Threat to Democracy* (New York: Seven Stories, 1997), 17–20.

14. Raúl Kraiselburd and Julio Muñoz, "Economic and Editorial Self-Sufficiency," in *Media and Democracy in Latin America and the Caribbean*, ed. Rosa M. González (Mayenne, France: UNESCO, 1996), 146–47.

15. Raul Gallegos, "Periodismo Feudal" (Feudal Journalism), *El Diario de Hoy* (San Salvador), 7 May 1998, 112.

16. Marylene Smeets, "Speaking Out: Postwar Journalism in Guatemala

and El Salvador," in *Attacks on the Press in 1999*, ed. Richard Murphy (New York: Committee to Protect Journalists, 2000), 225.

17. Kraiselburd and Muñoz, "Economic and Editorial Self-Sufficiency," 146.

Chapter 1: Honduras and the Media Oligarchy

1. Roy Hoffman, "A Year after Hurricane Mitch—Honduran Official: Our Country Has Lost What It Took Us 30 to 40 Years to Build," Newhouse News Service, in *Seattle Times*, 27 Oct. 1999, A3. See also Joan Treadway, "Honduras Struggles to Rebuild, Mitch's Toll Expensive but Country Is Focused," *New Orleans Times-Picayune*, 1 Dec. 1999, A23. Treadway notes the storm destroyed ninety bridges, seven hospitals, thousands of classrooms, and dozens of medical centers, along with damaging 70 percent of the nation's road and highway network.

2. James Dunkerley, *Power in the Isthmus: A Political History of Modern Central America* (London: Verso, 1988), 526–28.

3. Alison Acker, *Honduras: The Making of a Banana Republic* (Boston: South End, 1988), 74.

4. Thomas E. Skidmore and Peter H. Smith, *Modern Latin America* (New York: Oxford University Press, 2001), 340.

5. J. Mark Ruhl, "Doubting Democracy in Honduras," *Current History*, Feb. 1997, 81.

6. Ibid., 82.

7. Norman Roy Hernandez, chairman of CONATEL, the Honduran Communications Commission, interview with Rick Rockwell, Mar. 1998, Tegucigalpa, Honduras.

8. Associated Press, "International News," news capsule, 17 Dec. 1997.

9. "Corte Deniega Recurso de Inconstitucionalidad de Canal Seis" (Court denies recourse of unconstitutionality for Channel 6), *El Tiempo* (San Pedro Sula, Honduras), 17 Mar. 1998, 3.

10. Associated Press, "International News," 17 Dec. 1997.

11. Notimex, "Sancionan a Televisora Hondurena por Difusión Ilegal de Senales de EU" (Sanctioning a Honduran broadcaster for illegally transmitting signals from the United States), 22 Apr. 1998.

12. Notimex, "Ordenan Cierre Temporal de Televisora Hondurena por 'Pirateria'" (Ordering the temporary closure of Honduran broadcaster for piracy), 23 Apr. 1998.

13. Ibid.

14. Inforpress Centroamericana, "Principales Medios de Comunicación (Honduras, El Salvador y Guatemala)" (Principal communication media: Honduras, El Salvador, and Guatemala), Apr. 1998, 11.

15. Jorge Canahuati III, interview with Rick Rockwell, Mar. 1998, San Pedro Sula, Honduras.

16. Donald E. Schulz and Deborah Sundloff Schulz, *The United States, Honduras, and the Crisis in Central America* (Boulder, Colo.: Westview, 1994), 117.

17. Ibid., 8–10.

18. Dunkerley, *Power in the Isthmus*, 545.

19. Marvin Alisky, "Central American Radio," *Quarterly of Film, Radio, and TV* 10 (1955–56): 62.

20. The Economist Intelligence Unit, "Country Report: Nicaragua/Honduras," first quarter (London: The Economist Intelligence Unit, 2000), 30.

21. Schulz and Sundloff Schulz, *Crisis in Central America*, 204. See also Dunkerley, *Power in the Isthmus*, 566–67.

22. Rodolfo Dumas Castillo, telephone interview with Rick Rockwell, Mar. 1998, San Pedro Sula, Honduras.

23. Schulz and Sundloff Schulz, *Crisis in Central America*, 239.

24. The Economist Intelligence Unit, "Country Report: Nicaragua/Honduras," fourth quarter (London: The Economist Intelligence Unit, 2000), 29.

25. Inforpress Centroamericana, "Principales Medios de Comunicación," 11–12.

26. Francisco Medina, editor of *El Periodico*, interview with Rick Rockwell, Mar. 1998, Tegucigalpa, Honduras.

27. Inforpress Centroamericana, "Principales Medios de Comunicación," 12.

28. Edward S. Herman and Noam Chomsky, *Manufacturing Consent: The Political Economy of the Mass Media* (New York: Pantheon Books, 1988), 2.

29. Edgardo Benitez, editor of *El Nuevo Dia*, interview with Rick Rockwell, Mar. 1998, San Pedro Sula, Honduras.

30. "Con Protesta Busca Nodarse Evitar Cumplimiento de Ley" (With protest Nodarse seeks to avoid fulfillment of the law), *La Prensa* (San Pedro Sula, Honduras), 22 Mar. 1998, A7.

31. Committee to Protect Journalists, *Attacks on the Press in 1998*, ed. Alice Chasan (New York: Committee to Protect Journalists, 1999), 182.

32. Raul Valladares, radio news director at HRN, interview with Rick Rockwell, Mar. 1998, Tegucigalpa, Honduras.

33. Juan Ramon Martinez, columnist at *La Tribuna*, interview with Rick Rockwell, Mar. 1998, Tegucigalpa, Honduras.

34. Chasan, ed., *Attacks on the Press*, 182.

35. Ruhl, "Doubting Democracy," 83.

36. Freddy Cuevas, "Honduran President Fires Military Officials, Denies Coup Attempt," Associated Press, 31 July 1999.

37. Committee to Protect Journalists, *Attacks on the Press in 1999*, ed. Richard Murphy (New York: Committee to Protect Journalists, 2000), 198.

38. "Corte Deniega Recurso," 3.

39. John Shattuck and J. Brian Atwood, "Defending Democracy: Why Democrats Trump Autocrats," *Foreign Affairs* 77, no. 2 (Mar.–Apr. 1998): 168.

40. Inforpress Centroamericana, "Principales Medios de Comunicación," 10.

41. John Virtue, ed., *Latin American Media Directory* (North Miami: International Media Center, Florida International University, 1998), 225.

42. Dumas Castillo interview.

43. Inforpress Centroamericana, "Principales Medios de Comunicación," 10.

44. Marvin Alisky, *Latin American Media: Guidance and Censorship* (Ames: Iowa State University Press, 1981), 214. Alisky puts the rate of illiteracy at 75 percent in 1981; the rate was thus cut in half over a generation, while the population doubled.

45. Elizabeth Fox, *Latin American Broadcasting: From Tango to Telenovela* (Luton, U.K.: John Libbey Media, University of Luton, 1997), 131.

Chapter 2: El Salvador's Newly Respun Corporatism

1. Mireya Navarro, "Man in the News: Francisco Guillermo Flores Perez; New Salvadoran Puzzle," *New York Times,* 9 Mar. 1999, A10.

2. Juanita Darling, "*Mas* for the Masses," *IPI Report,* on-line edition of the quarterly journal of the International Press Institute (Summer 1999), <http://www.freemedia.at/publicat.html>.

3. Enrique Altamirano, director of *El Diario de Hoy,* interview with Noreene Janus, May 1998, San Salvador, El Salvador.

4. Robert Armstrong and Janet Shenk, *El Salvador: The Face of Revolution* (Boston: South End, 1982), 3–9. The authors credit *Time* with creating this reference to the oligarchy.

5. David Browning, *El Salvador: Landscape and Society* (Oxford: Clarendon, 1971), 222–23.

6. Liisa North, *Bitter Grounds: Roots of Revolt in El Salvador* (Westport, Conn.: Lawrence Hill, 1985), 22.

7. Paul P. Kennedy, *The Middle Beat: A Correspondent's View of Mexico, Guatemala, and El Salvador* (New York: Teachers College Press, Columbia University, 1971), 174–75.

8. North, *Bitter Grounds,* 24.

9. Browning, *El Salvador,* 147.

10. William M. LeoGrande, *Our Own Backyard: The United States in Central America, 1977–1992* (Chapel Hill: University of North Carolina Press, 1998), 159, 627.

11. Lafitte Fernandez Rojas, managing editor of *El Diario de Hoy,* interview with Noreene Janus, May 1998, San Salvador, El Salvador.

12. The Associated Press, "Salvadoran President Vows Jobs," *Boston Globe,* 2 June 1999, A14.

13. Marvin Alisky, *Latin American Media: Guidance and Censorship* (Ames: Iowa State University Press, 1981), 217.

14. Noreene Janus, Harold Moore Jr., and Danielle Rodriguez-Schneider, *Media and Campaign Coverage Assessment: El Salvador Presidential Elections, March 1999* (Washington, D.C.: USAID, 1999).

15. Juan Bosco, editor at *El Diario de Hoy,* interview with Noreene Janus, Apr. 1999, San Salvador, El Salvador.

16. Janus, Moore, and Rodriguez-Schneider, *Media and Campaign Coverage.*

17. James Dunkerley, *Power in the Isthmus: A Political History of Modern Central America* (London: Verso, 1988), 348.

18. Rick Rockwell, Noreene Janus, and Kristin Neubauer, "Exposé Could Signal End of El Salvador TV News Magazine," Pacific News Service, 24 May 2001, available at <http://www.pacificnews.org/content/pns/2001/may/0524expose.html>.

19. Janus, Moore, and Rodriguez-Schneider, *Media and Campaign Coverage.*

20. Dunkerley, *Power in the Isthmus*, 345–47.

21. Janus, Moore, and Rodriguez-Schneider, *Media and Campaign Coverage.*

22. Edward S. Herman and Noam Chomsky, *Manufacturing Consent: The Political Economy of the Mass Media* (New York: Pantheon Books, 1988), 97. See also Francisco Valencia, "El Poder Economico y los Medios de Comunicación" (Economic power and the communication media), in *Periodismo, Derechos Humanos y Control de Poder Politico en Centroamerica* (Journalism, human rights and the control of political power in Central America), ed. Jaime Ordóñez (San José, Costa Rica: InterAmerican Institute of Human Rights, 1994), 69.

23. John Shattuck and J. Brian Atwood, "Defending Democracy: Why Democrats Trump Autocrats," *Foreign Affairs* 77, no. 2 (Mar.–Apr. 1998): 168.

24. Herman and Chomsky, *Manufacturing Consent*, 171.

25. Inforpress Centroamericana, "Principales Medios de Comunicación (Honduras, El Salvador y Guatemala)" (Principal communication media: Honduras, El Salvador and Guatemala), Apr. 1998, 9.

26. Roberto Castañeda Alas, Radio Sonora owner, interview with Noreene Janus, Apr. 1999, San Salvador, El Salvador.

27. Ibid.

28. Janus, Moore, and Rodriguez-Schneider, *Media and Campaign Coverage.*

29. Castañeda interview.

30. Roger Atwood, "Peace of Mind," *New Republic*, 22 Mar. 1999.

31. Nery Mabel Reyes, news director of YSKL Radio, interview with Noreene Janus, Apr. 1999, San Salvador, El Salvador.

32. Inforpress Centroamericana, "Principales Medios de Comunicación," 9.

33. Ignacio "Nacho" Castillo, news director at RCS Radio, interview with Noreene Janus, Apr. 1999, San Salvador, El Salvador.

34. Jo Dallas, "Thin Bit of America," *Multichannel News International* 3, no. 4 (Apr. 1997): 26.

35. Marco Antonio Rivera, producer at Canal 12, interview with Noreene Janus, May 1998, San Salvador, El Salvador.

36. Marvin Alisky, "Central American Radio," *Quarterly of Film, Radio, and TV* 10 (1955–56): 57–58.

37. Dunkerley, *Power in the Isthmus*, 348.

38. Dallas, "Thin Bit of America." After interviewing experts in the region, Dallas estimates that El Salvador and the remainder of the region will approach double-digit cable penetration only after 2002.

39. Rivera interview. See also "Principales Medios de Comunicación," 8.

40. Inforpress Centroamericana, "Principales Medios de Comunicación," 8.

41. Andrew Paxman, "Ghostly Titan Works below Radar," *Variety*, 31 May 1999, 23.

42. Mauricio Funes, anchor at Canal 12, interview with Noreene Janus, May 1998, San Salvador, El Salvador.

43. Janus, Moore and Rodriguez-Schneider, *Media and Campaign Coverage*. Interestingly, Funes took issue with this report and questioned its methodology and reasoning; he was one of the few in Salvadoran media to react negatively to the findings. In his criticism, Funes openly questioned the journalistic ideal of objectivity, which seemed to be the basis for the study.

44. Jorge G. Castañeda, "Limits to Apertura: Prospects for Press Freedom in the New Free-Market Mexico," in *A Culture of Collusion: An Inside Look at the Mexican Press,* ed. William A. Orme Jr. (Miami: North-South Center Press, the University of Miami, 1997), 135.

45. Michael Shifter, "Tensions and Trade-Offs in Latin America," *Journal of Democracy* 8, no. 2 (Apr. 1997): 116.

Chapter 3: *Panama's Media Civil War*

1. James Aparicio, "Gerente de La Prensa Maltrata y Amenaza a su Mujer e Hijos" (Manager of *La Prensa* mistreats and threatens his wife and children), *La Estrella de Panama,* 23 Aug. 1998, A1.

2. Jean Gilbreath Niemeier, *The Panama Story* (Portland, Ore.: Metropolitan, 1968), 138–39, 256.

3. Mireya Navarro, "Woman in the News: Mireya Elisa Moscoso; Earnest Icon for Panama," *New York Times,* 4 May 1999, A11.

4. Niemeier, *The Panama Story,* 196–99.

5. Frederick Kempe, *Divorcing the Dictator: America's Bungled Affair with Noriega* (New York: Putnam's, 1990), 45.

6. Niemeier, *The Panama Story,* 198–200.

7. Ibid., 204–5.

8. Thomas E. Skidmore and Peter H. Smith, *Modern Latin America,* 5th ed. (New York: Oxford University Press, 2001), 328–29.

9. "Dejando Huella" (Leaving a mark), *El Cambio,* special edition of *El Panamá América,* 17 Mar. 1994, 2.

10. Kempe, *Divorcing the Dictator,* 62.

11. Tom Barry, John Lindsay-Poland, Marco Gandásegui, and Peter Simonson, *Inside Panama* (Albuquerque, N.M.: Resource Center, 1995), 108.

12. Marvin Alisky, *Latin American Media: Guidance and Censorship* (Ames: Iowa State University Press, 1981), 223–24.

13. Barry et al., *Inside Panama,* 108.

14. I. Roberto Eisenmann Jr. and Herasto Reyes, *La Prensa de Panama: La Creacion de un Diario Sin Dueño* (*La Prensa* of Panama: the creation of a daily without an owner) (Colombia: Carvajal, 1995), 34–35.

15. Rosental Calmon Alves, "Vanguard Newspapers in Latin America" (unpublished paper presented at the International Communication Association Conference, Montreal, 1997), 11.

16. Juan Luis Correa Esquivel, general manager of *La Prensa,* interview with Rick Rockwell, Aug. 1998, Panama City, Panama.

17. James Aparicio, editor of *La Estrella de Panama*, interview with Rick Rockwell, Aug. 1998, Panama City, Panama.

18. Rosario Arias de Galindo, publisher of *El Panamá América* and *Crítica*, interview with Rick Rockwell, Aug. 1998, Panama City, Panama.

19. Diana Martáns, publisher of *Pauta*, interview with Rick Rockwell, Aug. 1998, Panama City, Panama. See also the only independent review of newspaper circulation, "Los Periodicos: En Busca de la Lealtad Perdida" (The newspapers: in search of lost loyalty), *Pauta*, June 1992, 26–33.

20. Jaime Padilla Beliz, publisher of *El Siglo*, interview with Rick Rockwell, Aug. 1998, Panama City, Panama.

21. Aparicio interview.

22. Indalecio Rodriguez, ombudsman at *El Universal*, interview with Rick Rockwell, Aug. 1998, Panama City, Panama.

23. Barry et al., *Inside Panama*, 109.

24. Kempe, *Divorcing the Dictator*, 220.

25. Andrew Bounds, "Political Squalls as the 'Mireya Effect' Hits Panama," *Financial Times* (London), 6 Oct. 2000, 7.

26. Kempe, *Divorcing the Dictator*, 30.

27. Jo Dallas, "Thin Bit of America," *Multichannel News International* 3, no. 4 (Apr. 1997): 26.

28. Nicolás González Revilla, president of MEDCOM Holdings, interview with Rick Rockwell, Aug. 1998, Panama City, Panama.

29. Jon Mitchell, "U.S. Slams Panama for Investor Policies; Cable TV Decision Spurs America to Take Action," *Journal of Commerce*, 2 Apr. 1997, 3A.

30. Barry et al., *Inside Panama*, 110.

31. Gustavo Gorriti, associate editor of *La Prensa*, interview with Rick Rockwell, Aug. 1998, Panama City, Panama.

32. Correa Esquivel interview.

33. Dallas, "Thin Bit of America," 26.

34. Ana Teresa Benjamín, "El Mayor Problema es el Desempleo" (The major problem is unemployment), *La Prensa* (Panama City), 22 Aug. 1998, A17.

35. Fernando Correa Jolly, "La Necesidad de un Sistema de Mercadeo para la Radio en Panama" (The necessity of a market system for radio in Panama) (Master's thesis, University of St. Maria La Antigua, Panama City, 1992), 111. Correa Jolly is a manager at Radio KW Continente, one of Panama's leading radio networks.

36. Fernando Correa Jolly, executive vice-president, Radio KW Continente, interview with Rick Rockwell, Aug. 1998, Panama City, Panama.

37. Ibid.

38. Kathia Martinez, "New Panamanian President Annuls Press Gag Laws," Associated Press, 20 Dec. 1999.

Chapter 4: The Return of the Conservatives in Nicaragua

1. Paul B. Goodwin Jr., ed., *Global Studies: Latin America* (Guilford, Conn.: Dushkin/McGraw-Hill, 2000), 41–44. Other sources rank poverty in some of

the region's other countries as equally bad or worse. See Isabel Sanchez, "Latin America's Achilles Heel: Poverty, Inequality, Lack of Democracy," Agence France-Press, 29 June 2000. Sanchez ranks Guatemala's poverty rate and misery index higher than Nicaragua's. The discrepancies in the poverty rankings may stem from the different sources of information. Goodwin relies on information from the U.S. government, including CIA reports, while Sanchez cites United Nations statistical information.

2. Thomas E. Skidmore and Peter H. Smith, *Modern Latin America*, 5th ed. (New York: Oxford University Press, 2001), 321.

3. Jenny Pearce, "The Eagle Rises," in *Nicaragua: Unfinished Revolution*, ed. Peter Rosset and John Vandermeer (New York: Grove, 1986), 146.

4. Skidmore and Smith, *Modern Latin America*, 335.

5. Bernabe Somoza, "Start of Something Much Better for Nicaragua," *Houston Chronicle*, 4 Nov. 1996, A23.

6. Ilene O'Malley, "Play It Again, Ron," in *Nicaragua: Unfinished Revolution*, ed. Rosset and Vandermeer, 157.

7. John Spicer Nichols, "The Issue of Censorship," in *Nicaragua: Unfinished Revolution*, ed. Rosset and Vandermeer, 108.

8. Jeffery M. Paige, *Coffee and Power: Revolution and the Rise of Democracy in Central America* (Cambridge, Mass.: Harvard University Press, 1997), 4, 26.

9. Violeta Barrios de Chamorro, with Sonia Cruz de Baltodano and Guido Fernández, *Dreams of the Heart* (New York: Simon and Schuster, 1996), 17.

10. Nichols, "Issue of Censorship," 108.

11. George Black, "The 1972 Earthquake and After: *Somocismo* in Crisis," in *Nicaragua: Unfinished Revolution*, ed. Rosset and Vandermeer, 189–91.

12. Nichols, "Issue of Censorship," 109.

13. Henri Weber, "The Struggle for Power," in *Nicaragua: Unfinished Revolution*, ed. Rosset and Vandermeer, 197.

14. Harold E. Moore Jr., *Democracy, the Media and Politics in Nicaragua* (Miami: Latin American Journalism Program, Florida International University, 1995), 22.

15. M. L. Stein, "A Lone Free Voice in Nicaragua," *Editor and Publisher*, 19 May 1984, 16, as noted in Nichols, "Issue of Censorship," 110.

16. Barrios de Chamorro, Cruz de Baltodano, and Fernández, *Dreams of the Heart*, 240.

17. Moore, *Democracy*, 26.

18. Barrios de Chamorro, Cruz de Baltodano, and Fernández, *Dreams of the Heart*, 11.

19. Cristiana Chamorro, former director of *La Prensa*, interview with Noreene Janus, Kristin Neubauer, and Rick Rockwell, Aug. 2001, Managua, Nicaragua.

20. Hugo Holmann Chamorro, general manager of *La Prensa*, interview with Noreene Janus, Kristin Neubauer, and Rick Rockwell, Aug. 2001, Managua, Nicaragua.

21. David Hume, subdirector of *La Prensa*, interview with Rick Rockwell, Aug. 2001, Managua, Nicaragua.

22. M&R Consultores, with Price Waterhouse Coopers, *Auditoria de Circulacion* (Audit of circulation) (Managua, Nicaragua: M&R Consultores, 2001).

23. Juanita Darling, "Sandinista Paper Returns, but Ex-Staffers Aren't Impressed," *Los Angeles Times,* 22 July 2000, A1.

24. Glenn Garvin, "Newspaper Wars Heat Up in Nicaragua," *Miami Herald,* 19 Feb. 1998, A14.

25. Tomás Borge, former director of *Barricada* and former interior minister of Nicaragua, interview with Noreene Janus, Kristin Neubauer, and Rick Rockwell, Aug. 2001, Managua, Nicaragua.

26. Joel Gutiérrez, former director of *La Tribuna* and anchor for Canal 2, interview with Noreene Janus and Rick Rockwell, Aug. 2001, Managua, Nicaragua.

27. Francisco Chamorro, managing editor of *El Nuevo Diario,* interview with Rick Rockwell, Aug. 2001, Managua, Nicaragua.

28. M&R Consultores, with Price Waterhouse Coopers, *Auditoria de Circulacion.*

29. Goodwin, ed., *Global Studies,* 41.

30. Moore, *Democracy,* 9.

31. Universidad Centroamericana, *Encuesta sobre preferencia de Medios* (Poll on media preference) (Managua: Faculty of Communication Science, Universidad Centroamericana, 1998), 22.

32. Alfonso Chardy, "U.S. Found to Skirt Ban on Aid to Contras," *Miami Herald,* 24 June 1985, qtd. in *Nicaragua: Unfinished Revolution,* ed. Rosset and Vandermeer, 260.

33. Oswaldo Zuñiga, producer at Radio Catolica, interview with Noreene Janus, July 1998, Managua, Nicaragua.

34. Barrios de Chamorro, Cruz de Baltodano, and Fernández, *Dreams of the Heart,* 11.

35. Carlos Briceño, owner and general manager of TeleNica 8, interview with Noreene Janus, July 1998, Managua, Nicaragua.

36. Danilo Lacayo, former anchor and host of "Buenas Dias Nicaragua," Canal 2, interview with Noreene Janus, July 1998, Managua, Nicaragua.

37. David R. Dye, Jack Spence, and George Vickers, *Patchwork Democracy: Nicaraguan Politics Ten Years after the Fall* (Cambridge, Mass.: Hemisphere Initiatives, 2000), 20.

38. Carlos Chamorro, director of *Confidencial* (Managua) and host of "Este Semana," Canal 2, interview with Noreene Janus, Kristin Neubauer, and Rick Rockwell, Aug. 2001, Managua, Nicaragua.

39. Andrew Paxman, "Ghostly Titan Works below Radar," *Variety,* 31 May 1999, 23.

40. Moore, *Democracy,* 79.

41. Adolfo Pastrán, "La Situacion de la Prensa en Nicaragua" (The situation of the press in Nicaragua), *La Red* (the magazine of Periodistas de Investigacion [Investigative reporters and editors of Mexico]), Aug.–Sept. 1997, 5.

42. Thomas W. Walker, *Nicaragua: The Land of Sandino,* 3d ed. (Boulder, Colo.: Westview, 1991), 146.

43. Darling, "Sandinista Paper Returns," A1.

44. Moore, *Democracy*, 84.

45. Dye, Spence, and Vickers, *Patchwork Democracy*, 24.

46. Dennis Schwartz Galo, general manager of Radio Ya, interview with Noreene Janus, Aug. 2001, Managua, Nicaragua.

47. Milo Gadea Pantoja, co-owner of Radio Corporación, interview with Rick Rockwell, Aug. 2001, Managua, Nicaragua.

48. Universidad Centroamericana, *Encuesta*, 7.

49. Sanchez, "Latin America's Achilles Heel."

Chapter 5: Guatemala's Struggle with Manipulation

1. Florencio Simòn Chuy, director of Mayan language programs at Radio Nuevo Mundo, interview with Rick Rockwell, July 1998, Guatemala City, Guatemala.

2. Blancanivea Bendfeltd, media director at APCU Thompson Asociados, interview with Rick Rockwell, July 1998, Guatemala City, Guatemala.

3. Larry Rohter, "Report's Bluntness Shocks, Gratifies," *Montreal Gazette*, 28 Feb. 1999, B8. See also "Year after Gerardi's Murder, Case Still Unresolved," *New Catholic Times*, 25 Apr. 1999, 9. These sources base their estimate of 200,000 casualties on the UN-mandated Guatemalan Truth Commission report and the Catholic church's report *Guatemala: Nunca Mas*.

4. Simòn Chuy interview.

5. Robert McChesney, *Corporate Media and the Threat to Democracy* (New York: Seven Stories, 1997), 6.

6. Jon Vanden Heuvel and Everette E. Dennis, *Changing Patterns: Latin America's Vital Media* (New York: Freedom Forum Media Studies Center, 1995), 56.

7. Mark Fitzgerald, "Press Freedom in Latin America: A Survey," *Editor and Publisher*, 10 Apr. 2000, 42.

8. Vanden Heuvel and Dennis, *Changing Patterns*, 56.

9. Bendfeltd interview.

10. Andrew Paxman, "Ghostly Titan Works below Radar," *Variety*, 31 May 1999, 23.

11. John Virtue, ed., *Latin American Media Directory* (Miami: International Media Center, School of Journalism and Mass Communication, Florida International University, 1998), 215.

12. Bendfeltd interview.

13. Ibid.

14. Ileana Alamilla, Joáquin Pérez, and Ruth Taylor, eds., *The Guatemalan Media: The Challenge of Democracy* (Guatemala City: Cerigua, 1996), 9–10.

15. Inforpress Centroamericana, "Principales Medios de Comunicación (Honduras, El Salvador y Guatemala)" (Principal communication media: Honduras, El Salvador, and Guatemala), Apr. 1998, 4.

16. Bendfeltd interview.

17. Ibid.

18. Alamilla, Pérez, and Taylor, *Guatemalan Media*, 8.

19. J. Arthur Heise and Charles H. Green, "An Unusual Approach in the United States to Latin American Journalism Education," in *Communication in Latin America: Journalism, Mass Media and Society*, ed. Richard R. Cole (Wilmington, Del.: Scholarly Resources, 1996), 74.

20. Oscar Marroquín Rojas, publisher of *La Hora*, interview with Rick Rockwell, July 1998, Guatemala City, Guatemala.

21. Estuardo Zapeta, columnist, *Siglo Veintiuno*, interview with Rick Rockwell, July 1998, Guatemala City, Guatemala.

22. Bendfeltd interview.

23. Marylene Smeets, "Speaking Out: Postwar Journalism in Guatemala and El Salvador," in *Attacks on the Press in 1999*, ed. Richard Murphy (New York: Committee to Protect Journalists, 2000), 221.

24. Alamilla, Pérez, and Taylor, *Guatemalan Media*, 1–2.

25. Marvin Alisky, *Latin American Media: Guidance and Censorship* (Ames: Iowa State University Press, 1981), 212.

26. Jim Handy, *Gift of the Devil: A History of Guatemala* (Boston: South End, 1984), 105.

27. Bendfeltd interview.

28. Gerardo Jiménez, director of *Al Día*, interview with Rick Rockwell, July 1998, Guatemala City, Guatemala.

29. Joan Mower, "Newspapers Called Vital in Advancing Democracy in Latin America," in *free!* 15 July 1999, available at <http://www.freedomforum.org/international/1997/7/15pagina.asp>.

30. Haroldo Shetemul, former director of *Crónica*, interview with Rick Rockwell, July 1998, Guatemala City, Guatemala.

31. James Painter, *Guatemala: False Hope, False Freedom* (London: Catholic Institute for International Relations, 1987), 54–55.

32. Ibid., 42–44.

33. Ibid., 75.

34. Bendfeltd interview.

35. Committee to Protect Journalists, *Attacks on the Press in 1998*, ed. Alice Chasan (New York: Committee to Protect Journalists, 1999), 180–81.

36. Silvio R. Waisbord, "Investigative Journalism and Political Accountability in South American Democracies," *Critical Studies in Mass Communication* 13 (1996): 347–48.

37. Darrel R. Eglin, "The Economy," in *Guatemala: A Country Study*, ed. Richard F. Nyrop (Washington, D.C.: U.S. Army, 1983), 87.

38. Handy, *Gift of the Devil*, 65–66.

39. James Dunkerley, *Power in the Isthmus: A Political History of Modern Central America* (London, Verso, 1988), 457–62.

40. The Economist Intelligence Unit, "Country Profile: Guatemala/El Salvador" (London: The Economist Intelligence Unit, 2000), 22.

41. Painter, *Guatemala*, 38–41.

Chapter 6: Costa Rica, the Exception That Proves the Rule

1. Cynthia H. Chalker, "Elections and Democracy in Costa Rica," in *Elections and Democracy in Central America, Revisited*, ed. Mitchell A. Seligson and John A. Booth (Chapel Hill: University of North Carolina Press, 1995), 103–4.

2. Lowell Gudmundson, *Costa Rica before Coffee* (Baton Rouge: Louisiana State University Press, 1986), 67–69.

3. Jeffery M. Paige, *Coffee and Power: Revolution and the Rise of Democracy in Central America* (Cambridge, Mass.: Harvard University Press, 1997), 220.

4. Jon Vanden Heuvel and Everette E. Dennis, *Changing Patterns: Latin America's Vital Media* (New York: Freedom Forum Media Center, 1995), 62.

5. Bruce M. Wilson, *Costa Rica: Politics, Economics, and Democracy* (Boulder, Colo.: Lynne Rienner, 1998), 2.

6. Rolando Angulo Zeledón, independent radio journalist, interview with Dylana Segura of *La Nación* (San José, Costa Rica), June 2000, San José, Costa Rica.

7. Andrés Borrasé Sanou, director of *La Prensa Libre*, interview with Dylana Segura of *La Nación* (San José, Costa Rica), June 2000, San José, Costa Rica.

8. John A. Booth, *Costa Rica: Quest for Democracy* (Boulder, Colo.: Westview, 1998), 47.

9. Paige, *Coffee and Power*, 24.

10. Ibid., 149.

11. Shirley Saborío, editor of *Actualidad Economica*, interview with Dylana Segura of *La Nación* (San José, Costa Rica), May 2000, San José, Costa Rica.

12. Eduardo Ulibarri, editor of *La Nación*, interview with Dylana Segura of *La Nación*, May 2000, San José, Costa Rica.

13. Ana Cristina Rojas, "Television Sin Arbitraje" (Television without Arbitration), *Actualidad Economica* (May 2000): 30.

14. Wilson, *Costa Rica*, 1–2. See also "Progress and Inertia in Central America," *Swiss Review of World Affairs*, 3 Nov. 1997.

15. William Gómez, director of "Diario Extra," Extra TV, and Radio America, interview with Dylana Segura of *La Nación* (San José, Costa Rica), May 2000, San José, Costa Rica.

16. John Virtue, ed., *Latin American Media Directory* (Miami: International Media Center, School of Journalism and Mass Communication, Florida International University, 1998), 155.

17. Enrique Villalobos Quirós, professor at the Universidad Estatal a Distancia and Universidad Autonoma de CentroAmerica, interview with Noreene Janus, July 1998, San José, Costa Rica.

18. Jo Dallas, "Thin Bit of America," *Multichannel News International* 3, no. 4 (Apr. 1997): 26.

19. Enrique Villalobos Quirós, *El Derecho a la Información* (The right to information) (San José: La Editorial Universidad Estatal a Distancia, 1997), 108.

20. Andrew Paxman, "Ghostly Titan Works below Radar," *Variety*, 31 May 1999, 23. See also Rojas, "Television Sin Arbitraje," 28. Rojas sets González's ownership at thirty stations throughout Latin America.

21. Rojas, "Television Sin Arbitraje," 32.

22. Ana Cristina Rojas, reporter at *Actualidad Economica*, interview with Dylana Segura of *La Nación* (San José, Costa Rica), May 2000, San José, Costa Rica.

23. Luis Rojas Coles, "El Periodismo es mi Vida" (Journalism is my life), *Teleguia*, magazine insert of *La Nación*, 17 Jan. 1999, 10–11.

24. Rojas, "Television Sin Arbitraje," 34.

25. Ibid.

26. Elbert Durán Hidalgo, director of "Radio Periodicos Reloj," interview with Dylana Segura of *La Nación* (San José, Costa Rica), June 2000, San José, Costa Rica.

27. Vanden Heuvel and Dennis, *Changing Patterns*, 63–64.

28. Paige, *Coffee and Power*, 181. See also Chalker, "Elections and Democracy," 110.

29. Wilson, *Costa Rica*, 157–58.

30. Rojas, "Television Sin Arbitraje," 29.

Chapter 7: *State Power, the Static in the System*

1. Silvio Waisbord, *Watchdog Journalism in South America: News, Accountability, and Democracy* (New York: Columbia University Press, 2000), 5.

2. Silvio Waisbord and Nancy Morris, "Introduction: Rethinking Media Globalization and State Power," in *Media and Globalization: Why the State Matters*, ed. Nancy Morris and Silvio Waisbord (Lanham, Md.: Rowman and Littlefield, 2001), xii.

3. José Rolando Sarmiento, independent radio journalist at Radio X, interview with Rick Rockwell, Mar. 1998, Tegucigalpa, Honduras.

4. Raul Valladares, radio news director at HRN, interview with Rick Rockwell, Mar. 1998, Tegucigalpa, Honduras.

5. Committee to Protect Journalists, *Attacks on the Press in 1998*, ed. Alice Chasan (New York: Committee to Protect Journalists, 1999), 182–83.

6. Brian McNair, "Power, Profit, Corruption, and Lies: The Russian Media in the 1990s," in *De-Westernizing Media Studies*, ed. James Curran and Myung-Jin Park (London: Routledge, 2000), 88–89.

7. Leo Valladares Lanza and Susan C. Peacock, *The Search for Hidden Truths* (Tegucigalpa, Honduras: National Commission of Human Rights/CNDH, 1998), 4–5.

8. Freddy Cuevas, "Honduras Says It Has Evidence of Secret Graves at U.S.-built Base," Associated Press, 8 Aug. 1999.

9. The Associated Press, "Honduras' Army Chief Admits Shielding Fugitive Officers," *Miami Herald*, 17 Aug. 1998, A4.

10. Freddy Cuevas, "Honduras Compensates Families of People Killed by Death Squads," Associated Press, 2 Nov. 2000.

11. Rossana Guevara, "Factores de Poder y Autocensura: El Caso de Honduras" (Factors of power and self-censorship: the case of Honduras), in *Periodismo, Derechos Humanos y Control de Poder Politico en Centroamerica* (Journalism, human rights and the control of political power in Central America), ed. Jaime Ordóñez (San José, Costa Rica: InterAmerican Institute of Human Rights, 1994), 94.

12. Jon Vanden Heuvel and Everette E. Dennis, *Changing Patterns: Latin America's Vital Media* (New York: Freedom Forum Media Center, 1995), 14.

13. John Keane, "The Crisis of the Sovereign State," in *Media, Crisis and Democracy: Mass Communication and the Disruption of Social Order*, ed. Marc Raboy and Bernard Dagenais (London: Sage, 1992), 20.

14. Joseph Straubhaar, "Brazil: The Role of the State in World Television," in *Media and Globalization*, ed. Morris and Waisbord, 139.

15. Marco Antonio Rivera, producer at Canal 12, interview with Noreene Janus, May 1998, San Salvador, El Salvador.

16. Francisco Valencia, "El Poder Economico y los Medios de Comunicación" (Economic power and the communication media), in *Periodismo*, ed. Ordóñez, 69.

17. Robert W. McChesney, *Corporate Media and the Threat to Democracy* (New York: Seven Stories, 1997), 23.

18. Nery Mabel Reyes, news director of YSKL Radio, interview with Noreene Janus, May 1998, San Salvador, El Salvador.

19. David Rivas, president of APES, interview with Noreene Janus, May 1998, San Salvador, El Salvador.

20. Daniel C. Hallin, "Media, Political Power, and Democratization in Mexico," in *De-Westernizing Media Studies*, ed. Curran and Park, 99.

21. Joseph D. Straubhaar, "The Electronic Media in Brazil," in *Communication in Latin America: Journalism, Mass Media and Society*, ed. Richard R. Cole (Wilmington, Del.: Scholarly Resources, 1996), 225–26.

22. Boris Zelada, editor at *La Prensa Grafica*, interview with Noreene Janus, May 1998, San Salvador, El Salvador.

23. Mauricio Funes, anchorman at Canal 12, interview with Noreene Janus, May 1998, San Salvador, El Salvador.

24. Rick Rockwell, Noreene Janus, and Kristin Neubauer, "Exposé Could Signal End of El Salvador TV News Magazine," Pacific News Service, 24 May 2001, available at <http://www.pacificnews.org/content/pns/2001/may/0524expose.html>.

25. Rick Rockwell and Kristin Neubauer, "Media Feel Government Pressure," *Baltimore Sun*, 29 July 2001, C1, C6.

26. Rockwell, Janus, and Neubauer, "Exposé."

27. Marcos Alfredo Valladares Melgar, letter to Carlos Rosales, press sec-

retary, San Salvador, 22 Jan. 2001. Copy via fax from the Office of Information and Press of the President of the Republic of El Salvador.

28. Marylene Smeets, "El Salvador," *Attacks on the Press in 2000*, ed. Richard Murphy (New York: Committee to Protect Journalists, 2001), 149.

29. Keane, "Crisis of the Sovereign State," 17–21.

30. Will Weissert, "Congressmen Quit in Guatemala; Former Ruling Party in Disarray," Associated Press, in *The News* (Mexico City), 7 June 2000, 13.

31. Haroldo Shetemul, former director of *Crónica*, interview with Rick Rockwell, July 1998, Guatemala City, Guatemala, .

32. Inforpress CentroAmericana, "President Accused of 'Killing the Media,'" *Central America Report* 25, no. 12 (26 Mar. 1998): 2.

33. Jared Kotler, "Guatemala's New War—of Words," *Washington Post*, 19 Apr. 1998, A20.

34. Estuardo Zapeta, columnist at *Siglo Veintiuno*, interview with Rick Rockwell, July 1998, Guatemala City, Guatemala.

35. Chasan, ed., *Attacks on the Press in 1998*, 181.

36. Marylene Smeets, "Speaking Out: Postwar Journalism in Guatemala and El Salvador," in *Attacks on the Press in 1999*, ed. Richard Murphy (New York: Committee to Protect Journalists, 2000), 221. See also Rick Rockwell, "Vote Points to More Trouble," *Baltimore Sun*, 14 Nov. 1999, C6.

37. Mark Fitzgerald, "Press Freedom in Latin America: A Survey," *Editor and Publisher*, 10 Apr. 2000, 42.

38. Ileana Alamilla, Joáquin Pérez, and Ruth Taylor, eds., *The Guatemalan Media: The Challenge of Democracy* (Guatemala City: Cerigua, 1996), 5–6.

39. Committee to Protect Journalists, *Attacks on the Press in 1997*, ed. Alice Chasan (New York: Committee to Protect Journalists, 1998), 195.

40. Inforpress CentroAmericana, "Principales Medios de Comunicación (Honduras, El Salvador y Guatemala)" (Principal communication media: Honduras, El Salvador, and Guatemala), Apr. 1998, 5.

41. Fitzgerald, "Press Freedom," 42.

42. Rockwell, "Vote Points to More Trouble," C1.

43. Efe News Service, "Llega Relator de la OEA para la Libertad de Expresion" (OAS ombudsman for free expression arrives), 12 Apr. 2000. See also Andrew Paxman, "Ghostly Titan Works below Radar," *Variety*, 31 May 1999, 23.

44. Andrew Bounds, Robin Emmott, and Andy Webb-Vidal, "Press Finds It a Struggle to Stay Free in Latin America," *Financial Times* (London), 4 July 2001, 3.

45. "Nuevo Golpe á la Libertad de Prensa" (New coup against press liberty), *Prensa Libre* (Guatemala City), 4 Feb. 2000.

46. Paxman, "Ghostly Titan," 23.

47. The Associated Press, "Guatemala Sends Soldiers into Streets," *The News* (Mexico City), 9 June 2000, 10. See also Will Weissert, "Guatemalan

President's Family Evacuated as Fear Grips Nation," *The News* (Mexico City), 22 June 2000, 11.

48. Keane, "Crisis of the Sovereign State," 16.

49. Bounds, Emmott, and Webb-Vidal, "Press Finds It a Struggle," 3.

50. Harold E. Moore Jr., *Democracy, the Media and Politics in Nicaragua* (Miami: Latin American Journalism Program, Florida International University, 1995), 62.

51. Cristiana Chamorro, former director of *La Prensa*, interview with Noreene Janus, July 1998, Managua, Nicaragua.

52. Adolfo Pastrán, "La Situacion de la Prensa en Nicaragua" (The situation of the press in Nicaragua), *La Red* (the magazine of Periodistas de Investigacion [Investigative reporters and editors of Mexico]), Aug.–Sept. 1997, 5.

53. Brian J. Buchanan, "News Media Called Critical to Democracy, Reforms in Central America," *free!* 10 Sept. 1999, report available at <http://www.freedomforum.org/international/1999/9/10mediaatmill4.asp>.

54. Adolfo Pastrán, radio *noticiero*, interview with Noreene Janus, July 1998, Managua, Nicaragua.

55. Joel Gutierrez, former senior editor at *La Tribuna* (Managua), interview with Noreene Janus, July 1998, Managua, Nicaragua.

56. Committee to Protect Journalists, *Attacks on the Press in 1999*, ed. Richard Murphy (New York: Committee to Protect Journalists, 2000), 203.

57. Xavier Reyes, managing editor of *La Noticia* (Managua), interview with Noreene Janus, Aug. 2001, Managua, Nicaragua.

58. M&R Consultores, with Price Waterhouse Coopers, *Auditoria de Circulacion* (Audit of circulation) (Managua, Nicaragua: M&R Consultores, 2001).

59. Efe News Service, "*La Noticia*, Cuarto Diario Escrito del Pais, Circula desde Hoy" ("*La Noticia*, fourth daily written in the country, circulates from today"), 4 May 1999.

60. "Caso END es Malversación de los Bienes del Estado" (The case of *El Nuevo Diario* is embezzlement of state goods), *El Nuevo Diario* (Managua), 6 July 2001.

61. Rockwell and Neubauer, "Media Feel Government Pressure."

62. Fitzgerald, "Press Freedom," 42. See also Pastrán, "Situacion de la Prensa," 5; Buchanan, "News Media Called Critical."

63. Xavier Reyes, managing editor of *La Noticia* and former director of "Sesenta Minutos," Cadena de Oro, interview with Noreene Janus, July 1998, Managua, Nicaragua.

64. Fitzgerald, "Press Freedom," 42. See also Murphy, ed., *Attacks on the Press in 1999*, 203.

65. James Curran and Myung-Jin Park, "Beyond Globalization Theory," in *De-Westernizing Media Studies*, ed. James Curran and Myung-Jin Park (London: Routledge, 2000), 14.

66. John A. Booth, *Costa Rica: Quest for Democracy* (Boulder, Colo.: Westview, 1998), 120.

67. Martha Honey, *Hostile Acts: U.S. Policy in Costa Rica in the 1980s* (Gainesville: University Press of Florida, 1994), 203, 245, 313–17, as noted in Booth, *Costa Rica*, 120.

68. Violeta Barrios de Chamorro, with Sonia Cruz de Baltodano and Guido Fernández, *Dreams of the Heart* (New York: Simon and Schuster, 1996), 240.

69. Lezak Shallat, "AID and the Secret Parallel State," in *The Costa Rica Reader,* ed. Marc Edelman and Joanne Kenen (New York: Grove Weidenfeld, 1989), 223.

70. Jean Hopfensperger, "U.S. and Contras Find Ally in Costa Rica's Three Major Dailies," in *The Costa Rica Reader,* ed. Edelman and Kenen, 294; repr. from *The Christian Science Monitor,* 18 Aug. 1986.

71. Rolando Angulo Zeledón, radio *noticiero,* interview with Dylana Segura of *La Nación* (San José, Costa Rica), June 2000, San José, Costa Rica.

72. "Hank González Controversy Strains Mexico-U.S. Relations," *The News* (Mexico City), 22 June 1999. See also Agence France-Press, "Mexico Denounces Backlash in Costa Rica over Hank Affair," 10 June 1999; Associated Press, "International News," 12 June 1999.

73. Nefer Muñoz, "Suspendido Director de *La Republica*" (Director of *La Republica* suspended), *La Nación,* 9 Jan. 1999, A11.

74. Elbert Durán Hidalgo, director of "Radio Periodicos Reloj," interview with Dylana Segura of *La Nación* (San José, Costa Rica), June 2000, San José, Costa Rica.

75. Vanden Heuvel and Dennis, *Changing Patterns,* 63.

76. Armando González, director of *Al Día,* interview with Dylana Segura of *La Nación* (San José, Costa Rica), July 2000, San José, Costa Rica.

77. Vanden Heuvel and Dennis, *Changing Patterns,* 63, 69.

78. Committee to Protect Journalists, *Attacks on the Press in 1993,* ed. Anne Newman (New York: Committee to Protect Journalists, 1994), 112.

79. Pilar Cisneros Gallo, anchor at Canal 7, interview with Dylana Segura of *La Nación* (San José, Costa Rica), May 2000, San José, Costa Rica.

80. Eduardo Ulibarri, editor of *La Nación,* interview with Dylana Segura of *La Nación,* May 2000, San José, Costa Rica.

81. Committee to Protect Journalists, *Attacks on the Press in 1996,* ed. Alice Chasan (New York: Committee to Protect Journalists, 1997), 106–7.

82. Vanden Heuvel and Dennis, *Changing Patterns,* 64.

83. Efe News Service, "Condenan a Diario *La Nación* por Segunda Vez en Tres Semanas" (*La Nación* condemned for the second time in three weeks), 13 Nov. 1999.

84. Marcela Angulo Grillo, editor of *El Financiero,* interview with Dylana Segura of *La Nación,* June 2000, San José, Costa Rica.

85. Chasan, ed., *Attacks on the Press in 1998,* 172.

Chapter 8: The Threats to Central American Journalism

1. Dr. Santiago A. Canton, *Report of the Office of the Special Rapporteur for the Freedom of Expression,* vol. 3 (Washington, D.C.: Organization of American States, 1999), 3.

2. Committee to Protect Journalists, *Attacks on the Press in 1997,* ed. Alice Chasan (New York: Committee to Protect Journalists, 1998), 195.

3. Committee to Protect Journalists, *Attacks on the Press in 1998*, ed. Alice Chasan (New York: Committee to Protect Journalists, 1998), 180.

4. Reporters sans Frontières, "Ninth Ibero-American Summit in Havana, Cuba," available at <http://www.rsf.fr/indexuk.html>.

5. Chasan, ed., *Attacks on the Press in 1998*, 180.

6. Rick Rockwell, "Shining Light on a Shadowy Legal System," *Baltimore Sun*, 4 July 1999, C1.

7. Committee to Protect Journalists, *Attacks on the Press in 1994*, ed. Jeanne Sahadi (New York: Committee to Protect Journalists, 1995), 67–68. See also John A. Booth, *Costa Rica: Quest for Democracy* (Boulder, Colo.: Westview, 1998), 92.

8. Marcela Angulo Grillo, editor of *El Financiero*, interview with Dylana Segura of *La Nación*, June 2000, San José, Costa Rica.

9. Chasan, ed., *Attacks on the Press in 1998*, 187–88.

10. Carlos Briceño, owner and general manager of TeleNica 8, interview with Noreene Janus, July 1998, Managua, Nicaragua.

11. Ramiro McDonald Jr., former news director and principal anchor of "Guatemala Flash," interview with Rick Rockwell, July 1998, Guatemala City, Guatemala. See also Edgardo Benitez, editor of *El Nuevo Dia*, interview with Rick Rockwell, Mar. 1998, San Pedro Sula, Honduras; Chasan, *Attacks on the Press in 1998*, 180.

12. Canton, *Report*, 3:29–30.

13. Juanita Darling, "Panama: Looking for Ways to Silence Editors," *IPI Report* (Fall 1997): 22.

14. Gustavo Gorriti, associate editor of *La Prensa*, interview with Rick Rockwell, Nov. 1998, Washington, D.C.

15. Chasan, ed., *Attacks on the Press in 1997*, 202.

16. "Gadfly Won't Fly Away: An Expose-Minded Editor Vows to Resist Panama's Expulsion Threat," *Los Angeles Times*, 14 Aug. 1997, B8.

17. Suzanne Bilello, "Central American News Media: Independent but Shadowed by Threats," *free!* 27 Aug. 1999, report available at <http://www.freedomforum.org/international/1999/8/27mediaatmill.asp>.

18. Gustavo Gorriti, associate editor of *La Prensa*, interview with Rick Rockwell, Aug. 1998, Panama City, Panama.

19. Gorriti interview, Nov. 1998, Washington, D.C.

20. Committee to Protect Journalists, "Powerful Panamanians Conspire to Smear Local Editor," 26 Oct. 1999, available at <http://www.cpj.org/news/1999/Panama26Oct99.html>.

21. Mark Schapiro, "The Man without a Country," *Salon.com* (internet magazine), 7 Nov. 2000, available at <http://www.salon.com/news/feature/2000/11/07/montesinos/index2.html>.

22. Rick Rockwell, "Canal Control No Guarantee of Stability for Panama," *Baltimore Sun*, 15 Aug. 1999, C1.

23. Committee to Protect Journalists, *Attacks on the Press in 1999*, ed. Richard Murphy (New York: Committee to Protect Journalists, 2000), 204–5.

24. Kathia Martinez, "New Panamanian President Annuls Press Gag Laws," Associated Press, 20 Dec. 1999.

25. Timoteo Tobar Salazar, president of COOPEDEGUA, interview with Rick Rockwell, July 1998, Guatemala City, Guatemala.

26. Ileana Alamilla, Joáquin Pérez, and Ruth Taylor, eds., *The Guatemalan Media: The Challenge of Democracy* (Guatemala City, Guatemala: Cerigua, 1996), 7.

27. Chasan, ed., *Attacks on the Press in 1997,* 196–97.

28. Efe News Service, "Periodistas Han Vivido Entre Voragine del Terror y la Violencia" (Journalists have lived in the whirlpool of terror and violence), 29 Apr. 2000.

29. Rick Rockwell, "Vote Points to More Trouble," *Baltimore Sun,* 14 Nov. 1999, C1, C6.

30. Chasan, ed., *Attacks on the Press in 1997,* 194–96.

31. Ibid., 196.

32. Committee to Protect Journalists, *Attacks on the Press in 1993,* ed. Anne Newman (New York: Committee to Protect Journalists, 1994), 132–33. See also Germán Quintanilla, "La Policia y Los Medios de Comunicación: El Caso de Honduras" (The police and the media of communication: the case of Honduras), in *Periodismo, Derechos Humanos y Control de Poder Politico en Centroamerica* (Journalism, human rights and the control of political power in Central America), ed. Jaime Ordóñez (San José, Costa Rica: Inter-American Institute of Human Rights, 1994), 83–84.

33. Donald E. Schulz and Deborah Sundloff Schulz, *The United States, Honduras, and the Crisis in Central America* (Boulder, Colo.: Westview, 1994), 310.

34. Marcello Scarone, "Freedom and Restrictions: Perspectives," in *Media and Democracy in Latin America and the Caribbean,* ed. Rosa M González (Mayenne, France: UNESCO, 1996), 32–33.

35. Murphy, ed., *Attacks on the Press in 1999,* 198.

36. Committee to Protect Journalists, *Attacks on the Press in 1996,* ed. Alice Chasan (New York: Committee to Protect Journalists, 1997), 119.

37. Murphy, ed., *Attacks on the Press in 1999,* 198.

38. Efe News Service, "Matan Supuesto Pandillero Asesino á Periodista Television" (Killing of suspected gang member, assassin of a television journalist), 6 Dec. 1998.

39. Silvio Waisbord, "Investigative Journalism and Political Accountability in South American Democracies," *Critical Studies in Mass Communication* 13 (1996): 349.

Chapter 9: Corruption and Corporate Censorship

1. Thelma Mejia, "Smuggling Cases Reveal Rampant Corruption," Inter Press News Service, 26 Nov. 1999.

2. Inforpress CentroAmericana, "Contraband Coffee Sales Rise," *Central America Report* 25, no. 12 (26 Mar. 1998): 7.

3. Donald E. Schulz and Deborah Sundloff Schulz, *The United States, Honduras, and the Crisis in Central America* (Boulder, Colo.: Westview, 1994), 204–6.

4. Andrew Bounds, "Panama's Politicians Seek to Emerge from Noriega's Long Shadow," *Financial Times* (London), 25 Aug. 2000, 3.

5. Douglas W. Payne, *Storm Watch: Democracy in the Western Hemisphere into the Next Century* (Washington, D.C.: Center for Strategic and International Studies, 1998), 9.

6. James Wilson and Richard Lapper, "Confessed Killer Leads Race to Become Guatemalan President," *Financial Times* (London), 21 Sept. 1999, 9.

7. Maria Luisa Mackay, "Magic Realism in Latin America," *Media Studies Journal* 9, no. 3 (Summer 1995): 67.

8. Jerry Kammer, "Mexican Press Becoming Activist," *Arizona Republic,* 18 June 2000, J1.

9. Maurice Fliess, "Honduran Press Called Tarnished by Corruption," *free!* 13 Sept. 1999, available at <http://www.freedomforum.org/international/1999/9/13mediaatmill.asp>.

10. Rossana Guevara, "Factores de Poder y Autocensura: El Caso de Honduras" (Factors of power and self-censorship: the case of Honduras), in *Periodismo, Derechos Humanos y Control de Poder Politico en Centroamerica* (Journalism, human rights and the control of political power in Central America), ed. Jaime Ordóñez (San José, Costa Rica: InterAmerican Institute of Human Rights, 1994), 92.

11. Maria Antonia Martinez, managing editor of *La Prensa,* interview with Rick Rockwell, Mar. 1998, San Pedro Sula, Honduras.

12. Fliess, "Honduran Press Called Tarnished."

13. Mejia, "Smuggling Cases."

14. John Nerone, "Lessons from American History," *Media Studies Journal* 10, no. 4 (Fall 1996): 150, 154–56.

15. Alina Guerrero, "Las Relaciones Peligrosas" (Dangerous Relations), *Pulso,* Apr.–July 1995, 16–17.

16. Gustavo Berganza, "La Informacion Como un Derecho Humano, El Caso de Guatemala" (How information is a human right: the case of Guatemala), in *Periodismo,* ed. Ordóñez, 60.

17. Gustavo Berganza, managing editor of *Siglo Veintiuno,* interview with Rick Rockwell, July 1998, Guatemala City, Guatemala.

18. Isabel Sanchez, "Latin America's Achilles Heel: Poverty, Inequality, Lack of Democracy," Agence France-Press, 29 June 2000.

19. José Eduardo Zarco, former director of "Temas de Noche," interview with Rick Rockwell, July 1998, Guatemala City, Guatemala.

20. Marylene Smeets, "Speaking Out: Postwar Journalism in Guatemala and El Salvador," in *Attacks on the Press in 1999,* ed. Richard Murphy (New York: Committee to Protect Journalists, 2000), 225.

21. Fliess, "Honduran Press Called Tarnished."

22. Lafitte Fernandez Rojas, managing editor of *El Diario de Hoy,* interview with Noreene Janus, May 1998, San Salvador, El Salvador.

23. Ricardo Chacón, former managing editor of *La Prensa Grafica,* interview with Noreene Janus, May 1998, San Salvador, El Salvador.

24. Rolando Monterrosa, chief of public information for *El Diario de Hoy*, interview with Noreene Janus, May 1998, San Salvador, El Salvador.

25. Transparency International, "1999 Transparency International Corruption Perceptions Index," available at <www.transparency.de/documents/cpi/index.html>.

26. Michael Kanell, "Latin America: BellSouth's New Frontier," *Atlanta Constitution*, 22 Feb. 1998, H7.

27. Harold Moore, internal memo to Gary Russell of USAID, U.S. Embassy, Managua, 1996.

28. Mario F. Espinoza, journalism educator and journalist formerly with *Barricada*, interview with Noreene Janus, July 1998, Managua, Nicaragua.

29. Mauricio Funes, news anchor at Canal 12, interview with Noreene Janus, May 1998, San Salvador, El Salvador.

30. Jo Dallas, "Thin Bit of America," *Multichannel News International* 3, no. 4 (Apr, 1997): 26.

31. Silvio Waisbord, *Watchdog Journalism in South America: News, Accountability, and Democracy* (New York: Columbia University Press, 2000), 4.

32. Edward S. Herman and Noam Chomsky, *Manufacturing Consent: The Political Economy of the Mass Media* (New York: Pantheon Books, 1988), 3–4, 16–18.

33. Cristiana Chamorro, former director of *La Prensa*, interview with Noreene Janus, July 1998, Managua, Nicaragua.

34. Rick Rockwell and Noreene Janus, "Vertical Integration and Media Oligarchy in Central America," in *Proceedings of the International Mass Communications Symposium*, ed. Judy B. Oskam, vol. 1 (Lubbock: Texas Tech University, 1999), 122.

35. Espinoza interview.

36. David Rivas, president of APES, interview with Noreene Janus, May 1998, San Salvador, El Salvador.

37. Rolando Angulo Zeledón, radio *noticiero*, interview with Dylana Segura of *La Nación* (San José, Costa Rica), June 2000, San José, Costa Rica.

38. Berganza, "Informacion Como un Derecho," 59.

39. Guevara, "Factores de Poder," 92.

40. James Aparicio, editor of *La Estrella de Panama*, interview with Rick Rockwell, Aug. 1998, Panama City, Panama.

41. Nery Mabel Reyes, news director at Radio YSKL, interview with Noreene Janus, May 1998, San Salvador, El Salvador.

42. Nery Mabel Reyes, "Grupos Economicos e Influencia en los Medios de Comunicación" (Economic groups and influence in the communication media), in *Periodismo*, ed. Ordóñez, 65.

43. Funes interview.

44. Fernandez Rojas interview.

45. Rivas interview.

46. Gonzalo Marroquín Godoy, director of *Prensa Libre*, interview with Rick Rockwell, July 1998, Guatemala City, Guatemala.

Chapter 10: The Postwar Evolution

1. Robert McChesney, *Corporate Media and the Threat to Democracy* (New York: Seven Stories, 1997), 23.

2. Leo Bogart, "Media and Democracy," *Media Studies Journal* 9, no. 3 (Summer 1995): 2, 6.

3. John Shattuck and J. Brian Atwood, "Defending Democracy: Why Democrats Trump Autocrats," *Foreign Affairs* 77, no. 2 (Mar.–Apr. 1998): 168.

4. Colin Sparks, "Media Theory after the Fall of European Communism: Why the Old Models from East and West Won't Do Any More," in *De-Westernizing Media Studies*, ed. James Curran and Myung-Jin Park (London: Routledge, 2000), 47.

5. David Escobar Galindo, dean of the School of Communication, University of José Matías Delgado, interview with Noreene Janus, May 1998, San Salvador, El Salvador.

6. Thomas Carothers, "Democracy without Illusions," *Foreign Affairs* 76, no. 1 (Jan.–Feb. 1997): 85.

7. William I. Robinson, "Polyarchy: Coercion's New Face in Latin America," *NACLA Report on the Americas* 34, no. 3 (Nov.–Dec. 2000): 43.

8. Elizabeth Fox, *Latin American Broadcasting: From Tango to Telenovela* (Luton, U.K.: John Libbey Media, University of Luton, 1997), 129.

9. Silvio Waisbord, *Watchdog Journalism in South America: News, Accountability, and Democracy* (New York: Columbia University Press, 2000), 4.

10. Joan Mower, "Newspapers Called Vital in Advancing Democracy in Latin America," *free!* 15 July 1999, available at <http://www.freedomforum.org/international/1999/7/15pagina.asp>.

11. Joseph Straubhaar, "Brazil: The Role of the State in World Television," in *Media and Globalization: Why the State Matters*, ed. Nancy Morris and Silvio Waisbord (Lanham, Md.: Rowman and Littlefield, 2001), 133–34.

12. Rosental Calmon Alves, "Vanguard Newspapers in Latin America" (unpublished paper presented at the International Communication Association Conference, Montreal, 1997), 22.

13. Silvio Waisbord, "Media in South America: Between the Rock of the State and the Hard Place of the Market," in *De-Westernizing Media Studies*, ed. Curran and Park, 50–51.

14. Charles H. Green, Gerardo Bolaños, Francisco Vásquez, and Ana Cecilia With, *Finding Their Role: Nicaraguan News Media Grapple with Freedom* (North Miami: Florida International University, 1991), 12.

15. Fox, *Latin American Broadcasting*, 130.

16. Gustavo Gorriti, farewell message to *La Prensa* (Panama), 2 Mar. 2001, copy via electronic mail.

17. Gustavo Gorriti, electronic message to Rick Rockwell, 24 Oct. 2001, copy via electronic mail.

BIBLIOGRAPHY

Books

Acker, Alison. *Honduras: The Making of a Banana Republic.* Boston: South End, 1988.

Alisky, Marvin. *Latin American Media: Guidance and Censorship.* Ames: Iowa State University Press, 1981.

Armstrong, Robert, and Janet Shenk. *El Salvador: The Face of Revolution.* Boston: South End, 1982.

Barrios de Chamorro, Violeta, with Sonia Cruz de Baltodano and Guido Fernández. *Dreams of the Heart.* New York: Simon and Schuster, 1996.

Barry, Tom, John Lindsay-Poland, Marco Gandásegui, and Peter Simonson. *Inside Panama.* Albuquerque, N.M.: Resource Center, 1995.

Booth, John A. *Costa Rica: Quest for Democracy.* Boulder, Colo.: Westview, 1998.

Browning, David. *El Salvador: Landscape and Society.* Oxford: Clarendon, 1971.

Chasan, Alice, ed. *Attacks on the Press in 1996.* New York: Committee to Protect Journalists, 1997.

———. *Attacks on the Press in 1997.* New York: Committee to Protect Journalists, 1998.

———. *Attacks on the Press in 1998.* New York: Committee to Protect Journalists, 1999.

Cole, Richard R., ed. *Communication in Latin America: Journalism, Mass Media and Society.* Wilmington, Del.: Scholarly Resources, 1996.

Curran, James, and Myung-Jin Park, eds. *De-Westernizing Media Studies.* London: Routledge, 2000.

Dunkerley, James. *Power in the Isthmus: A Political History of Modern Central America.* London: Verso, 1988.

Edelman, Marc, and Joanne Kenen, eds. *The Costa Rica Reader.* New York: Grove Weidenfeld, 1989.

Edmisten, Patricia Taylor. *Nicaragua Divided: La Prensa and the Chamorro Legacy.* Pensacola: University of West Florida Press, 1990.

Eisenmann, I. Roberto, Jr., and Herasto Reyes. *La Prensa de Panama: La Creacion de un Diario Sin Dueño.* Colombia: Carvajal, 1995.

Fox, Elizabeth. *Latin American Broadcasting: From Tango to Telenovela.* Luton, U.K.: John Libbey Media, University of Luton, 1997.

González, Rosa M., ed. *Media and Democracy in Latin America and the Caribbean*. Mayenne, France: UNESCO, 1996.

Goodman, Louis W., William M. LeoGrande, and Johanna Mendelson Forman. *Political Parties and Democracy in Central America*. Boulder, Colo.: Westview, 1992.

Goodwin, Paul B., Jr., ed. *Global Studies: Latin America*. Guilford, Conn.: Dushkin/McGraw-Hill, 2000.

Gudmundson, Lowell. *Costa Rica before Coffee*. Baton Rouge: Louisiana State University Press, 1986.

Handy, Jim. *Gift of the Devil: A History of Guatemala*. Boston: South End, 1984.

Herman, Edward S., and Noam Chomsky. *Manufacturing Consent: The Political Economy of the Mass Media*. New York: Pantheon Books, 1988.

Kempe, Frederick. *Divorcing the Dictator: America's Bungled Affair with Noriega*. New York: Putnam's, 1990.

Kennedy, Paul P. *The Middle Beat: A Correspondent's View of Mexico, Guatemala, and El Salvador*. New York: Teachers College Press, Columbia University, 1971.

Knowlton, Steven R., and Patrick Parsons, eds. *The Journalist's Moral Compass: Basic Principles*. Westport, Conn.: Praeger, 1995.

Leiken, Robert S., and Barry Rubin, eds. *The Central American Crisis Reader*. New York: Summit Books, 1987.

LeoGrande, William M. *Our Own Backyard: The United States in Central America, 1977–1992*. Chapel Hill: University of North Carolina Press, 1998.

McChesney, Robert W. *Corporate Media and the Threat to Democracy*. New York: Seven Stories, 1997.

Morris, Nancy, and Silvio Waisbord, eds. *Media and Globalization: Why the State Matters*. Lanham, Md.: Rowman and Littlefield, 2001.

Murphy, Richard, ed. *Attacks on the Press in 1999*. New York: Committee to Protect Journalists, 2000.

———. *Attacks on the Press in 2000*. New York: Committee to Protect Journalists, 2001.

Newman, Anne, ed. *Attacks on the Press in 1993*. New York: Committee to Protect Journalists, 1994.

Niemeier, Jean Gilbreath. *The Panama Story*. Portland, Ore.: Metropolitan, 1968.

North, Liisa. *Bitter Grounds: Roots of Revolt in El Salvador*. Westport, Conn.: Lawrence Hill, 1985.

Nyrop, Richard F., ed. *Guatemala: A Country Study*. Washington: U.S. Army, 1983.

Ordóñez, Jaime, ed. *Periodismo, Derechos Humanos y Control de Poder Politico en Centroamerica*. San José, Costa Rica: InterAmerican Institute of Human Rights, 1994.

Orme, William A., Jr., ed. *A Culture of Collusion: An Inside Look at the Mexican Press*. Miami: North-South Center, the University of Miami, 1997.

Paige, Jeffery M. *Coffee and Power: Revolution and the Rise of Democracy in Central America.* Cambridge, Mass.: Harvard University Press, 1997.

Painter, James. *Guatemala: False Hope, False Freedom.* London: Catholic Institute for International Relations, 1987.

Raboy, Marc, and Bernard Dagenais, eds. *Media, Crisis and Democracy: Mass Communication and the Disruption of Social Order.* London: Sage, 1992.

Rosset, Peter, and John Vandermeer, eds. *Nicaragua: Unfinished Revolution.* New York: Grove, 1986.

Sahadi, Jeanne, ed. *Attacks on the Press in 1994.* New York: Committee to Protect Journalists, 1995.

Schulz, Donald E., and Deborah Sundloff Schulz. *The United States, Honduras, and the Crisis in Central America.* Boulder, Colo.: Westview, 1994.

Seligson, Mitchell A., and John A. Booth, eds. *Elections and Democracy in Central America, Revisited.* Chapel Hill: University of North Carolina Press, 1995.

Skidmore, Thomas E., and Peter H. Smith. *Modern Latin America.* New York: Oxford University Press, 2001.

Valladares Lanza, Leo, and Susan C. Peacock. *The Search for Hidden Truths.* Tegucigalpa, Honduras: National Commission of Human Rights/CNDH, 1998.

Vanden Heuvel, Jon, and Everette E. Dennis. *Changing Patterns: Latin America's Vital Media.* New York: Freedom Forum Media Studies Center, 1995.

Villalobos Quirós, Enrique. *El Derecho a la Información.* San José, Costa Rica: La Editorial Universidad Estatal a Distancia, 1997.

Virtue, John, ed. *Latin American Media Directory.* North Miami: International Media Center, Florida International University, 1998.

Waisbord, Silvio. *Watchdog Journalism in South America: News, Accountability, and Democracy.* New York: Columbia University Press, 2000.

Walker, Thomas W. *Nicaragua: The Land of Sandino.* Boulder, Colo.: Westview, 1991.

Wilson, Bruce M. *Costa Rica: Politics, Economics, and Democracy.* Boulder, Colo.: Lynne Rienner, 1998.

Magazine and Journal Articles

Alisky, Marvin. "Central American Radio." *Quarterly of Film, Radio and TV* 10 (1955–56): 59–62.

Atwood, Roger. "Peace of Mind." *The New Republic,* 22 March 1999.

Aumente, Jerome. "Struggles for Independent Journalism." *Media Studies Journal* 13, no. 3 (Fall 1999): 166–75.

Bogart, Leo. "Media and Democracy." *Media Studies Journal* 9, no. 3 (Summer 1995): 1–10.

Carothers, Thomas. "Democracy without Illusions." *Foreign Affairs* 76, no. 1 (January–February 1997): 85.

Dallas, Jo. "Thin Bit of America," *Multichannel News International* 3, no. 4 (April 1997): 26.

Darling, Juanita. "Panama: Looking for Ways to Silence Editors." *IPI Report* (Fall 1997): 22.

Fitzgerald, Mark. "Press Freedom in Latin America: A Survey." *Editor and Publisher*, 10 April 2000, 41–42.

Guerrero, Alina. "Las Relaciones Peligrosas." *Pulso*, April–July 1995, 16–17.

Inforpress CentroAmericana. "President Accused of 'Killing the Media.'" *Central America Report* 25, no. 12 (26 March 1998): 1–2.

———. "Contraband Coffee Sales Rise." *Central America Report* 25, no. 12 (26 March 1998): 7.

Mackay, Maria Luisa. "Magic Realism in Latin America." *Media Studies Journal* 9, no. 3 (Summer 1995): 61–68.

Nerone, John. "Lessons from American History." *Media Studies Journal* 10, no. 4 (Fall 1996): 149–58.

Pastrán, Adolfo. "La Situacion de la Prensa en Nicaragua." *La Red*, August–September 1997, 5.

Paxman, Andrew. "Ghostly Titan Works below Radar." *Variety*, 31 May 1999, 23.

"Los Periodicos: En Busca de la Lealtad Perdida." *Pauta* (Panama City), June 1992, 26–33.

"Progress and Inertia in Central America." *Swiss Review of World Affairs*, 3 November 1997.

Robinson, William I. "Polyarchy: Coercion's New Face in Latin America." *NACLA Report on the Americas* 34, no. 3 (November–December 2000): 42–48.

Rojas, Ana Cristina. "Television Sin Arbitraje." *Actualidad Economica* (San José, Costa Rica) (May 2000): 28–35.

Ruhl, J. Mark. "Doubting Democracy in Honduras." *Current History*, February 1997, 81–86.

Shattuck, John, and J. Brian Atwood. "Defending Democracy: Why Democrats Trump Autocrats." *Foreign Affairs* 77, no. 2 (March–April 1998): 167–80.

Shifter, Michael. "Tensions and Trade-Offs in Latin America." *Journal of Democracy* 8, no. 2 (April 1997): 114–28.

Waisbord, Silvio. "Investigative Journalism and Political Accountability in South American Democracies." *Critical Studies in Mass Communication* 13 (1996): 343–63.

———. "The Ties That Still Bind: Media and National Culture in Latin America." *Canadian Journal of Communication* 23, no. 3 (Summer 1998): 381.

Reports

Alamilla, Ileana, Joáquin Pérez, and Ruth Taylor, eds. *The Guatemalan Media: The Challenge of Democracy.* Guatemala City: Cerigua, 1996.

Alves, Rosental Calmon. "Vanguard Newspapers in Latin America." Unpublished paper presented at the International Communication Association Conference, Montreal, 1997.

Canton, Santiago A. *Report of the Office of the Special Rapporteur for the Freedom of Expression.* Vol. 3. Washington, D.C.: Organization of American States, 1999.

Dye, David R., with Jack Spence and George Vickers. *Patchwork Democracy: Nicaraguan Politics Ten Years after the Fall.* Cambridge, Mass.: Hemisphere Initiatives, 2000.

The Economist Intelligence Unit. "Country Profile 2000: Guatemala/El Salvador." London: The Economist Intelligence Unit, 2000.

———. "Country Report: Nicaragua/Honduras." First Quarter. London: The Economist Intelligence Unit, 2000.

———. "Country Report: Nicaragua/Honduras." Fourth Quarter. London: The Economist Intelligence Unit, 2000.

Green, Charles H., Gerardo Bolaños, Francisco Vásquez, and Ana Cecilia With. *Finding Their Role: Nicaraguan News Media Grapple with Freedom.* North Miami: Florida International University, 1991.

Janus, Noreene, Harold Moore Jr., and Danielle Rodriguez-Schneider. *Media and Campaign Coverage Assessment: El Salvador Presidential Elections, March 1999.* Washington, D.C.: USAID, 1999.

Moore, Harold E., Jr. *Democracy, the Media and Politics in Nicaragua.* Miami: Latin American Journalism Program, Florida International University, 1995.

M&R Consultores, with Price Waterhouse Coopers. *Auditoria de Circulacion.* Managua, Nicaragua: M&R Consultores, S.A., 2001.

Payne, Douglas W. *Storm Watch: Democracy in the Western Hemisphere into the Next Century.* Washington: Center for Strategic and International Studies, 1998.

Universidad Centroamericana. *Encuesta sobre preferencia de Medios.* Managua: Faculty of Communication Science, Universidad Centroamericana, 1998.

Newspaper Articles

Aparicio, James. "Gerente de *La Prensa* Maltrata y Amenaza a su Mujer e Hijos." *La Estrella de Panama,* 23 August 1998, A1.

The Associated Press. "Honduras' Army Chief Admits Shielding Fugitive Officers." *Miami Herald,* 17 August 1998, A4.

———. "Salvadoran President Vows Jobs." *Boston Globe,* 2 June 1999, A14.

———. "Guatemala Sends Soldiers into Streets." *The News* (Mexico City), 9 June 2000, 10.

Benjamín, Ana Teresa. "El Mayor Problema es el Desempleo." *La Prensa* (Panama City), 22 August 1998, A17.

Bounds, Andrew. "Panama's Politicians Seek to Emerge from Noriega's Long Shadow." *Financial Times* (London), 25 August 2000, 3.

———. "Political Squalls as the 'Mireya Effect' Hits Panama." *Financial Times* (London), 6 October 2000, 7.

Bounds, Andrew, Robin Emmott, and Andy Webb-Vidal. "Press Finds It a

Struggle to Stay Free in Latin America." *Financial Times* (London), 4 July 2001, 3.

"Caso END es Malversación de los Bienes del Estado." *El Nuevo Diario* (Managua), 6 July 2001.

"Con Protesta Busca Nodarse Evitar Cumplimiento de Ley." *La Prensa* (San Pedro Sula, Honduras), 22 March 1998, A7.

"Corte Deniega Recurso de Inconstitucionalidad de Canal Seis." *El Tiempo* (San Pedro Sula, Honduras), 17 March 1998, 3.

Darling, Juanita. "Sandinista Paper Returns, but Ex-Staffers Aren't Impressed." *Los Angeles Times,* 22 July 2000, A1.

"Dejando Huella." *El Panamá América* (Panama City), special ed., 17 March 1994, 2.

"Gadfly Won't Fly Away: An Expose-Minded Editor Vows to Resist Panama's Expulsion Threat." *Los Angeles Times,* 14 August 1997, B8.

Gallegos, Raul. "*Periodismo Feudal.*" *El Diario de Hoy* (San Salvador) 7 May 1998, 112.

Garvin, Glenn. "Newspaper Wars Heat Up in Nicaragua." *Miami Herald,* 19 February 1998, 14A.

"Hank González Controversy Strains Mexico-U.S. Relations." *The News* (Mexico City), 22 June 1999.

Hoffman, Roy. "A Year after Hurricane Mitch—Honduran Official: Our Country Has Lost What It Took Us 30 to 40 Years to Build." Newhouse News Service, *Seattle Times,* 27 October 1999, A3.

Kammer, Jerry. "Mexican Press Becoming Activist." *Arizona Republic,* 18 June 2000, J1.

Kanell, Michael. "Latin America: BellSouth's New Frontier." *Atlanta Constitution,* 22 February 1998, 7H.

Kotler, Jared. "Guatemala's New War—of Words." *Washington Post,* 19 April 1998, A20.

Mitchell, Jon. "U.S. Slams Panama for Investor Policies; Cable TV Decision Spurs America to Take Action." *Journal of Commerce,* April 2, 1997, 3A.

Muñoz, Nefer. "Suspendido Director de *La Republica.*" *La Nación* (San José), 9 January 1999, A11.

Navarro, Mireya. "Man in the News: Francisco Guillermo Flores Perez; New Salvadoran Puzzle." *New York Times,* 9 March 1999, A10.

———. "Woman in the News: Mireya Elisa Moscoso; Earnest Icon for Panama." *New York Times,* 4 May 1999, A11.

"Nuevo Golpe á la Libertad de Prensa." *Prensa Libre* (Guatemala City), 4 February 2000.

Rockwell, Rick. "Shining Light on a Shadowy Legal System." *Baltimore Sun,* 4 July 1999, C1.

———. "Canal Control No Guarantee of Stability for Panama." *Baltimore Sun,* 15 August 1999, C1.

———. "Vote Points to More Trouble." *Baltimore Sun,* 14 November 1999, C1, C6.

Rockwell, Rick, and Kristin Neubauer. "Media Feel Government Pressure." *Baltimore Sun,* 29 July 2001, C1, C6.

Rohter, Larry. "Report's Bluntness Shocks, Gratifies." *Montreal Gazette*, 28 February 1999, B8.

Rojas Coles, Luis. "El Periodismo es mi Vida." *Teleguia* (San José), 17 January 1999, 10–11.

Somoza, Bernabe. "Start of Something Much Better for Nicaragua." *Houston Chronicle*, 4 November 1996, A23.

Treadway, Joan. "Honduras Struggles to Rebuild, Mitch's Toll Expensive but Country Is Focused." *New Orleans Times-Picayune*, 1 December 1999, A23.

Weissert, Will. "Congressmen Quit in Guatemala; Former Ruling Party in Disarray." The Associated Press, *The News* (Mexico City), 7 June 2000, 13.

———. "Guatemalan President's Family Evacuated as Fear Grips Nation," *The News* (Mexico City), 22 June 2000, 11.

Wilson, James, and Richard Lapper. "Confessed Killer Leads Race to Become Guatemalan President." *Financial Times* (London), 21 September 1999, 9.

"Year after Gerardi's Murder, Case Still Unresolved." *New Catholic Times*, 25 April 1999, 9.

News Service Reports

Agence France-Press. "Mexico Denounces Backlash in Costa Rica over Hank Affair." 10 June 1999.

Associated Press. "International News." 17 December 1997.

———. "International News." 12 June 1999.

Cuevas, Freddy. "Honduran President Fires Military Officials, Denies Coup Attempt." Associated Press, 31 July 1999.

———. "Honduras Says It Has Evidence of Secret Graves at U.S.-built Base." Associated Press, 8 August 1999.

———. "Honduras Compensates Families of People Killed by Death Squads." Associated Press, 2 November 2000.

Efe News Service. "Matan Supuesto Pandillero Asesino á Periodista Television." 6 December 1998.

———. "*La Noticia*, Cuarto Diario Escrito del Pais, Circula desde Hoy." 4 May 1999.

———. "Condenan a Diario *La Nación* por Segunda Vez en Tres Semanas." 13 November 1999.

———. "Llega Relator de la OEA para la Libertad de Expresion." 12 April 2000.

———. "Periodistas Han Vivido Entre Voragine del Terror y la Violencia." 29 April 2000.

Inforpress Centroamericana. "Principales Medios de Comunicación (Honduras, El Salvador y Guatemala)." April 1998.

Martinez, Kathia. "New Panamanian President Annuls Press Gag Laws." Associated Press, 20 December 1999.

Mejia, Thelma. "Smuggling Cases Reveal Rampant Corruption." Inter Press News Service, 26 November 1999.

Notimex. "Sancionan a Televisora Hondurena por Difusion Ilegal de Senales de EU." 22 April 1998.

———. "Ordenan Cierre Temporal de Televisora Hondurena por 'Pirateria.'" 23 April 1998.

Sanchez, Isabel. "Latin America's Achilles Heel: Poverty, Inequality, Lack of Democracy." Agence France-Press, 29 June 2000.

Electronic Documents

Bilello, Suzanne. "Central American News Media: Independent but Shadowed by Threats." *free!* 27 August 1999. On-line journal of the Freedom Forum. Available via internet.

Buchanan, Brian J. "News Media Called Critical to Democracy, Reforms in Central America." *free!* 10 September 1999. On-line journal of the Freedom Forum. Available via internet.

Committee to Protect Journalists. "Powerful Panamanians Conspire to Smear Local Editor." 26 October 1999. On-line database. Available via internet.

Darling, Juanita. "*Mas* for the Masses." *IPI Report* (Summer 1999). On-line version of the quarterly journal of the International Press Institute. Available via internet.

Fliess, Maurice. "Honduran Press Called Tarnished by Corruption." *free!* 13 September 1999. On-line journal of the Freedom Forum. Available via internet.

Mower, Joan. "Newspapers Called Vital in Advancing Democracy in Latin America." *free!* 15 July 1999. On-line journal of the Freedom Forum. Available via internet.

Reporters sans Frontières. "Ninth Ibero-American Summit in Havana, Cuba." On-line database. Available via internet.

Rockwell, Rick, Noreene Janus, and Kristin Neubauer. "Exposé Could Signal End of El Salvador TV News Magazine." Pacific News Service, 24 May 2001. On-line content database of the news service. Available via internet.

Schapiro, Mark. "The Man without a Country." *Salon.com*, 7 November 2000. On-line magazine. Available via internet.

Transparency International. "1999 Transparency International Corruption Perceptions Index." On-line database. Available via internet.

Other Documents

Correa Jolly, Fernando. "La Necesidad de un Sistema de Mercadeo para la Radio en Panama." Master's thesis, University of St. Maria La Antigua, Panama City, 1992.

Gorriti, Gustavo. Farewell message to *La Prensa*, Panama, 2 March 2001. Copy via electronic mail.

————. Electronic message to Rick Rockwell, 24 October 2001. Copy via electronic mail.

Moore, Harold E., Jr. Internal memo to Gary Russell of USAID. U.S. Embassy, Managua, 1996.

Valladares Melgar, Marcos Alfredo. Letter to Carlos Rosales, press secretary, San Salvador, 22 January 2001. Copy via fax from the Office of Information and Press of the President of the Republic of El Salvador.

Interviews

Altamirano, Enrique, director, *El Diario de Hoy* (San Salvador). Interview by Noreene Janus, May 1998, San Salvador, El Salvador. Tape-recorded.

Angulo Grillo, Marcela, editor, *El Financiero* (San José). Interview by Dylana Segura of *La Nación* (San José, Costa Rica), June 2000, San José, Costa Rica. Tape-recorded.

Angulo Zeledón, Rolando, independent radio journalist. Interview by Dylana Segura of *La Nación* (San José, Costa Rica), June 2000, San José, Costa Rica. Tape-recorded.

Aparicio, James, editor, *La Estrella de Panama* (Panama City). Interview by Rick Rockwell, August 1998, Panama City, Panama. Tape-recorded.

Arias de Galindo, Rosario, publisher, *El Panamá América* and *Crítica* (Panama City). Interview by Rick Rockwell, August 1998, Panama City, Panama. Tape-recorded.

Bendfeltd, Blancanivea, media director, APCU Thompson Asociados. Interview by Rick Rockwell, July 1998, Guatemala City, Guatemala. Transcript notes.

Benitez, Edgardo, editor, *El Nuevo Dia* (San Pedro Sula, Honduras). Interview by Rick Rockwell, March 1998, San Pedro Sula, Honduras. Tape-recorded.

Berganza, Gustavo, managing editor, *Siglo Veintiuno* (Guatemala City). Interview by Rick Rockwell, July 1998, Guatemala City, Guatemala. Tape-recorded.

Borge, Tomás, former director of *Barricada* and former interior minister of Nicaragua. Interview by Noreene Janus, Kristin Neubauer, and Rick Rockwell, August 2001, Managua, Nicaragua. Tape-recorded.

Borrasé Sanou, Andrés, director, *La Prensa Libre* (San José). Interview by Dylana Segura of *La Nación* (San José, Costa Rica), June 2000, San José, Costa Rica. Tape-recorded.

Bosco, Juan, editor, *El Diario de Hoy* (San Salvador). Interview by Noreene Janus, April 1999, San Salvador, El Salvador. Transcript notes.

Briceño, Carlos, owner and general manager, TeleNica 8. Interview by Noreene Janus, July 1998, Managua, Nicaragua. Tape-recorded.

Canahuati, Jorge, III. Interview by Rick Rockwell, March 1998, San Pedro Sula, Honduras. Tape-recorded.

Castañeda Alas, Roberto, owner, Radio Sonora. Interview by Noreene Janus, April 1999, San Salvador, El Salvador. Transcript notes.

Castillo, Ignacio "Nacho," news director, RCS Radio. Interview by Noreene Janus, April 1999, San Salvador, El Salvador. Transcript notes.

Chacón, Ricardo, former managing editor, *La Prensa Grafica* (San Salvador). Interview by Noreene Janus, May 1998, San Salvador, El Salvador. Tape-recorded.

Chamorro, Carlos, director, *Confidencial* (Managua), and host of "Este Semana," Canal 2. Interview by Noreene Janus, Kristin Neubauer, and Rick Rockwell, August 2001, Managua, Nicaragua. Tape-recorded.

Chamorro, Cristiana, former director, *La Prensa* (Managua). Interview by Noreene Janus, July 1998, Managua, Nicaragua. Tape-recorded.

———. Interview by Noreene Janus, Kristin Neubauer, and Rick Rockwell, August 2001, Managua, Nicaragua. Transcript notes.

Chamorro, Francisco, managing editor, *El Nuevo Diario* (Managua). Interview by Rick Rockwell, Managua, Nicaragua. Tape-recorded.

Cisneros Gallo, Pilar, anchor, Canal 7. Interview by Dylana Segura of *La Nación* (San José, Costa Rica), June 2000, San José, Costa Rica. Tape-recorded.

Correa Esquivel, Juan Luis, general manager, *La Prensa* (Panama City). Interview by Rick Rockwell, August 1998, Panama City, Panama. Tape-recorded.

Correa Jolly, Fernando, executive vice-president, Radio KW Continente. Interview by Rick Rockwell, August 1998, Panama City, Panama. Tape-recorded.

Dumas Castillo, Rodolfo. Interview by Rick Rockwell, March 1998, San Pedro Sula, Honduras. Transcript notes.

Durán Hidalgo, Elbert, director, "Radio Periodicos Reloj." Interview by Dylana Segura of *La Nación* (San José, Costa Rica), June 2000, San José, Costa Rica. Tape-recorded.

Escobar Galindo, David, dean of the School of Communication, University of José Matias Delgado. Interview by Noreene Janus, May 1998, San Salvador, El Salvador. Tape-recorded.

Espinoza, Mario F., journalism educator and journalist formerly with *Barricada* (Managua). Interview by Noreene Janus, July 1998, Managua, Nicaragua. Tape-recorded.

Fernandez Rojas, Lafitte, managing editor, *El Diario de Hoy* (San Salvador). Interview by Noreene Janus, May 1998, San Salvador, El Salvador. Tape-recorded.

Funes, Mauricio, anchor, Canal 12. Interview by Noreene Janus, May 1998, San Salvador, El Salvador. Tape-recorded.

Gadea Pantoja, Milo, co-owner, Radio Corporación. Interview by Rick Rockwell, August 2001, Managua, Nicaragua. Tape-recorded.

Gómez, William, director, "Diario Extra" (San José), Extra TV, and Radio America. Interview by Dylana Segura of *La Nación* (San José, Costa Rica), May 2000, San José, Costa Rica. Tape-recorded.

González, Armando, director, *Al Día* (San José). Interview by Dylana Segura of *La Nación* (San José, Costa Rica), July 2000, San José, Costa Rica. Tape-recorded.

González Revilla, Nicolás, president of MEDCOM Holdings. Interview by Rick Rockwell, August 1998, Panama City, Panama. Tape-recorded.

Gorriti, Gustavo, associate editor, *La Prensa* (Panama City). Interview by Rick Rockwell, August 1998, Panama City, Panama. Tape-recorded.

———. Interview by Rick Rockwell, November 1998, Washington, D.C. Transcript notes.

Gutierrez, Joel, former senior editor, *La Tribuna* (Managua). Interview by Noreene Janus, July 1998, Managua, Nicaragua. Tape-recorded.

———. Interview by Noreene Janus and Rick Rockwell, August 2001, Managua, Nicaragua. Transcript notes.

Hernandez, Norman Roy, chairman of CONATEL, the Honduran Communications Commission. Interview by Rick Rockwell, March 1998, Tegucigalpa, Honduras. Tape-recorded.

Holmann Chamorro, Hugo, general manager, *La Prensa* (Managua). Interview by Noreene Janus, Kristin Neubauer, and Rick Rockwell, August 2001, Managua, Nicaragua. Tape-recorded.

Hume, David, subdirector, *La Prensa* (Managua). Interview by Rick Rockwell, August 2001, Managua, Nicaragua. Tape-recorded.

Jiménez, Gerardo, director, *Al Día* (Guatemala City). Interview by Rick Rockwell, July 1998, Guatemala City, Guatemala. Transcript notes.

Lacayo, Danilo, former anchor and host of "Buenas Dias Nicaragua," Canal 2. Interview by Noreene Janus, July 1998, Managua, Nicaragua. Tape-recorded.

Marroquín Godoy, Gonzalo, director, *Prensa Libre* (Guatemala City). Interview by Rick Rockwell, July 1998, Guatemala City, Guatemala. Tape-recorded.

Marroquín Rojas, Oscar, publisher, *La Hora* (Guatemala City). Interview by Rick Rockwell, July 1998, Guatemala City, Guatemala. Tape-recorded.

Martáns, Diana, publisher, *Pauta* (Panama City). Interview by Rick Rockwell, August 1998, Panama City, Panama. Tape-recorded.

Martinez, Juan Ramon, columnist, *La Tribuna* (Tegucigalpa). Interview by Rick Rockwell, March 1998, Tegucigalpa, Honduras. Tape-recorded.

Martinez, Maria Antonia, managing editor, *La Prensa* (San Pedro Sula, Honduras). Interview by Rick Rockwell, March 1998, San Pedro Sula, Honduras. Tape-recorded.

McDonald, Ramiro, Jr., former news director and principal anchor, "Guatemala Flash." Interview by Rick Rockwell, July 1998, Guatemala City, Guatemala. Tape-recorded.

Medina, Francisco, editor, *El Periodico* (Tegucigalpa). Interview by Rick Rockwell, March 1998, Tegucigalpa, Honduras. Tape-recorded.

Monterrosa, Rolando, chief of public information, *El Diario de Hoy* (San Salvador). Interview by Noreene Janus, May 1998, San Salvador, El Salvador. Tape-recorded.

Padilla Beliz, Jaime, publisher, *El Siglo* (Panama City). Interview by Rick Rockwell, August 1998, Panama City, Panama. Tape-recorded.

Pastrán, Adolfo, independent radio journalist. Interview by Noreene Janus, July 1998, Managua, Nicaragua. Tape-recorded.

Reyes, Nery Mabel, news director, YSKL Radio. Interview by Noreene Janus, May 1998, San Salvador, El Salvador. Tape-recorded.
———. Interview by Noreene Janus, April 1999, San Salvador, El Salvador. Transcript notes.
Reyes, Xavier, former producer, "Sesenta Minutos," Cadena de Oro, and managing editor, *La Noticia* (Managua). Interview by Noreene Janus, July 1998, Managua, Nicaragua. Tape-recorded.
———. Interview by Noreene Janus, August 2001, Managua, Nicaragua. Transcript notes.
Rivas, David, president of APES. Interview by Noreene Janus, May 1998, San Salvador, El Salvador. Tape-recorded.
Rivera, Marco Antonio, producer, Canal 12. Interview by Noreene Janus, May 1998, San Salvador, El Salvador. Tape-recorded.
Rodriguez, Indalecio, ombudsman, *El Universal* (Panama City). Interview by Rick Rockwell, August 1998, Panama City, Panama. Tape-recorded.
Rojas, Ana Cristina, reporter, *Actualidad Economica* (San José). Interview by Dylana Segura of *La Nación* (San José, Costa Rica), May 2000, San José, Costa Rica. Tape-recorded.
Saborío, Shirley, editor, *Actualidad Economica* (San José). Interview by Dylana Segura of *La Nación* (San José, Costa Rica), May 2000, San José, Costa Rica. Tape-recorded.
Sarmiento, José Rolando, independent radio journalist, Radio X. Interview by Rick Rockwell, March 1998, Tegucigalpa, Honduras. Tape-recorded.
Schwartz Galo, Dennis, general manager, Radio Ya. Interview by Noreene Janus, August 2001, Managua, Nicaragua. Transcript notes.
Shetemul, Haroldo, former director, *Crónica* (Guatemala City). Interview by Rick Rockwell, July 1998, Guatemala City, Guatemala. Tape-recorded.
Simòn Chuy, Florencio, director, Mayan language programs, Radio Nuevo Mundo. Interview by Rick Rockwell, July 1998, Guatemala City, Guatemala. Transcript notes.
Tobar Salazar, Timoteo, president, COOPEDEGUA. Interview by Rick Rockwell, July 1998, Guatemala City, Guatemala. Transcript notes.
Ulibarri, Eduardo, editor, *La Nación* (San José). Interview by Dylana Segura of *La Nación* (San José, Costa Rica), May 2000, San José, Costa Rica. Tape-recorded.
Valladares, Raul, news director, HRN Radio. Interview by Rick Rockwell, March 1998, Tegucigalpa, Honduras. Transcript notes.
Villalobos Quirós, Enrique, professor, Universidad Estatal a Distancia and Universidad Autonoma de CentroAmerica. Interview by Noreene Janus, July 1998, San José, Costa Rica. Transcript notes.
Zapeta, Estuardo, columnist, *Siglo Veintiuno* (Guatemala City). Interview by Rick Rockwell, July 1998, Guatemala City, Guatemala. Transcript notes.
Zarco, José Eduardo, former director, "Temas de Noche." Interview by Rick Rockwell, July 1998, Guatemala City, Guatemala. Transcript notes.
Zelada, Boris, editor, *La Prensa Grafica* (San Salvador). Interview by Noreene Janus, May 1998, San Salvador, El Salvador. Tape-recorded.
Zuñiga, Oswaldo, producer, Radio Catolica. Interview by Noreene Janus, July 1998, Managua, Nicaragua. Tape-recorded.

INDEX

RICK ROCKWELL teaches journalism at American University, in Washington, D.C., and has more than two decades of experience in the media as a reporter, TV producer, and news manager. In addition to his work for ABC News, the Discovery Channel, and PBS, he has covered the last two Mexican presidential elections and the 2001 Nicaraguan elections for various news organizations, including the Associated Press. He is a contributor to the book *Latin Politics, Global Media* and to publications such as the *Baltimore Sun* and *In These Times.*

NOREENE JANUS earned a Ph.D. in communications from Stanford University and has been a telecommunications consultant since 1983, specializing in projects in Latin America and in computer and communications training and development for nonprofit organizations in the Caribbean, Africa, and Latin America. She is Communications for Development advisor for Latin America and Caribbean at the Academy for Educational Development (AED) and has also served as head of communications research for the Latin American Institute for Transnational Studies in Mexico City.

The University of Illinois Press
is a founding member of the
Association of American University Presses.

Composed in 9.5/12.5 Trump Mediaeval
by Jim Proefrock
at the University of Illinois Press
Manufactured by Thomson-Shore, Inc.

University of Illinois Press
1325 South Oak Street
Champaign, IL 61820-6903
www.press.uillinois.edu